Abortion Decisions of the Supreme Court

Abortion Decisions
of the Supreme Court,
1973 through 1989

A Comprehensive Review
with Historical Commentary

by
Dan Drucker

McFarland & Company, Inc., Publishers
Jefferson, North Carolina, and London

British Library Cataloguing-in-Publication data are available

Library of Congress Cataloguing-in-Publication Data

Drucker, Dan, 1943–
    Abortion decisions of the Supreme Court, 1973 through 1989 : a
comprehensive review with historical commentary / by Dan Drucker.
        p.   cm.
    [Includes index.]
    Includes bibliographical references.
    ISBN 0-89950-459-0 (lib. bdg. : 50# alk. paper) ∞
    1. Abortion — Law and legislation — United States — Cases.
I. Title.
    KF3771.A7D78   1990
    344.73'04192 — dc20
    [347.3044192]   89-43620
                                                                        CIP

Manufactured in the United States of America

McFarland & Company, Inc., Publishers
  Box 611, Jefferson, North Carolina 28640

*This book is dedicated to
the women of the United States who every day
must face the long arm of "man-made" laws
that go so far as to invade their innermost sanctity.*

*And it is also dedicated to three specific women, each one different
but together providing me with the encouragement
and motivation to complete this work.
First, my mom Mitzi, who taught me
that love is much deeper than life itself.
Second, Sura, who taught me that
no matter how tough the odds, one should continue
fighting for one's principles and never give up
until one's last breath!
Finally, there is Karen,
who has proven to me that there exists
a higher level of love, compassion and sensitivity
which is attainable if one works to achieve it.*

Table of Contents

A Note to the Reader   xiii

Introduction   1
    Defining Abortion   1
    Interpretation of the Constitution   3
    Methods and Restrictions of Abortion   3
    Medical Judgments   6
    Public Funding   6

1: The United States Supreme Court   8

2: Texas Statutes on Abortion [Enacted 1857]   10
Roe vs. Wade   11
    Right to Privacy   11
    Regulation of Abortion   12
Opinion of the Court: Read by Justice Blackmun   13
Viewpoint: Selected Concurring Views of Justice Stewart   13
Viewpoint: Selected Dissenting Views of Justice Rehnquist   14
The Court's Decision   15

3: Georgia Statutes on Abortion [Enacted 1968]   17
American Law Institute Model Penal Code [Section 230.3 Abortion]   19
Doe vs. Bolton   20
    Judgment of the Physician   22
    Hospital Accreditation   22
    Hospital Committee   23
    Physician's Approval   24
    Residency Requirement   24
Opinion of the Court: Read by Justice Blackmun   24
Viewpoint: Selected Concurring Views of Chief Justice Burger   25
Viewpoint: Selected Concurring Views of Justice Douglas   26
Viewpoint: Selected Dissenting Views of Justice White   28
Viewpoint: Selected Dissenting Views of Justice Rehnquist   28
The Court's Decision   28

4: Missouri Statutes on Abortion [Enacted 1974]   30

Planned Parenthood of Central Missouri vs. Danford   33
    Viability   34
    Consent of the Pregnant Woman   35
    Consent of the Spouse   35
    Parental Consent   36
    The Saline Amniocentesis Abortion Method   37
    Preserving the Life of the Fetus   37
    Retaining Medical Records and Information   38
Opinion of the Court: Read by Justice Blackmun   39
Viewpoint: Selected Concurring Views of Justice Stewart   40
Viewpoint: Selected Views of Justice Stevens, Concurring in Part,
    Dissenting in Part   41
Viewpoint: Selected Views of Justice White, Concurring in Part,
Dissenting in Part   42
The Court's Decision   45

5: Massachusetts Abortion Statute [Sec. 12P] [Enacted 1974]   47

Bellotti, Attorney General of Massachusetts vs. Baird   47
    Parental Consent   48
Opinion of the Court: Read by Justice Blackmun   49
The Court's Decision   50

6: The Connecticut Welfare Department Abortion Regulation [Sec. 275] [Enacted 1975]   51

Maher, Commissioner of Social Services of Connecticut vs. Roe   51
    Medicaid Payments for Abortions   52
    Medicaid Payments to Indigent Pregnant Women   52
    Prohibiting Abortion for Indigent Women   53
    Abortion for the Indigent: Obligations and Concerns   53
Opinion of the Court: Read by Justice Powell   54
Viewpoint: Selected Concurring Views of Chief Justice Burger   55
Viewpoint: Selected Dissenting Views of Justice Brennan   55
The Court's Decision   57

7: Massachusetts Abortion Statute [Sec. 12S(P)] [Enacted 1974(77)]   58

Bellotti, Attorney General of Massachusetts vs. Baird (II)   58
    Constitutional Rights of Adolescents   59
    The Adolescent and the Abortion Decision   60
Opinion of the Court: Read by Justice Powell   62

Viewpoint: Selected Concurring Views of Justice Rehnquist 64
Viewpoint: Selected Concurring Views of Justice Stevens 64
Viewpoint: Selected Dissenting Views of Justice White 65
The Court's Decision 66

8: Pennsylvania Abortion Control Act [Enacted 1974] 68

Colautti, Secretary of Welfare of Pennsylvania vs. Franklin 68
    The Ambiguity of Viability 69
    Standard-of-Care Provision Concerning Abortions 71
Opinion of the Court: Read by Justice Blackmun 72
Viewpoint: Selected Dissenting Views of Justice White 73
The Court's Decision 75

9: State of Utah Annotated Code 76

H.L. vs. Matheson, Governor of Utah 76
    Questions Concerning Mature Consent 77
    Clarifying the Law 78
Opinion of the Court: Read by Chief Justice Burger 79
Viewpoint: Selected Concurring Views of Justice Powell 80
Viewpoint: Selected Concurring Views of Justice Stevens 81
Viewpoint: Selected Dissenting Views of Justice Marshall 81
The Court's Decision 85

10: The City of Akron (Ohio) Ordinance No. 160-1978 [Enacted 1978] 87

City of Akron vs. Akron Center for Reproductive Health 90
    Limiting a State's Abortion Concern 90
    Hospitalization for Post–First-Trimester Abortions 91
    Adolescent Maturity 92
    Informed Decision 92
    Twenty-Four–Hour Waiting Period 93
    Disposing of Fetal Remains 93
Opinion of the Court: Read by Justice Powell 94
Viewpoint: Selected Dissenting Views of Justice O'Connor 95
The Court's Decision 99

11: Missouri (Kansas City) Statutes on Abortion 100

Planned Parenthood of Kansas City vs. Ashcroft 102
    Second Physician 102
    Pathologist's Report 103
    Hospitalization for Second-Trimester Abortions 103
    Substitute Consent 104
Opinion of the Court: Read by Justice Powell 104

Viewpoint: Selected Views of Justice Blackmun, Concurring in Part,
   Dissenting in Part   105
Viewpoint: Selected Views of Justice O'Connor, Concurring in Part,
   Dissenting in Part   108
The Court's Decision   109

12: The State of Virginia Abortion Ordinance Sec. 18.2–71   110

Simopoulos vs. The State of Virginia   110
   Regulating Second-Trimester Abortion Procedures   111
Opinion of the Court: Read by Justice Powell   112
Viewpoint: Selected Concurring Views of Justice O'Connor   113
Viewpoint: Selected Dissenting Views of Justice Stevens   113
The Court's Decision   114

13: Pennsylvania Abortion Control Act [Enacted 1982]   115

Thornburgh, Governor of Pennsylvania vs. American College of Obstetricians and
   Gynecologists   123
   Influencing Informed Consent   124
   Postviability Abortions and the Second-Physician Requirement   125
   Maintaining Records on Abortion   126
Opinion of the Court: Read by Justice Blackmun   126
Viewpoint: Selected Concurring Views of Justice Stevens   129
Viewpoint: Selected Dissenting Views of Chief Justice Burger   132
Viewpoint: Selected Dissenting Views of Justice White   134
Viewpoint: Selected Dissenting Views of Justice O'Connor   142
The Court's Decision   145

14: Conservatism: Ushering In a New Era in Jurisprudence   147

15: Missouri Regulation of Abortions   154

Modified, Amended and Repealed Statutes   161
Rulings of the Circuit Court of Appeals   162
Rulings of the United States Supreme Court   162
Webster vs. Reproductive Health Services   163
   Post–First-Trimester Hospitalization   165
   Determining Viability   165
   Public Funding   167
   Public Employees Assisting in Abortion   170
Opinion of the Court: Read by Chief Justice Rehnquist   171
Viewpoint: Selected Views of Justice O'Connor, Concurring in Part   177
Viewpoint: Selected Views of Justice Blackmun, Concurring in Part, Dissenting
   in Part   180

Viewpoint: Selected Concurring Views of Justice Scalia 190
*Viewpoint: Selected Views of Justice Stevens, Concurring in Part, Dissenting
    in Part* 193
The Court's Decision 197

16: Pending Cases 199

References 201

Index 203

A Note to the Reader

For clarity to the lay reader, this book presents paraphrases of Supreme Court opinions; statutes have been lightly edited. Substance, tone, and memorable diction in the opinions have been retained. Those who wish to read the opinions in their entirety will find relevant citations in the References.

Introduction

One dictionary defines *abortion* as "the expulsion of the fetus before it is viable or able to survive outside the womb." In legal terms abortion is an "intentionally induced miscarriage." The procedure may be accomplished in one of several ways: through the use, for instance, of any instrument, surgical or otherwise, including the hand, that applies external force; or through the administering of any drug, chemical substance, or potion.

After many months of expert testimony, the United States Supreme Court determined in 1973 that "there is no medical or scientific proof that life is present from conception." The belief is solely a religious concept, based on ancient philosophies and recorded in 430 B.C. as part of the ancient Hippocratic Oath. The Court further concluded that, "we need not resolve the difficult question of when life begins, when those trained in the respective fields of medicine, philosophy and theology are unable to arrive at any consensus. The judiciary at this point in the development of man's knowledge is not in a position to speculate as to the answer."

The relevant argument over the abortion issue is strictly a question of its constitutionality. Is the Constitution deficient on issues pertaining to women, and specifically abortion? Do women have the inalienable constitutional right to procure an abortion?

In the landmark abortion decision of 1973, did the justices of the Supreme Court act properly by invalidating century-old abortion laws in effect in many states? Prior to 1973 the only "legal" abortion procedure performed was to save the life of the mother. Under no circumstances could abortion be performed legally for any other reason. Since forbidding abortion is based solely on religious and philosophical feelings of morality, there remains no scientific or legal basis for banning the procedure. Based on that reasoning, the Court handed down its landmark decision.

Prior to the Supreme Court ruling on abortion, "back alley" abortion clinics flourished, literally victimizing thousands of desperate women who wished to terminate unwanted pregnancies. An estimated 750,000 illegal abortions were performed annually in the United States, under conditions best described as deplorable and unsanitary. Many women were permanently maimed and in some cases even died under the hands of untrained practitioners.

On January 22, 1973, the United States Supreme Court, in a landmark decision, ruled on the constitutionality of abortion by handing down judgments on two "test" abortion cases. The first, *Roe vs. Wade,* challenged abortion laws of the state of Texas, enacted in 1857 and never amended. The second case, *Doe vs. Bolton,* questioned the constitutionality of Georgia's abortion statutes, enacted in 1876 and slightly modified in 1968. The Court replaced the invalidated statutes with a uniform system clearly identifying stages of pregnancy in trimesters and the "legal" enforcement one can expect during each trimester. During the first trimester (up to the 12th week of pregnancy), the abortion decision is left to the pregnant woman in consultation with her physician; the state is powerless to intrude in the decision or procedure. The state can require a written consent from the pregnant woman, certifying that she is of a certain age and maturity in giving informed consent. During the second trimester (from the 13th to the 24th week of pregnancy), the state has a justifiable interest in the abortion procedure and may impose regulations if necessary; however, the regulation cannot be overly restrictive and must be related to interests of maternal health. Sometime during the 24th to the 27th week, at the beginning of the third trimester, viability occurs (the fetus is capable of independent survival outside the womb). It is primarily because of viability that the state has a compelling interest in the abortion decision, and may choose either to regulate the procedure strictly or completely proscribe it, unless the health of the pregnant woman is in danger. However, even at this late stage of pregnancy, the state is forbidden from making any medical determination as to the probability of fetal viability; that remains a medical judgment. Essentially the Court stipulated that abortion should be a medical decision, regardless of the stage of pregnancy. However, states were allowed to retain an interest in the procedure, but the interest of the state would be limited to concerns of maternal health, and if restrictions were imposed, they could not be overly burdensome.

The landmark Supreme Court ruling on abortion was a complete overhaul of abortion laws in effect in a number of states, which allowed abortion only to save the life of the mother. A few of the states had previously granted permission for an abortion if the pregnancy was a result of rape or incest, but elective abortion was not permitted.

In the years following the landmark ruling on abortion, there have been many challenges made by fundamentalist religious groups and conservatives, but the basic structure of the original judgment stands as firm as it did in 1973. This can be attributed primarily to the philosophical balance of the Court, virtually unchanged in the years following the abortion decision. However, in recent years some of the moderate justices have retired from the bench, many of whom had played a major role in the landmark abortion decision. Many of the justices today are "new breed" jurists who follow a more fundamental, conservative philosophy. The shift in the Court's ideology could have a profound effect on future challenges to current abortion laws.

Interpretation of the Constitution

The United States Constitution is written in a manner allowing for broad interpretations; a good example of this is applying the wording of the Fourteenth Amendment's Due Process Clause to a woman's right in terminating an unwanted pregnancy. The manner in which a particular law is defined depends largely on the individual's interpretation. There are often no correct or incorrect ways of defining a point of law. For instance, on the issue of abortion and the application of the wording contained within the Fourteenth Amendment's Due Process Clause ("nor shall any state deprive any persons of life, liberty or property, without due process of law"), three justices interpret the clause differently: Justice Blackmun avers that the right said to be possessed by the pregnant woman to choose to terminate her pregnancy, would be found in the concept of personal liberty, embodied within the Fourteenth Amendment's Due Process Clause; Justice Stevens says that the Constitution does not specify or mention the right of personal choice in matters of family life (abortion); and Justice Rehnquist has written that the only conclusion possible is that the drafters of the Constitution did not intend to have the Fourteenth Amendment withdraw from the states the power to legislate with respect to the issue of abortion. Challenges to abortion laws also have been based on violations of the Fourth Amendment (adopted 1791), which states, "The right of the people to be secure in their persons, houses, papers, and effects, against unreasonable searches and seizures, shall not be violated and no warrants shall issue, but upon probable cause, supported by oath or affirmation, and particularly describing the place to be searched, and the persons or things to be seized," and the Ninth Amendment (adopted 1791), which proclaims, "The enumeration in the Constitution, of certain rights, shall not be construed to deny or disparage others retained by the people."

Methods and Restrictions of Abortion

Methods of producing abortion became a hotly debated issue in 1973. On this issue the United States Supreme Court commented that states have a legitimate interest in seeing the abortion procedure treated in the same manner as any other surgical procedure, that it be performed under circumstances insuring for maximum safety for the patient.

Because of concern over safety, many states banned the use of saline amniocentesis, even though it had been used successfully in a majority of post–first-trimester abortions. Critics of saline were concerned with some serious side effects associated with the procedure, including (1) disruption of the body's blood-clotting function, (2) increased sodium levels in the body, leading to convulsions and perhaps death, (3) water intoxication due to high levels of sodium, which could cause abnormality in the functioning of the central nervous system, and (4) tissue damage to the inside wall of the uterus, which saline is known to have caused.

Regardless of the concern over side effects, saline amniocentesis was proven to be safer than normal childbirth and was the most widely accepted medical procedure in accomplishing abortion. Critics of saline have claimed that the alternative method of prostaglandin amnio infusion is safer than saline. However, critics of prostaglandin, in a counterchallenge, claimed that aside from the method's being almost unavailable in America, it too has some very serious side effects, which include nausea, vomiting, headaches, and diarrhea. In addition, the claim was made that prostaglandin was dangerous to women who also suffered from such other ailments as asthma, glaucoma, hypertension, epilepsy, and any cardiovascular disease.

In 1973 there was strong support in requiring the hospitalization of second-trimester abortion patients, but with advances in medical technology in the late 1970s and early 1980s, it is no longer an area of concern. The most widely used method for second trimester abortions (up to the 16th week of pregnancy) is dilation and evacuation (D & E). In 1973 the method was used in first-trimester abortions only, but it is now the method of choice for most second-trimester procedures. The most common method used in first-trimester procedures is oxytocin induction, otherwise referred to as dilation and curettage (D & C) or dilation suction. The method is considered to be safer than normal childbirth and can be used up to the 13th week of pregnancy, but rarely afterward. The method most recommended by physicians for third-trimester abortions is hysterotomy, a surgical procedure carrying all of the risks associated with any surgical procedure. The only drawback to this procedure is that any future childbirth would have to be accomplished by cesarean section (C-section).

Prior to 1973, in some states a woman did not have the "right" to have an abortion without first obtaining permission from her husband. During the debate of this issue, the Court cited the Missouri case of *Planned Parenthood vs. Danford* (1976) as a prime example of denying a woman her right to have an abortion. The Missouri law under discussion required that the woman's husband first give his approval if the procedure was to be performed during the first twelve weeks of pregnancy, unless the procedure was needed to save her life. The statute was ruled unconstitutional by the Supreme Court. When the Missouri legislators enacted the statute, they reasoned that most of the important decisions in a marriage are agreed to by both husband and wife, including family planning, artificial insemination, and voluntary sterilization. Also, adopting a child requires joint consent. Since so many decisions require joint consent, why should abortion be treated differently, when it is perhaps the only decision that is irreversible? The opposition argued that there could be problems if the father of the child could not be located at the time of the abortion procedure.

Planned Parenthood vs. Danford was again cited for the argument over restricting minor children from seeking an abortion without parental permission. The abortion restriction in the Missouri case included all minors, regardless of their maturity.

For their argument in favor of restricting abortion for adolescents, the state legislature reasoned that minors are prohibited from purchasing firearms, tobacco, or alcoholic beverages without parental permission, as well as viewing sexually explicit material. Since abortion is irreversible, the Missouri legislature felt that it should be added to the list of restrictions adolescents must face.

Lawmakers, however, displayed an even deeper concern in restricting abortion for minors because they felt that an immature wrong decision could lead to lifelong emotional and physical problems.

But the opposition argued that minors could be tested for venereal disease and treated for drug abuse without parental knowledge. The statute was ruled unconstitutional because it failed to separate "mature" minors from "immature" ones; some adolescents are emotionally ready to make rational decisions at earlier ages than others; individuals must be judged independently. Emancipated and married minors must be given separate consideration.

In *H.L. vs. Matheson* (1981), Utah also required parental or husband approval before an abortion could be performed on a minor, but when this law was challenged, it was ruled constitutional because it did not interfere with the abortion decision; it was strictly an informational requirement to assist the physician with a complete and concise medical history of his minor patient.

Prior to 1973, many states had preconditional hospital requirements before an abortion procedure could be performed. The state of Georgia had the severest of requirements. All women desiring to terminate an unwanted pregnancy had to appear before a hospital committee charged with the responsibility of approving the abortion after certain requirements were met. Approval or denial was a result of majority vote of the committee. In addition to the approval of the hospital committee, the woman had to obtain as many as six consensual opinions before the procedure could be performed. All of these legalities were problematic for a procedure where timing was of the utmost importance.

Medical Judgments

Viability is a medical concept that specifies a certain time within the gestation cycle when the fetus is capable of independent survival outside the mother's womb. Viability of the fetus varies with each patient but can be expected somewhere between the 24th and the 28th week of pregnancy. Fetal viability is a matter of great concern for the medical and legal community because of the serious ramifications that occur if a viable fetus is aborted. It is essential for physicians to approximate the date viability will occur. One method is in estimating the size of fetal growth by determining the size of the patient's uterus.

In the 1973 case of *Roe vs. Wade,* the United States Supreme Court held that when viability is reached, a state may exercise concern over safeguarding fetal survival by preventing the abortion procedure, unless it can be proved the health of the mother is in jeopardy. Even in this late stage of pregnancy, a state is forbidden from making any determination as to the viability of the fetus; that remains a medical decision.

Public Funding

Critics of abortion thought it highly improper to use public funds by allowing Medicaid recipients to have elective abortions. Legislation designed to restrict abortions for indigent women on welfare was introduced into Congress in 1976 by Congressman Hyde. The bill and subsequent law became known as the Hyde Amendment. The amendment gave Congress the power to prohibit the use of federal funds to reimburse costs of elective abortions to indigent women under the Medicaid program by adjusting the annual budget of the Department of Health, Education, and Welfare, with exceptions based on individual appeals. Medicaid, however, continues to provide funding for natural childbirth. The Equal Rights Clause of the Fourteenth Amendment does not require states participating in the Medicaid program to pay for elective abortions, even though they have a policy of providing funding for natural childbirth. In 1980 the language of the Hyde Amendment was amended and broadened to include emergency abortion funding for pregnancy that was a result of rape or incest, or placing a woman's life in jeopardy.

The Supreme Court acknowledged that providing funds for natural childbirth but refusing it for abortion is an attractive incentive for natural childbirth. A question over the constitutionality of the use of public funds which provide benefits to some while at the same time refusing them to others is raised.

In conclusion, the Supreme Court stipulated that states have a legitimate interest in seeing to it that abortion like any other surgical procedure is performed under circumstances ensuring maximum safety for the patient. The interest extends to the performing physician and his staff, the facilities involved, the availability of after-care, and adequate provisions for any complications or emergency that may occur. The risk to a woman's health increases as the pregnancy advances to full term. Thus, states retain a definite interest in protecting the woman's health when an abortion is proposed at a later stage of pregnancy. A state's interest also extends to protection of prenatal life. Only when the life of the mother is at stake, balanced against the life she carries within her, should the interest of the embryo or fetus not prevail.

Statistics on abortion released in 1983 showed that nearly 63 percent of the women seeking abortion were between the ages of 15 and 24. Women who had never given birth represented almost 58 percent of those who had had abortions, with the percentage dropping to 20 percent for women who had had at least one child. Approximately 81 percent were not married at the time of the abortion procedure, and unmarried women were twice as likely to have an abortion as their married contemporaries.

1: The United States Supreme Court

The structure of the federal government consists of three branches: legislative (enacts laws), executive (enforces laws), and judicial (interprets laws). The Supreme Court, within the judicial division of the federal system, functions as an appellate court (court of appeals). It was empowered by the Constitution to review constitutional deficiencies of lower-court judgments that are relevant to individual rights and court procedure.

The Supreme Court was authorized by Article III of the Constitution in 1787.

[Section 1.] The judicial Power of the United States, shall be vested in one supreme Court, and in such inferior Courts as the Congress may from time to time ordain and establish. The Judges, both of the supreme and inferior Courts, shall hold their Offices during good Behavior, and shall, at stated Times, receive for their Services, a Compensation, which shall not be diminished during Continuance in Office.

[Section 2.] The judicial Power shall extend to all Cases, in Law and Equity, arising under this Constitution, the Laws of the United States, and Treaties made, or which shall be made, under their Authority; — to all Cases affecting Ambassadors, other public Ministers and Consuls; — to all cases of admiralty and maritime Jurisdiction; — to Controversies to which the United States shall be a party; — to Controversies between two or more States; — between a State and Citizens of another State; — between Citizens of different States; — between Citizens of the same State claiming Lands under Grants of different States, and between a State, or the Citizens thereof, and foreign States, Citizens or Subjects.

In all Cases affecting Ambassadors, other public Ministers and Consuls, and those in which a State shall be Party, the supreme Court shall have original Jurisdiction. In all the other cases beforementioned, the supreme Court shall have appellate Jurisdiction, both as to Law and Fact, with such Exceptions, and under such Regulations as the Congress shall make.

The Trial of all Crimes, except in Cases of Impeachment, shall be by Jury; and such Trial shall be held in the State where the said Crimes shall have been committed; but when not committed within any State, the Trial shall be at such Place or Places as the Congress may by Law have directed.

Two years later (1789), in the Judiciary Act, Congress established procedures and the basic organization of the Court. The first panel of nine jurists was nominated by President George Washington. The Court was convened for the first time in October 1790. During the following years, the number of justices ranged from four to nine, until 1948, when Congress set the number at its present eight associate judges and one chief justice.

Approximately 10 million cases are tried annually in federal and state courts. Nearly 4,500 are approved by the Supreme Court for review, of which the Court acts on approximately 250, or 5 percent of the accepted cases. There are two acceptable procedures in presenting appeals to the Court, by direct appeal or writ of certiorari (a request made by the Supreme Court to lower courts to submit information of a particular judgment in order that a determination can be made whether trial irregularities occurred). In the event no constitutional infirmities are found in a lower-court decision, the Court will convey the message in the form of a refusal to hear the appeal. A simple majority of six jurists must agree on cases to be selected for constitutional review.

The Court convenes on the first Monday of October and continues in session until approximately the middle of June. Fridays are usually conference days when justices confer on cases heard during the previous week and set the Court calendar for the following week. The Constitution requires a simple two-thirds majority in decisions it hands down. In cases of a tie vote, the decision of the lower court is sustained (upheld), with the option of filing another appeal for rearguments at a later date. Justices may express either concurring or dissenting views as part of their decision.

An invitation to argue a case before the Court is considered a high honor. Prior to the hearing, case briefs are presented, with oral arguments limited to 30 minutes. The Supreme Court is the final appeals court, which is why at times it is referred to as "the court of last resort." Once a ruling is handed down, there is no legal recourse, since a rehearing is very unlikely.

The president of the United States is charged with the responsibility of appointing justices to the Supreme Court, with the advice and consent of the Senate. In the selection of potential candidates, a president will traditionally consider the nominee's political point of view rather than judicial prowess. The term of the president is four years; the term of a Supreme Court jurist is for life or until he or she voluntarily retires from the bench. The system makes it possible for the political philosophy of an ex-president to have a profound effect on Court decisions for many years after he leaves office.

2: Texas Statutes on Abortion [Enacted 1857]

Article 1191 (Abortion)
If any person shall designedly administer to a pregnant woman or knowingly procure to be administered with her consent any drug or medicine, or shall use towards her any violence or means whatever externally or internally applied and thereby procure an abortion, [such person] shall be confined in the penitentiary not less than two nor more than five years, [and if such abortion] be done without the woman's consent, the punishment shall be double. By abortion is meant that life of the fetus or embryo shall be destroyed in the woman's womb or that a premature birth thereof be caused.

Article 1192 (Furnishing the Means)
Whoever furnishes the means for procuring an abortion knowing the purpose intended, is guilty as an accomplice.

Article 1193 (Attempt at Abortion)
If the means used shall fail to produce an abortion, the offender is nevertheless guilty of an attempt to produce abortion, provided it be shown that such means were calculated to produce that result, and shall be fined not less than one hundred nor more than one thousand dollars.

Article 1194 (Murder in Producing Abortion)
If the death of the mother is occasioned by an abortion so produced or by an attempt to effect the same, it is murder.

Article 1195 (Destroying the Unborn Child)
Whoever shall during parturition of the mother destroy the life in a child in a state of being born and before actual birth, which child would otherwise have been born alive, shall be confined in the penitentiary for life, or not less than five years.

Article 1196 (By Medical Advice)
[Restricts legal abortion to those procured or attempted by medical advice for the purpose of saving the mother's life.]

Since its enactment in 1857, the Texas abortion law was never amended. The only article not challenged in this action was 1195 (Destroying the Unborn Child).

Roe vs. Wade

Texas abortion statutes, enacted in 1857, restricted legal abortion to women who would place their own life in jeopardy if the pregnancy was carried to term. There were no exceptions or exclusions to the law.

Jane Roe (pseudonym for Norma McCorvey), the plaintiff, was a single woman living in Dallas, Texas, who was pregnant at the time of filing her action in federal court. She was unsuccessful in procuring an abortion because of the strict Texas law, even though the procedure would have been performed in a sanitary and safe facility with a competent physician in attendance.

Because of her inability in obtaining a legal abortion, Roe brought suit against the district attorney, Henry Wade. She asked the court to grant her a ruling that Texas abortion laws were unconstitutional on their face and to prevent the defendant (Wade) from enforcing the statutes.

A three-judge federal district court panel ruled the Texas abortion statutes unconstitutional; they violated the plaintiff's Ninth and Fourteenth Amendment rights. The court ruled in favor of the constitutionality question but rejected the issue of preventing the defendant from enforcing the statutes.

Because of the ruling by the lower court, the case was appealed to the United States Supreme Court, from the United States District Court for the Northern District of Texas (Docket #70-18). It was first argued on December 13, 1971, then reargued on October 11, 1972, and finally decided on January 22, 1973.

On the question of the constitutionality of the Texas abortion laws, the Supreme Court affirmed the finding of the lower court in stipulating that indeed the abortion statutes of the state of Texas were in violation of the Ninth Amendment and the Fourteenth Amendment's Due Process Clause.

For the first time in history, a state's abortion laws were successfully challenged. This decision marked the beginning of the end for the abortion laws of many states.

Right to Privacy

State abortion laws that exempt from criminal action only lifesaving procedures, without regard to the stage of pregnancy, are a violation of the Fourteenth Amendment's Due Process Clause, which protects from any government encroachment the right to privacy, including a woman's right to terminate her pregnancy.

The right to privacy, whether in the Fourteenth Amendment's definition of personal liberty, restricting government intrusion, or the Ninth Amendment's consignment of rights to the people, is broad enough to include the right to have an abortion. In denying a woman the choice of terminating an unwanted pregnancy, the state would create a hardship for the pregnant woman that could result in psychological harm. In addition, her mental and physical health would be severely affected by the stress of bearing an unwanted child.

Regulation of Abortion

Although the right to privacy cannot be overruled by the state, the state does retain an interest in the protection of the health of the pregnant woman and the potential life she carries.

In recognizing a woman's right to privacy, the Supreme Court also acknowledged that the state is entitled to regulate abortion to some degree. During the pregnancy, a state may assert its interest in maintaining the health and standards of medical care for the pregnant woman and the potential life she carries. As the pregnancy advances to term, the interest of the state increases so that during the first twelve weeks of pregnancy, the first trimester, the abortion decision must be left to the medical judgment of the woman's physician. Although abortions performed during the first trimester are not without risk, they are considered safer than normal childbirth. The risk factor is so minimal that no state intervention is required.

For the period following the end of the first trimester, continuing through the second trimester (12th to the 24th week of pregnancy), the interest of the state in the abortion procedure is more constraining but is limited to matters relating to maternal health: the qualifications of the attending physician, the facility where the abortion is to be performed (a clinic or a full-service hospital), to prenatal and postnatal care, and whether the facility is properly licensed for abortions.

Viability, the stage of pregnancy when the fetus is capable of independent survival outside the womb, usually occurs between the 24th and 27th week of pregnancy. During this stage, the state may choose to limit the abortion procedure to women with medical emergencies, where continued pregnancy would place the mother's life in jeopardy. The state has the authority to prohibit the abortion but can do so only after proper medical judgment is made by the woman's physician. Even at this late stage in pregnancy, the state is powerless to make any determination of viability.

[Although the right to privacy as cited in the Fourteenth Amendment does give women the right to have an abortion, the right is not absolute and must be weighed against other factors.]

Physicians performing abortions may be required to be licensed in the state in which the abortion is being performed. Those who do not meet the requirement may be prohibited from performing abortions in that state.

The Court defined *physician* to mean a person who is specifically licensed by the state to perform abortions in the state.

As the pregnancy continues to term, the state has the authority to impose additional restrictions "as it sees fit" on the abortion procedure but must remain within the guidelines of its avowed interest. The physician is morally free in providing medical judgment to the point of intervention by the state. If the physician abuses his trust by improper conduct, judicial remedies are available.

Opinion of the Court:
Read by Justice Blackmun (Paraphrase)

The Texas abortion statutes under attack here are typical of those that have been in effect for nearly a century. . . .

Acknowledged is our awareness of the sensitive and emotional nature of the abortion controversy, of our vigorous opposing views, even among physicians, and the deep, absolute beliefs that the subject inspires. One's philosophies, one's experience of the raw edges of human experience, one's religious training, one's attitude toward life and family and their values, and the moral standards one establishes and seeks to observe are likely to influence and color one's thinking and conclusions about abortion.

Our task, of course, is to resolve the issue by constitutional evaluation, free of emotion and prejudice. The principal attack on the Texas statutes is that they improperly invade a right said to be possessed by the pregnant woman to choose to terminate her pregnancy. One would find this right in the concept of personal liberty embodied in the Fourteenth Amendment's Due Process Clause.

Where certain fundamental rights are involved, limiting these rights is justified only by an asserted state interest.

If a state must enact a statute, it must be made to express the legitimate interest of the state.

We therefore conclude that the right to privacy includes the abortion decision but that that right is not unqualified and must be considered against state interests in regulation.

Viewpoint: Selected Concurring Views
of Justice Stewart (Paraphrase)

In a Constitution for a free people there can be no doubt that the meaning of liberty must be broad. Though the language of the Constitution does not include specific wording mentioning rights of personal choice in concerns of marriage and family life, the liberty protected by the Due Process Clause of the Fourteenth Amendment is broader than those freedoms named in the Bill of Rights. Several decisions of the Court have made it clear that the freedom of personal choice in matters of family life and marriage is one of the liberties protected by the Fourteenth Amendment's Due Process Clause. That right includes the right of a woman to decide whether or not to terminate her pregnancy.

Clearly, therefore, the Court today is correct in holding that the right asserted by the plaintiff is embraced within a personal liberty protected by the Fourteenth Amendment's Due Process Clause. It is evident that the Texas abortion statute infringes that right directly. Indeed it is difficult to imagine a more complete abridgment of a constitutional freedom than that worked by the inflexible criminal statute now in force in Texas.

Protection of the health and safety of the pregnant woman and the potential life she carries within her is the only proper interest of the state. The objectives are important enough to permit a state to regulate the abortion procedure only as it does other surgical procedures. Perhaps in later stages of pregnancy the state should be permitted to restrict the abortion procedure or even to prohibit it.

But such legislation is not before us today, and I think the Court has thoroughly demonstrated that these state interests cannot constitutionally support the broad abridgment of personal liberty worked by existing Texas law. Accordingly, I join the Court's decision holding that the law is invalid under the Due Process Clause of the Fourteenth Amendment.

Viewpoint: Selected Dissenting Views of Justice Rehnquist (Paraphrase)

The Court's opinion brings to the decision of this troubling question both extensive historical fact and a wealth of legal scholarship. While the opinion thus commands my respect, I find myself nonetheless in fundamental disagreement with those parts of it that invalidate the Texas statutes in question, and therefore I dissent.

The Court has decided that during the first trimester of pregnancy, a state is virtually powerless in restricting the abortion procedure. I have difficulty in concluding that the right of privacy is involved in this case. A transaction resulting in an operation such as this is not private in the ordinary usage of that word. Nor is the privacy that the Court finds here a distant relative of freedom from searches and seizures protected by the Fourth Amendment, which the Court has referred to as embodying a right to privacy. If the Court means by the term *privacy* no more than that a claim of a person to be free from un-wanted state regulation of consensual transactions may be a form of liberty protected by the Fourteenth Amendment, there is no doubt that similar claims have been upheld in our earlier decisions on the basis of that liberty. But that liberty is not guaranteed absolutely against deprivation without due process of law.

The fact that a majority of states have had restrictions on abortions for at least a century is a strong indication that the asserted right to an abortion is not so rooted in traditions and conscience of our people as to be ranked fundamental. Even today, when society's views are changing on abortion, the very existence of debates on the issue is evidence that the right to an abortion is not so universally accepted as one would have us believe.

Abortion laws in the United States date back to 1821 when the Connecticut legislature enacted laws that restricted abortion. In 1868, the year the Four-teenth Amendment was adopted, 36 states and territories had already imposed limitations on the abortion procedure.

The Texas abortion statutes invalidated by the Court had been in effect since 1857 and were never amended, while approximately 21 states had laws restricting abortion that were enacted in 1858 and still remained in effect.

At the time the Fourteenth Amendment was adopted, no one questioned the constitutionality of abortion, or any other state-legislated, law.

The only conclusion possible from this history is that the drafters of the Constitution did not intend to have the Fourteenth Amendment withdraw from the states the power to legislate with respect to the issue of abortion.

The Texas abortion statutes are struck down even though the Court apparently concedes that at later periods of pregnancy Texas might impose identical statutes limiting abortion. My understanding of past practice is that a statute found to be invalid as applied to a particular plaintiff, but unconstitu-tional as a whole, is not simply struck down but instead is declared unconstitu-tional as applied to the fact situation before the Court.

The Court's Decision

On January 22, 1973, the Supreme Court voted to affirm in part and to reverse in part the ruling of the district court.

In the opinion of the Court: The Texas abortion statute identified as Ar-ticle 1196 (By Medical Advice) makes no distinction between abortions per-formed earlier or later in pregnancy and limits to a single reason, saving the life of the mother, legal justification for the procedure. Therefore, Article 1196 is ruled unconstitutional, so that Texas abortion laws must fall as a unit; other-wise, the state would be left with statutes that would prohibit all abortions, no matter what the medical emergency. In essence, the Court ruled that only Article 1196 was unconstitutional; however, if the other articles were left in effect without the presence of Article 1196, abortion would be completely banned in the state of Texas. Thus with the invalidation of Article 1196 had to come the voiding of all the remaining Texas abortion statutes.

The opinion of the Court was read by Justice Blackmun and joined by Chief Justice Burger and Justices Douglas, Brennan, Stewart, Marshall, and Powell.

A concurring opinion was read by Justice Stewart. Justice Rehnquist filed the dissenting opinion, in which Justice White joined.

3: Georgia Statutes on Abortion [Enacted 1968]

26-1201 (Criminal Abortion)
Except as otherwise provided in section 26-1202, a person commits criminal abortion when he administers any medicine, drug, or other substance whatever to any woman or when he uses any instrument or other means whatever upon any woman with intent to produce a miscarriage or abortion.

26-1202 (Exception)
(a) Section 26-1201 shall not apply to an abortion performed by a duly licensed physician based on his best clinical judgment that an abortion is necessary because:

(1) Continuation of pregnancy would endanger the life of the pregnant woman or would seriously and permanently injure her health; or,

(2) The fetus would very likely be born with grave, permanent and irremediable mental or physical defect; or,

(3) The pregnancy resulted from forcible or statutory rape.

(b) No abortion is authorized or shall be performed under this section unless each of the following conditions is met:

(1) The pregnant woman requesting the abortion certifies in writing under oath and subjects to the penalties of false swearing to the physician who proposes to perform the abortion that she is a bona-fide legal resident of the state of Georgia.

(2) The physician certifies that he believes the woman is a bona-fide resident of this state and that he has no information which would lead him to believe otherwise.

(3) Such physician's judgment is reduced to writing and concurred in by at least two other physicians duly licensed to practice medicine and surgery, who certify in writing that based on their separate personal medical examination of the pregnant woman, the abortion is in their judgment, necessary, because of one or more of the reasons enumerated above.

(4) Such abortion is performed in a hospital licensed by the State Board of Health and accredited by the Joint Commission on Accreditation of Hospitals (JCAH).

(5) The performance of the abortion has been approved in advance by a committee of the medical staff of the hospital in which the operation is to be performed. This committee must be one established and maintained in accordance with the standards set forth by the Joint Commission on Accreditation

of Hospitals, and its approval must be by a majority vote of membership of not less than three members of the hospital staff; the physician proposing to perform the operation may not be counted as a member of the committee for this purpose.

(6) The proposed abortion is considered necessary because the woman has been raped, the woman makes a written statement under oath, and is subject to the penalties of false swearing, of the date, time and place of rape and the name of the rapist, if known. There must be attached to this statement a certified copy of any report of rape made by any law enforcement officer or agency . . . that according to his best information, there is probable cause to believe that the rape did occur.

(7) Such written opinions, statements, certificates and concurrences are maintained in permanent files of such hospital and are available at all reasonable times to the solicitor general of the judicial circuit in which the hospital is located.

(8) A copy of written opinions, statements, certificates and concurrences is filed with the director of the State Department of Public Health within 10 days after such operation is performed.

(9) All written opinions, statements, certificates and concurrences filed and maintained pursuant to paragraphs (7) and (8) of this subsection shall be confidential records and shall not be made available for public inspection at any time.

(c) Any solicitor general of the judicial circuit in which the abortion is to be performed under this section, or any person who would be a relative of the child within the second degree of kinship, may petition the superior court of the county in which the abortion is to be performed for a declaratory judgment whether the performance of such abortion would violate any constitutional or other legal rights of the fetus. Such solicitor general may also petition such court for the purpose of taking issue with compliance with the requirements of this section. The physician who proposes to perform the abortion and the pregnant woman shall be respondents. The petition shall be heard expeditiously and if the court rules that such abortion would violate the constitutional or other legal rights of the fetus, the court shall so declare and shall restrain the physician from performing the abortion.

(d) If an abortion is performed in compliance with this section, the death of the fetus shall not give rise to any claim for wrongful death.

(e) Nothing in this section shall require a hospital to admit any patient under the provisions hereof for the purpose of performing an abortion, nor shall any hospital be required to appoint a committee as contemplated under **subsection (b)(5)**. A physician, or any other person who is a member of or associated with the staff of a hospital, or any employee of a hospital in which an abortion has been authorized, who shall state in writing an objection to such abortion on moral or religious grounds, shall not be required to participate in the medical procedure. The refusal of any such person to participate therein shall not form the basis of any claim for damages on account of such refusal or for any disciplinary or recriminatory action against such person.

26–1203 (Punishment)
A person convicted of criminal abortion shall be punished by imprisonment for not less than one nor more than ten years.

Georgia's abortion laws, originally enacted in 1876, were modified and patterned after the American Law Institutes' Model Penal Code on Abortion, section 230.3, in 1968.

American Law Institute Model Penal Code [Section 230.3 Abortion]

1) Unjustified Abortion
A person who purposely and unjustifiably terminates the pregnancy of another otherwise than by a live birth commits a felony of the third degree or, where the pregnancy has continued beyond the twenty-sixth week, a felony of the second degree.

2) Justifiable Abortion
A licensed physician is justified in terminating a pregnancy if he believes there is substantial risk that continuance of the pregnancy would gravely impair the physical or mental health of the mother or that the child would be born with grave physical or mental defect, or that pregnancy resulted from rape, incest, or other felonious intercourse. All illicit intercourse with a girl below the age of sixteen years shall be deemed felonious for the purpose of this subsection. Justifiable abortions shall be performed only in a licensed hospital except in case of emergency when hospital facilities are unavailable.

3) Physicians' Certificates: Presumption from Non-Compliance
No abortion shall be performed unless two physicians, one of whom may be the person performing the abortion, shall have certified in writing the circumstances which they believe to justify the abortion. Such certificates shall be submitted before the abortion to the hospital where it is to be performed and in the case of abortion following felonious intercourse, to the prosecuting attorney or police. Failure to comply with any of the requirements of this subsection gives rise to a presumption that the abortion was unjustified.

4) Self Abortion
A woman whose pregnancy has continued beyond the twenty-sixth week commits a felony of the third degree if she purposely terminates her own pregnancy otherwise than by live birth, or if she uses instruments, drugs, or violence upon herself for the purpose of terminating her pregnancy otherwise than by live birth whether or not the pregnancy has continued beyond the twenty-sixth week.

5) Pretend Abortion
A person commits a felony of the third degree if, representing that it is his purpose to perform an abortion, he does an act adapted to cause abortion in a pregnant woman although the woman is in fact not pregnant, or the actor does not believe she is. A person charged with unjustified abortion under subsection (1) or an attempt to commit that offense may be convicted thereof upon proof of conduct prohibited by this subsection.

6) Distribution of Abortifacients
A person who sells, offers to sell, possesses with intent to sell, advertise or display for sale anything specially designed to terminate a pregnancy, or held out by the actor as useful for that purpose, commits a misdemeanor, unless;

(a) The sale, offer or display is to a physician or druggist or to an intermediary in a chain of distribution to physicians or druggists;

(b) The sale is made upon prescription or order of a physician;

(c) The possession is with intent to sell as authorized in **paragraphs (a) and (b)**;

(d) The advertising is addressed to persons named in **paragraph (a)** and confined to trade or professional channels not likely to reach the general public.

7) Section Inapplicable to Prevention of Pregnancy
Nothing in this section shall be deemed applicable to the prescription, administration or distribution of drugs or other substances for avoiding pregnancy, whether by preventing implantation of a fertilized ovum or by any other method that operates before, at or immediately after fertilization.

The ALI Model Penal Code on Abortion was first introduced in 1962 and shortly thereafter adopted in about a quarter of the states. After nearly 90 years, in 1968 the Georgia legislature reworked the state's abortion statutes, which closely reflected abortion laws of Texas, and patterned them after the ALI Model Penal Code on Abortion. Sections 26–1202(a), 26–1202(b) (3, 6), and 26–1202(c) were invalidated by the federal District Court of Northern Georgia. The wording of the statutes was invalidated because limiting the performance of abortion to specifics detailed in the statutes was unconstitutional. The court viewed the abortion statutes as inflexible.

In addition to the statutes ruled unconstitutional by the lower court, the Supreme Court ruled the following to be in violation of the Fourteenth Amendment's Due Process Clause: 26–1202(b), (1–5).

Doe vs. Bolton

The "companion case" to *Roe vs. Wade, Doe vs. Bolton,* which challenged the abortion laws of Georgia, was decided on the same day as *Roe vs. Wade,* January 22, 1973. But that is where the similarities end, because abortion laws in Georgia were much more restrictive than those challenged in Texas.

Abortion laws in Georgia were originally enacted in 1876, remaining in effect and not amended until 1968 when the Georgia Legislature modified many of the original laws by patterning them after the American Law Institute's Model Penal Code on Abortion, which prior to 1973 had been in effect in nearly 25 percent of the states.

The new Georgia abortion laws banned the abortion procedure unless it was performed by a physician licensed in the state of Georgia and in his "best clinical judgment," the life of the mother was in jeopardy or the fetus would be born with a serious defect, or the pregnancy was a result of rape or incest.

A challenge to Georgia's abortion statutes was filed in the federal District Court of Northern Georgia on April 16, 1970, by Mary Doe and 23 others, including physicians licensed to practice in Georgia, clergy, nurses, and social workers. The defendants in this action were the district attorney for Fulton County and the chief of police of Atlanta. Appellants petitioned the court for injunctive relief preventing the defendants from enforcing the abortion statutes and declaratory relief, asking the court for immediate invalidation of the strict abortion laws.

Mary Doe, an appellant in this action, was 22 years old, married, and the mother of three children, two of whom had been placed in foster homes and the third put up for adoption because of Doe's inability to provide for them. At the time she filed the court action, the young Georgia resident was an indigent and nine weeks pregnant. Because her husband had abandoned her and her financial status was poor, she was forced to live with her impoverished parents and their eight children.

It was learned later that Mary Doe and her husband had reconciled their differences and were living together. Her husband, however, worked sporadically as a construction worker, making it almost impossible for her to care for or support her "new" child. Because of all the stress in her life, it was learned, Doe was a patient at a Georgia state mental hospital. It was primarily for these reasons that Mary Doe applied for a therapeutic abortion at Grady Memorial Hospital in Atlanta, on March 25, 1970, under conditions cited in section 26–1202(a). Her request was denied 16 days later (April 10) by the Hospital Abortion Committee, on grounds that her situation was not covered in section 26–1202(a).

Mary Doe interpreted the rejection of her abortion request as an infringement of her constitutional rights to privacy and liberty as related to matters of family, marriage, and sex. In addition, Doe charged that she was deprived of her right to choose if and when she would have children, claiming the rejection of her request was an abridgment of rights guaranteed in the Fourth, Ninth, and Fourteenth Amendments. She contended that since the statutes were constitutionally vague, they discouraged hospitals and physicians from performing abortion procedures. Doe sued "on her own behalf and on behalf of others similarly situated."

The District Court of Northern Georgia granted the appellants declaratory relief by invalidating some of the restrictions for obtaining abortions in Georgia. Held by the court as unconstitutional were provisions restricting legal abortions to incidents of rape, by force or statutory, incest, or to cases in which continuing the pregnancy would place the life of the mother in jeopardy or the fetus would be born with a serious, irreversible mental or physical defect. In essence, the court, in removing a number of the restrictions, made abortion more attainable in Georgia.

Because of the partial victory in the lower court, the case was appealed to the Supreme Court. It was first argued on December 13, 1971, and reargued on October 11, 1972. The case was decided by a split decision on January 22, 1973, the same day *Roe vs. Wade* was decided.

The Court ruled that some provisions still in effect in Georgia violated the Fourteenth Amendment's Due Process Clause, reversing part of the lower-court ruling and invalidating a number of abortion statutes left standing by the lower court.

Judgment of the Physician

Performing an abortion in Georgia was considered a criminal act unless the physician was licensed to practice in Georgia. Section 26–1202 provided in part that a physician might perform abortion if in his best clinical judgment an abortion was necessary, because (1) continued pregnancy would endanger the mother's health, (2) the fetus would be born with a serious mental or physical defect, or (3) pregnancy was a result of rape (forced or statutory) or incest.

Appellants contended that the word "necessary" was related to "a physician's best clinical judgment" and was ambiguous in that it could be misconstrued in a variety of ways. Because appellants found the statute vague, they felt physicians would choose to be cautious in their diagnoses and might opt to make final abortion decisions based on impulse, rather than on their "best clinical judgment."

The Court felt that a physician's decision in performing an abortion based on "his best clinical judgment" was not vague, since the decision could be made in light of all accompanying circumstances. As stated in section 26–1202, "when an abortion is necessary," was considered a professional judgment that a physician would routinely make, no different from decisions physicians make on every patient requiring surgery.

Hospital Accreditation

It was required of the woman in the state of Georgia to have the abortion performed in a hospital that subscribed to the JCAH (Joint Commission on Accreditation of Hospitals). The state did not prove that hospitals with a JCAH accreditation met the required standards for fully protecting the interests of abortion patients. A hospital that did not exclude from preconditions first-trimester abortions would be in violation of the Fourteenth Amendment's Due Process Clause.

The Joint Commission on Accreditation of Hospitals is an organization without government sponsorship. Its primary purpose in accreditation of hospitals is setting high standards for quality patient care and maintaining the highest medical standards. Therefore, the Court stipulated the integrity of the organization was not in question. However, nowhere in the JCAH

Standards of Medical Ethics, was there a mention of abortion as a medical or surgical procedure. The Court considered this to be an infringement of fundamental rights; the JCAH did not address specifically the medical problems related to the abortion procedure.

Appellants presented the Court with a mass of data, showing that facilities other than full-service hospitals were adequate in performing first-trimester abortion procedures. The Court felt compelled to agree with the appellants since the state did not prove that only full-service hospitals were able to comply with state-mandated health and safety requirements.

Hospital Committee

As part of a requirement for an abortion, pregnant women were required to appear before a hospital committee on abortion. The state required the committee to be established and maintained by personnel approved by the JCAH. Before any final approval was made on the abortion procedure, the select committee was mandated to approve abortions only after a majority vote was given; otherwise it was denied. Georgia did not impose this restrictive rule for other surgical procedures performed in the state. Therefore, the Court felt this procedure to be unduly restrictive of patients' rights that were already protected by the physician.

The Court felt it worthy of note that the hospital committee was composed of members of the hospital medical staff. The staff was changed periodically, in order that responsibilities be shared, which in turn made the committee more creditable. The primary function of the committee, besides deciding on abortion procedures, was in protecting the hospital in legal and operational matters. In a modern complex society, with hospitals considered as modern business entities, they must be kept abreast of legal rights and obligations.

In reviewing the Georgia statutes, the Court found no justification for a hospital to have an advance-approval committee. Also, in regard to protection of potential life, which was one of the major reasons for hospitals to sanction such committees, the Court found that medical decisions protecting potential life were made long before any required appearance before a select committee. The Court specifically noted that in the state of Georgia, other surgical procedures did not require appearances before a committee prior to surgery. In addition, under Georgia law, hospitals were not required to admit patients who desired abortion, nor were physicians or other hospital employees required to participate in the abortion procedure if they had a moral or religious objection. If this be the case, the Court felt, then hospitals were likewise free in choosing whether to have a special hospital committee strictly as a precondition for abortion procedures.

Therefore, the Court ruled, the requirement of a special appearance before a committee prior to an abortion procedure was unduly restrictive of the pregnant woman's rights and needs.

Physician's Approval

The state of Georgia required approval by two physicians licensed in Georgia, in addition to the opinion of the woman's personal physician and the approval of three doctors on the hospital committee, a total of six consensual opinions mandated by the state prior to an abortion procedure.

The Court felt the best clinical judgment of the woman's personal physician should be sufficient in making a decision on abortion. Again, no other surgical procedure in the state of Georgia required so many consensual opinions prior to surgery. The Court pointed out that if the attending physician failed to exercise his best professional judgment, there were judicial remedies available.

Residency Requirement

In order for a woman to have an abortion in the state, she had to be a legal resident of Georgia. The Court found this requirement to be a blatant violation of constitutional privileges that protect residents of another state from being denied medical services in a neighboring state.

The argument over justifying the saving of a state's medical facilities for the exclusive use of its residents was not valid since the law included private hospitals as well as private physicians. If the constitutionality of this requirement was upheld, the door would be left open for other states to restrict their health care facilities for the exclusive use of their residents.

Opinion of the Court:
Read by Justice Blackmun (Paraphrase)

In this appeal, the criminal abortion statutes recently enacted in the state of Georgia are challenged on constitutional grounds. We today have struck down as constitutionally defective the Texas abortion statutes that are representative of provisions long in effect in a majority of our states. The Georgia legislation, however, is different and merits separate consideration. The 'new' Georgia provisions enacted in 1968 are patterned after the American Law Institute's

Model Penal Code. The ALI Code has served as the model for recent legislation in approximately one fourth of the states. The 'new' Georgia statutes replaced statutory law that had been in effect for more than ninety years. Georgia laws, 1876, paralleled the Texas laws that had made abortion a criminal act except to preserve the life of the mother.

Appellants in this action argued that present Georgia laws must be viewed historically, that prior to 1968 an abortion in Georgia was not criminal if it was performed for the sole purpose of saving the mother's life. It was suggested that the ALI statute, currently in effect, placed emphasis on the rights of the mother and none for the fetus. Appellants contended that Georgia's "new" abortion statutes were misleading. The newly adopted statutes, according to the appellants, were clear in giving little if any, and certainly not first, consideration to the unborn child; yet, it is the right of the unborn that Georgia asserted was the justification for legislating new guidelines for abortion.

The JCAH-hospital restriction, the hospital committee, the confirmation of two independent physicians, and the residency restriction are all in violation of rights guaranteed in the Fourteenth Amendment's Due Process Clause.

Viewpoint: Selected Concurring Views of Chief Justice Burger (Paraphrase)

I agree that under the Fourteenth Amendment of the Constitution, the abortion statutes of Georgia and Texas impermissibly limit the performance of abortion necessary to protect the health of the pregnant woman, using the term *health* in its broadest medical context. I am somewhat troubled that the Court has taken notice of the various scientific and medical data in reaching its conclusion. However, I do not believe that the Court has exceeded the scope of judicial notice accepted in other contexts. States must have broader power within the limits indicated in the opinions to regulate the subject of abortion, but where the consequences of state intervention are so severe, uncertainty must be avoided as much as possible. For my part, I would be inclined to allow states to require certification of two physicians to support an abortion. I do not believe that such a procedure is unduly burdensome as are the complex steps of the Georgia statute, which requires as many as six doctors and the use of a hospital certified by the JCAH.

The dissenting view discounts the reality that a vast majority of physicians observe standards of their profession and act only on basis of carefully deliberated medical judgments relating to life and health.

Plainly the Court today rejects any claim that the Constitution requires abortion on demand.

Viewpoint: Selected Concurring Views
of Justice Douglas (Paraphrase)

The questions presented in the present cases go far beyond the issue of vagueness. They involve the right of privacy, one aspect of which we considered when we held that various guarantees in the Bill of Rights create zones of privacy. (There is no specific mention of privacy in our Bill of Rights, but the Court's decisions have recognized it as one of the fundamental values those amendments were designed to protect.)

A few years ago, Justice Brandeis defined the right of privacy as the "right to be let alone." The right to privacy includes the right of individuals to plan their affairs without government intrusion. Outside areas of plainly harmful conduct, every American is left to shape his own life as he thinks best, do what he pleases, go where he pleases.

The Georgia statute is at war with the clear message of these cases; that a woman is free to make the basic decision whether to bear an unwanted child. Elaborate argument is hardly necessary to demonstrate that childbirth may deprive a woman of her preferred lifestyle and force upon her a radically different and undesired future. For example, rejected applicants under Georgia statutes are required to endure the discomforts of pregnancy.

Elective, voluntary abortion without restrictions and under questionable medical standards would infringe upon the concerns of many in our society. Part of that concern includes the health and safety of both the mother and the life of the fetus after the stage of viability is reached, not to mention the concerns of parents and loved ones. These concerns heighten a state's justification in treating abortion as it does any other surgical or medical procedure.

The unpredictability of life produces pregnancies which may be unwanted or impair health in the broad sense of the term, or may imperil the life of the mother. In some cases if the pregnancy is carried to term, it may cause suffering, dislocation, misery, or tragedy, which makes an abortion early in the pregnancy justifiable.

Surely there should be no argument over the qualifications of medical personnel and physicians who are involved in the abortion procedure. The legitimate objective of preserving the mother's life clearly supports state regulation of medical personnel. However, the recently adopted Georgia abortion statutes make performing abortions a criminal act, even in the earliest stages of pregnancy. In the light of modern medical evidence suggesting that an early abortion is safer healthwise than childbirth itself, it cannot be seriously urged that so comprehensive a ban is aimed at protecting the woman's health.

The present statute has struck the balance between the woman's and the state's interest wholly in favor of the latter. I am not prepared to hold that a state may equate, as Georgia has done, all phases of maturation preceding birth.

Under Georgia's abortion statutes, the woman's personal physician is not the "sole judge" in making the abortion decision; two other physicians must agree with his diagnosis. Additionally, the abortion must be performed in a licensed hospital, and the abortion must be approved in advance by a committee of the medical staff of that hospital. It is one thing for a patient to agree that her physician may consult with another physician about her case. It is quite a different matter for the state to make it compulsory, to impose another layer of physicians. The right of privacy, the right to care for one's health and person, and to seek out a physician of one's own choice, which is protected by the Fourteenth Amendment, becomes only a matter of theory, not a reality, when a multiple-physician approval system is mandated by the state.

If a licensed physician is derelict in his duty, there are judicial remedies available to punish him or remove his license to practice. Of critical concern is Georgia's imposed control over the medical decision whether an abortion should be performed. The physician whom the woman has placed her full trust in may have his decision overridden, with a "final" decision made by two physicians in whose selection the patient has no choice. This is a total destruction of the right of privacy between physician and patient, and the intimacy of the relation that entails.

The right to seek advice on one's health and the right to place reliance on the physician of one's choice are basic to Fourteenth Amendment values. We deal with fundamental rights and liberties, which as already noted can be contained or controlled only by discretely drawn legislation that preserves the "liberty" and regulates only those phases of the problem of compelling concern.

Abortion is the only medical procedure that the state has chosen to control by imposing restrictions over physician and patient and their decisions. Even if a surgery is more life threatening than abortion, the state imposes no such controls over the procedure. The supervision imposed on the physician and his patient involved in an abortion decision denies them the right to privacy.

The state of Georgia has a constitutional mandate to see that abortion is given the identical concern of any other medical problem. In addition, the state also has a legitimate concern in protecting a woman's right to privacy, but control of the situation must be left to her personal physician.

Protection of the fetus after it has reached viability is an interest that should be protected by the state. However, Georgia's "new" abortion laws make no observable definition on that issue. According to the wording embodied in the statute, the development of the fetus is of little interest to the state if the pregnancy was a result of rape, the fetus would be born with severe mental or physical defects, or the mother's life would be placed in jeopardy if she carried to term. When life is present is a question we do not try to resolve.

Viewpoint: Selected Dissenting Views of Justice White (Paraphrase)

The Court has the authority to do what it did today, but in my view its judgment is an improvident and extravagant exercise of power of judicial review that the Constitution extends this Court.

The Court apparently values the convenience of the pregnant mother more than the continued existence and development of the life or potential life she carries. Whether or not I might agree with that marshaling of values, I can in no event join the Court's judgment because I find no constitutional warrant for imposing such an order of priorities on the people and the legislatures of the states. In a sensitive area such as this, involving as it does issues over which reasonable men may easily and heatedly differ, I cannot accept the Court's exercise of its clear power of choice by interposing a constitutional barrier to state efforts to protect human life and by investing mothers and doctors with the constitutionally protected right to exterminate it. This issue for the most part should be left with the people and the political process the people have devised to govern their affairs.

It is my view therefore that the Georgia statute is not constitutionally infirm because it denies abortion to those who seek to serve only their convenience rather than to protect their life or health. Nor is this plaintiff who claims no threat to her mental or physical health entitled to assert the possible rights of those women whose pregnancies assertedly implicate their health.

Viewpoint: Selected Dissenting Views of Justice Rehnquist (Paraphrase)

The holding in *Roe vs. Wade* that state abortion laws can withstand constitutional scrutiny only if the state can demonstrate a compelling state interest apparently compels the Court's close scrutiny of various provisions in Georgia's abortion statute. Since, as indicated by my dissent in *Roe vs. Wade,* I view the compelling-state-interest standard as an inappropriate measure of the constitutionality of state abortion laws, I respectfully dissent from the majority's holdings.

The Court's Decision

The Court found that although the Texas criminal statutes on abortion were representative of laws that had been in effect in a number of states for nearly a century, Georgia enacted laws that differed, which merited separate consideration by the Court.

On January 22, 1973, the same day the ruling was handed down on *Roe vs. Wade, Doe vs. Bolton* was decided. The Court invalidated additional statutes that the lower court did not act upon. The opinion of the Court was read by Justice Blackmun and joined by Chief Justice Burger and Justices Douglas, Brennan, Stewart, Marshall, and Powell.

An opinion that concurred with the majority opinion was read by Chief Justice Burger and Justice Douglas. The opposing opinion was read to the assembled justices by Justice White; he was joined by Justice Rehnquist, who filed a brief dissenting opinion of his own.

4: Missouri Statutes on Abortion [Enacted 1974]

Section (1): It is the intention of the General Assembly of the state of Missouri to reasonably regulate abortion in conformance with the decisions of the Supreme Court of the United States.

Section (2): Unless the language or context clearly indicates a different meaning is intended, the following words or phrases for the purpose of this act shall be given the meaning ascribed them:

Part 1

"Abortion," the intentional destruction of the life of the embryo or fetus in his or her mother's womb or the intentional termination of pregnancy of a mother with an intention other than to increase the probability of a live birth or to remove a dead or dying unborn child.

Part 2

"Viability," that stage of fetal development when life of the unborn child may be continued outside the mother's womb indefinitely by natural or artificial life support systems.

Part 3

"Physician," any person licensed to practice medicine in this state by the state Board of Registration of the Healing Arts.

Section (3): No abortion shall be performed prior to the end of the first twelve weeks of pregnancy except:

Part 1

By a duly licensed consenting physician in the exercise of his best clinical judgment.

Part 2

After the woman, prior to submitting to the abortion, certifies in writing her consent to the abortion and that her consent is informed and freely given and is not the result of coercion.

Part 3

With the written consent of the woman's spouse, unless the abortion is certified by a licensed physician to be necessary in order to preserve the life of the mother.

Part 4

With written consent of one parent or guardian of the woman, if the woman is unmarried and under the age of eighteen years, unless the abortion is certified by a licensed physician as necessary to preserve the life of the mother.

Section (4): No abortion performed subsequent to the first twelve weeks of pregnancy shall be performed except where the provisions of **Section (3)** of this act are satisfied and in a hospital.

Section (5): No abortion not necessary to preserve the life or health of the mother shall be performed unless the attending physician first certifies with reasonable medical certainty that the fetus is not viable.

Section (6): [Requires the physician to exercise professional care to preserve the fetus life and health; failure to do so would result in filing of manslaughter charges against the physician.]

Part 1
No person who performs abortion or induces an abortion shall fail to exercise that degree of professional skill, care and diligence to preserve the life and health of the fetus which such person would be required to exercise in order to preserve the life and health of any fetus intended to be born and not aborted. Any physician or person assisting in the abortion who shall fail to take such measures to encourage or sustain life of the child and death results, shall be deemed guilty of manslaughter and upon conviction shall be punished as provided in Missouri Law Sec. 559–140. Further, such physician or other person shall be liable in an action for damages as provided in Missouri Law Sec. 537.000.

Part 2
Whoever with intent to do so shall take life of a premature infant aborted alive, shall be guilty of murder of the second degree.

Part 3
No person shall use any fetus or premature infant aborted alive for any type of scientific research, laboratory or other kind of experimentation either prior to or subsequent to any abortion procedure except as necessary to protect or preserve the life and health of such premature infant aborted alive.

Section (7): In every case where a live-born infant results from an attempted abortion which was not performed to save the life or health of the mother, such infant shall be an abandoned ward of the state under jurisdiction of the Juvenile Court wherein the abortion occurred, and the mother and father, if he has consented to the abortion of such infant, shall have no parental rights or obligations whatsoever relating to such infant, as if the parental rights had been terminated pursuant to Missouri Law Sec. 211.411. The attending physician shall forthwith notify said Juvenile Court of the existence of such live-born infant.

Section (8): Any woman seeking abortion in the state of Missouri shall be verbally informed of the provisions of **Section (7)** of this act by the attending physician and the woman shall certify in writing that she has been informed.

Section (9): The General Assembly finds that the method or technique of abortion known as saline amniocentesis whereby the amniotic fluid is withdrawn and a saline or other fluid is inserted into the amniotic sac for the purpose of killing the fetus and artificially inducing labor is deleterious to maternal health and is hereby prohibited after the first twelve weeks of pregnancy.

Section (10): Every health facility and physician shall be supplied with forms promulgated by the division of health, the purpose and function of which shall be the preservation of maternal health and life by adding to the sum of medical knowledge through the compilation of relevant maternal and life data and to monitor all abortions performed to assure that they are done under and in accordance with the provisions of the law.

Part 1

The forms shall be provided by the State Division of Health.

Part 2

All information obtained by the physician, hospital, clinic, or other health facility from a patient for the purpose of preparing reports to the Division of Health shall be confidential and shall be used only for statistical purposes. Such records however may be inspected and health data acquired by local, state, or national public health officers.

Section (11): All medical records and other documents required to be kept shall be maintained in the permanent files of the health facility in which the abortion was performed for a period of seven years.

Section (12): Any practitioner of medicine, surgery, or nursing, or other health personnel who shall willfully and knowingly do or assist any action made unlawful by this act shall be subject to having his license, application for license, or authority to practice his profession as physician, surgeon, or nurse in the State of Missouri, rejected or revoked by the appropriate state licensing board.

Section (13): Any physician or other person who fails to maintain the confidentiality of any records or reports required under this act shall be guilty of a misdemeanor and upon conviction shall be punished as provided by law.

Section (14): Any person who, contrary to the provisions of this act, knowingly performs or aids in the performance of any abortion or knowingly fails to perform any action required by this act shall be guilty of a misdemeanor and, upon conviction, shall be punished as provided by law.

Section (15): Any person who is not a licensed physician as defined in **Section (2)** of this act who performs or attempts to perform an abortion on another as defined in **Section (2), Part 1** of this act is guilty of a felony and upon conviction shall be imprisoned by the Department of Corrections for a term of not less than two years, nor more than seventeen years.

Section (16): Nothing in this act shall be construed to exempt any person, firm, or corporation from civil liability for medical malpractice for negligent acts or certification under this act.

Section (16A): Because of the necessity for immediate state action to regulate abortions to protect the lives and health of citizens of this state, this act is deemed necessary for the immediate preservation of the public health, welfare, peace and safety and is hereby declared to be an emergency act within the meaning of the Constitution and this act shall be in full force and effect upon its passage and approval.

Section (16B): If any provision of this act or the application thereof to any person or circumstances shall be held invalid, such invalidity does not affect the provisions or application of this act which can be given effect without invalid provisions or applications and to this end the provisions of this act are declared severable.

The United States district court, in a divided vote, invalidated sentence 1, section (6), part 1: "No person who performs or induces an abortion shall fail to exercise that degree of professional skill, care and diligence to preserve the life and health of the fetus which such person would be required to exercise in order to preserve the life and health of any fetus intended to be born and not aborted." The sentence was invalidated on grounds that it was overbroad in that it failed to exclude the stage of pregnancy prior to viability.

On July 1, 1976, the Supreme Court invalidated section (3), parts 3 and 4; section (9); and section (6); part 1.

Planned Parenthood of Central Missouri vs. Danford

This case did not involve the rights of an individual; it concerned issues that affected an entire class of people. Two prominent Missouri physicians became concerned with the overly restrictive nature of the abortion laws in the state of Missouri. They felt that because of the restrictions imposed by the strict law, they could not provide their patients with the highest medical standards when performing abortions. They viewed the law as an infringement of their constitutional rights.

The two physicians, one performing abortions at a local hospital, the other supervising abortions at the Planned Parenthood facility of Central Missouri, asked the federal district court for both injunctive and declarative relief. As part of the legal process, plaintiffs filed a class action suit against John C. Danford, attorney general of Missouri on their behalf and "on behalf of the entire class consisting of duly licensed physicians and surgeons presently performing or desiring to perform abortions and on behalf of the entire class consisting of their patients desiring the termination of pregnancy, all within the state of Missouri."

The plaintiffs charged that certain provisions of the law deprived them and their patients of various rights as guaranteed by the Constitution. Some of these rights included (1) the right to practice medicine as they saw fit in assuring their patients that they would receive the highest standard of care available; (2) the right of their female patients to choose whether to bear children; (3) a physician's right to give and a patient's right to expect safe and adequate medical advice and treatment, primarily pertaining to the decision of whether to carry a given pregnancy to term and if not, the method of terminating the pregnancy; and (4) the right of their female patients to be free from cruel and unusual punishment, forcing or coercing women to bear each embryo they conceive.

Provisions of the law plaintiffs found to be in violation of a woman's rights were (1) a requirement that women certify in writing that they were not coerced into an abortion decision, that they made their decision based on their own free will; (2) a precondition that required written permission of the woman's spouse prior to performing a first-trimester abortion; and (3) a requirement for adolescents who were unmarried and under the age of 18 to obtain permission of their parents for an abortion. This restriction did not apply to adolescents under 18 who were married. In addition, there were demands placed on the attending physician to use his best judgment in preserving the life of the fetus; failure to do so would result in criminal charges of manslaughter being filed against the physician. Missouri law also required a fetus that survived an abortion attempt to be made a ward of the court, thus denying the parents any claim to the "live-born" fetus.

The restrictive law also banned one of the most widely used post–first-trimester abortion methods, saline amniocentesis, because lawmakers felt the method was injurious to a woman's health.

The federal district court eliminated some of the language embodied in the provisions, but most of the provisions withstood the challenge, with the exception of sentence 1 of section 6, Standard of Care. The sentence was ruled invalid because it failed to exclude the stage of pregnancy prior to viability.

Because the lower court rejected most of the arguments of the plaintiffs, the case was appealed to the United States Supreme Court. First arguments were heard on March 23, 1976, a decision not being reached until July 1, 1976. By a split vote, the jurists voted to affirm in part and to reverse in part the decision of the lower court.

Of all the abortion cases presented before the Supreme Court, this one proved to be one of the most relevant and topical. The issues presented during the ensuing litigation, though temporarily settling the abortion question in one state, did very little toward finding permanent solutions to the overall problem.

Viability

Probably one of the most controversial and hotly debated topics pertaining to abortion is when life begins. Does it begin at conception, or does it begin at live birth and certainly not before viability is reached? The medical community has pretty much accepted the theory that "live" birth begins when the fetus is capable of independent survival outside the womb, or when the fetus becomes "viable." The point of when viability begins is neither a function of the judiciary or legislative branch of the government; it is exclusively a medical judgment made by the woman's physician.

The determination of viability is a medical concept that sets a specific point in the gestation cycle, usually between the 24th and 28th week of pregnancy. However, since each pregnancy is an individual matter, when viability is reached is variable, thus making it virtually impossible as well as unconstitutional to legislate a specific time when viability will be reached.

Consent of the Pregnant Woman

The Missouri law requires a woman who desires a first-trimester abortion to first certify in writing that her decision was made by her own free will. Primarily, the law was enacted to ensure that women who are understandably under a great deal of stress are made fully aware of their decision. For this reason, it is most important that a decision be made without coercion of any kind; making an error in the decision could lead to both constitutional and legal problems for the state and the attending physician.

The decision to terminate an unwanted pregnancy is not an easy one for most women; therefore, requiring a written consent prior to performing the abortion serves to strengthen their understanding and participation in the procedure. The Court viewed the law as important for any surgical procedure and entirely valid.

Consent of the Spouse

The Court viewed a requirement of approval by the spouse prior to a first-trimester abortion as unconstitutional. In its opinion the Court reiterated that states are powerless in delegating a veto power to a spouse that the state itself is absolutely prohibited from effectuating.

Defendants argued that the statute became law after the Missouri General Assembly went on record defining marriage as an "institution." The feeling was that a number of states required joint consent in respect to artificial insemination and the legitimacy of children so conceived. Similar legislation requires joint consent for voluntary sterilization and adoption of a child. A child requires changes within the family's structure, which are set into motion by mutual or joint consent. They felt that abortion should be treated in a like manner.

Plaintiffs counterargued that a situation might occur in which the father of the child could not be located to approve the abortion, which in some cases could lead to very serious consequences.

It was also felt that in marriages where both partners are so fundamentally divided on such a critical issue, this requirement could not be considered either ideal or successful.

Plaintiffs summed up their argument by stating that the requirement is vague and was enacted primarily to give the spouse the right to prevent or "veto" an abortion, whether or not he was the father of the fetus.

Parental Consent

In previous court decisions it had been stipulated that states are prohibited from imposing a "blanket" parental-consent requirement covering all minors regardless of maturity as a precondition for a first-trimester abortion procedure. The presumed interest of the state did not justify it "safeguarding" a family unit by requiring parental consent authority for an adolescent or unmarried pregnant woman. The ultimate decision maker must be the woman's personal physician because abortion is a medical judgment.

Missouri required parental consent for all pregnant women under the age of 18 years and not married prior to arranging for an abortion. The only exception allowed was where the abortion was certified as a necessity to save the life of the pregnant minor.

The law was defended by the appellees as solid legislation. They argued that certain decisions are considered to be outside the ability of a minor to react in his or her best interest or in the interest of the public. As examples they cited the fact that there are laws banning the sale of firearms, tobacco, and alcoholic beverages to minors. Additionally, minors are prohibited from purchasing or viewing sexually explicit or extremely violent material. Court records showed that minors as young as 11 years of age had sought abortion, making it a necessity to allow states to legislate making abortion impermissible to minors who want it on demand without the counsel of a responsible adult. They argued that to supply such abortion on demand would constitute an irresponsible renunciation of the duty of a state in protecting the welfare of minor children.

Plaintiffs argued that Missouri did not require consent of parents for a minor child who desired other surgical or medical treatment. The law specifically singled out abortion as its prime target. The contention of plaintiffs was that minors could legally consent to medical services pertaining to pregnancy, excluding abortion, and the treatment of venereal disease or drug abuse. The law was seen as discriminatory in that it did not apply to minors under 18 who were either married or emancipated.

The primary disagreement with this statute was that states were prohibited from imposing a "blanket" law requiring parental consent as a precondition to a first-trimester abortion. They explained that states do not have the authority to give a "third" party an absolute and possibly a discretionary veto over the abortion decision. Directing its comments toward this important issue, the Court stipulated that minors and adults are protected by constitutional rights.

But the Court did not want to suggest that every adolescent regardless of age or maturity may give effective consent for termination of pregnancy. The problem with Missouri's law is that it imposes a special consent provision by a person other than the woman or her physician. There is no justification for this form of restriction as a prerequisite for a teenager or unmarried woman to terminate her unwanted pregnancy.

The Saline Amniocentesis Abortion Method

In the 1970s, one of the most common methods of abortion for post–first-trimester procedures, up to the 16th week of pregnancy was saline amniocentesis. In the mid–1970s, however, this method was banned in the state of Missouri, even though the procedure was considered to be safer than continuing a pregnancy to term. It was theorized that if the restrictive law was enforced, physicians would be encouraged to use methods that were far more dangerous to the woman's health. The legislative banning of saline was felt by many to be an unreasonable regulation designed for no other purpose than to prevent the majority of abortions after the first 12 weeks of pregnancy.

In the saline-amniocentesis abortion, amniotic fluid is withdrawn, and saline or other fluid is inserted into the amniotic sac. Missouri law prohibits this method on grounds that it is harmful to maternal health. Plaintiffs argued that the provision virtually banned all post–first-trimester abortions. The argument was substantiated by the fact that nearly 70 percent of all abortions performed after the first trimester used the saline-amniocentesis method. Plaintiffs also pointed out that the method is safer than normal childbirth. It would be possible for the Missouri statute to withstand the challenge if there was a safer method of inducing abortion after the first 12 weeks.

Appellees managed to shove aside some very pertinent facts in their arguments in regard to saline. They failed to recognize that saline amniocentesis was one of the most widely accepted methods of abortion in this country. Saline was used in a majority (testimony from both sides showed that actual percentages ranged from 68 percent to 72 percent) of first-trimester abortions. Missouri's statute banned the use of saline while not prohibiting techniques that were considered to be many times more likely to result in maternal death. The banning of saline would force the pregnant woman and her physician to terminate her pregnancy by methods far more dangerous to her health than the outlawed method.

Preserving the Life of the Fetus

The debate over when life actually begins has been argued for centuries. The Supreme Court declared that it need not resolve the difficult question of when life begins, when those trained in the respective disciplines of medicine, philosophy, and theology are unable to arrive at any consensus. The judiciary at this point in the development of man's knowledge is not in a position to speculate as to the answer.

In essence, the statute required any physician who performed abortions to use his best professional skill and care in preserving the life and health of the fetus, which would be required of him if the fetus was intended to be born and not aborted. The statute further stated that if the physician failed in taking the above-described measures, resulting in the death of the fetus, charges of manslaughter could be filed against him.

The Court ruled the first sentence of section 6(1) to be unconstitutional because it failed to mention stages of pregnancy.

Appellees contended that the first sentence of the statute established the standard of care that applied to the person performing the abortion and that the second sentence described the conditions when that standard of care applies. Appellees further explained that despite reference to a fetus in sentence 1 of the statute, the standard of care mentioned is only conditional upon "live" birth.

The argument of the plaintiffs differed in that it focused more on the language of the statute, the manner in which it effectively banned abortions and imposed a standard of care without regard to the stage of pregnancy.

Retaining Medical Records and Information

In the view of the Court, the reporting and record-keeping requirement can be beneficial to a state's interest in protecting the health of its female citizens and may be of some medical value for future abortion procedures. The Court found this provision not constitutionally defective, especially if extra care was taken in maintaining the confidentiality of such records. The Court further found that this provision in no way interfered with the abortion decision of the patient and her doctor.

Missouri's statute requiring information on abortions had only one purpose — to assist in the preservation of maternal health and life, adding to the sum of medical knowledge by gathering pertinent data and monitoring abortions to assure they were being performed under the guidelines prescribed by law. The records and data had to remain confidential, used primarily for statistical purposes.

Plaintiffs argued that record keeping imposes yet another layer of regulation on the abortion decision. However, the Court completely rejected the plaintiffs' argument, stipulating that the reports and files would prove to be beneficial as a learning tool for abortions performed in the future. Finally, the Court agreed that the edicts of the statute were not an interference in performing abortions.

Opinion of the Court:
Read by Justice Blackmun (Paraphrase)

In *Roe vs. Wade,* we used the term *viable* properly to signify the point at which the fetus is "potentially able to live outside the womb." We noted that the point of viability is usually placed at about seven months or 28 weeks, but may occur earlier. We agree with the district court and conclude that the definition of viability as described in section 2(3) does not conflict with what we said and held in *Roe vs. Wade.*

(The Court agreed with the finding of the lower court in regard to requiring consent of the pregnant woman prior to an abortion procedure being performed because it "assured her control of the abortion procedure over the prudence of her consulting physician." In agreeing with the decision of the lower court, the Supreme Court commented that the requirement did not single out abortion but included all surgeries performed in Missouri hospitals. Because the Court did not find this provision to be constitutionally defective, it withstood the challenge made by the plaintiffs.)

(The Court held that a state is constitutionally prohibited from requiring the written consent of the woman's spouse prior to an abortion procedure being performed. Yet section 3(3) specified this procedure as a precondition to a first-trimester abortion procedure. However, the Court stipulated that a state cannot delegate to a spouse a veto power the state itself is prohibited from exercising.) We are fully aware of the deep concern and interest that a devoted husband has in his wife's pregnancy and in the development of the fetus she's carrying. This Court has not failed to recognize the importance of the marital relationship in our society. We additionally understand the profound effect that an abortion decision may have on the future of any marriage; however, despite those factors, we cannot give to the states the constitutional authority to bestow upon the spouse absolute power of veto in the decision of whether or not to terminate a pregnancy.

It would be ideal if the husband and wife could agree on a decision to terminate a pregnancy. The feelings of only one can prevail when both are fundamentally opposed to an abortion. However, since the woman bears all of the pain and physical discomforts of pregnancy, the decision should be hers.

It is difficult to conclude that providing a parent with absolute power to overrule a decision made by a physician and his minor patient to terminate her pregnancy would benefit in strengthening the family unit. It is not likely that placing a veto power in the hands of parents will enhance parental authority or control where the minor and nonconsenting parents are so fundamentally in conflict. (The Court, in invalidating the parental-consent provision, did not want its ruling to be misconstrued by other minors desiring abortion as the Court's condoning every minor's terminating her unwanted pregnancy.)

The defect found with section 3(4) was that it gave consent privileges to a person other than the pregnant woman and her physician. It clearly violates the strictures set by the Court in *Roe vs. Wade* and *Doe vs. Bolton*.

We held in *Roe vs. Wade* that after the first stage of pregnancy, the state may if it chooses, regulate the abortion procedure in ways that are related to maternal health. The question surrounding section 9 is whether the absolute prohibiting of saline amniocentesis as an abortion procedure is a restriction which relates to the preservation and protection of maternal life.

The district court, in sustaining Missouri's ban on the use of saline, made reference to "safer" methods of producing an abortion. The "safe" techniques included (1) hysterotomy and (2) prostaglandin infusion injection. (The Court, in commenting on the lower-court decision, cited the fact that the lower court failed to take into consideration that saline amniocentesis at the time of this litigation was an acceptable method for a majority of post–first-trimester abortion procedures, as well as being the method of choice for many physicians.) Evidence presented before the court showed that comparatively, maternal-related deaths were substantially higher for normal childbirth than saline amniocentesis. In addition, the lower court failed to acknowledge that the use of prostaglandin infusion injection was not well known or in wide use in this country, nor was it made known to the court whether the method was available to residents of Missouri. Also not considered by the lower court was the inherent idiosyncrasy of the statute, which bans the use of saline, a method proven to be safe, but fails to prohibit the use of methods that are far more injurious to maternal health.

The banning of saline amniocentesis as an acceptable abortion procedure was an unjust regulation designed only to inhibit the majority of post–first-trimester abortion procedures.

Viewpoint: Selected Concurring Views of Justice Stewart (Paraphrase)

Justice Stewart wrote the concurring opinion, in which Justice Powell joined.

While joining the Court's opinion, I write separately to indicate my understanding of some of the constitutional issues raised by this litigation.

The definition of viability in section 2(2) has almost no operative significance. The state has required physicians who perform abortions to certify in that the fetus to be aborted is not viable. For failure to issue a certification, the physician may face criminal charges. However, if he erroneously concludes that a fetus was not viable, there may be no charges filed.

Section 3(2), regarding a pregnant woman's consent to an abortion, regulates the abortion during all stages of pregnancy; however, I do not feel that it conflicts with what we held in *Roe vs. Wade*.

Regarding section 3(3), consent of the woman's husband, previous decisions have recognized that a man's right to father children and to enjoy the offspring is a constitutionally protected freedom. However, I concur with the Court, simply because it is the woman who physically bears the child, who is more directly affected by the pregnancy; the balance weighs in her favor.

With respect to laws requiring parental consent: The constitutional deficiency of the statute is that it allows for an absolute limitation of the minor's right to obtain an abortion. The question of whether to abort or not is a critical evaluation for a young minor female to make while under extreme emotional distress. She may be ill-equipped to make a proper decision without mature adult advice and emotional support. It seems very unlikely that she will obtain adequate counsel and support from the attending physician at an abortion clinic, a place where adolescents usually seek abortions.

Viewpoint: Selected Views of Justice Stevens, Concurring in Part, Dissenting in Part (Paraphrase)

If both abortion methods, saline and prostaglandin, had been equally available to the physician performing abortions, the Court would not have overturned the district court's ruling in banning the method it found to be less safe, even though proscribing the use of saline does not reflect the opinion of the medical community. A statute that called for the complete banning of saline would be equivalent to the complete proscription of second trimester abortions. A restriction of the magnitude statute section 9 would impose upon the women of Missouri would be inconsistent with the essential holding of *Roe vs. Wade* and therefore could not withstand a constitutional challenge.

In my opinion the parental consent requirement is consistent with the holding of *Roe vs. Wade*. A state's interest in the welfare of its younger citizens constitutes a justification for imposing a number of protective laws, primarily because many adolescents do not have the maturity or prudence required to understand the consequences involved in important decision making, especially a decision that is irreversible. For example, adolescents can't sign legally enforceable contracts, be employed in certain businesses, or view sexually explicit or extremely violent movies. In addition, they cannot get married legally without parental consent; this includes female adolescents who are pregnant. Protecting young people from physical and mental harm is a major concern of lawmakers, which justifies imposing restraints on certain activities they may engage in. However, placing similar constraints on adults would be unconstitutional. The Fourteenth Amendment's Due Process Clause protects a woman's right to have an abortion, but the conclusion should not be made that state legislatures are powerless to enact laws for the specific purpose of protecting young women from the severe consequences of an incorrect decision.

The decision to have an abortion is one of the most important resolutions for a young female to make. The reason why care must be taken to avoid a wrong decision is that unlike other decisions minors make, abortion is irreversible. The severity associated with making an error in an abortion decision justifies maximum interest by the state in seeing that the decision be made correctly and with full understanding of the consequences involved with either alternative.

The major concern of lawmakers is that the significant consequences of the abortion decision are not medical ones, which makes it logical for a state to insist on the proper counseling prior to an abortion being performed. Including a parent in any of the decision making process is surely not irrational thinking.

Presumably, if there were an absence of parental-consent requirements, minors would enter into agreements without informing their parents; this includes the abortion decision. Many adolescent females believe that their parents will react with anger when told of the pregnancy. It is an unrealistic assumption to make that every parent-child relationship is so ideal that parents will be understanding of their daughter's dilemma or that the parent-child relationship is so poor that there is no communication at all. I assume that parents will make errors in judgment in rejecting a daughter's decision to have an abortion, a decision which might have been beneficial to all had it been allowed. Similarly, doctors at times incorrectly conclude that a decision to abort would outweigh alternative decisions. Parents sometimes have the ability to evaluate the advantages and disadvantages from a different perspective.

The Court seems to assume that the capacity to conceive a child and the judgment of the attending physician are the only constitutionally acceptable regulations for determining whether a young woman can make the abortion decision. Each individual case contains factors many times more complicated than mere medical judgment. The overriding consideration is that the right to make a choice be exercised as wisely as possible.

I think the state has the power to legislate to select a minimum age for an independent abortion decision. In my opinion, that a state professes to have an interest in the welfare of its youth is sufficient to support a parental-consent requirement.

Viewpoint: Selected Views of Justice White Concurring in Part, Dissenting in Part (Paraphrase)

Justice White wrote the opinion, in which Chief Justice Burger and Justice Rehnquist joined.

In *Roe vs. Wade*, we held that until the fetus becomes viable, the interest of the state in potential life is outweighed by the interest of the mother in choosing whether or not to terminate her pregnancy. A Missouri statute prohibits the abortion from taking place unless the husband agrees to the procedure in writing. The entire statute was invalidated by the Court because of the wording of one sentence. The state is powerless in prohibiting abortions and is also barred from passing on the authority to another person, including the spouse. Nowhere does the statute mention that the state is attempting to delegate authority to another person; rather it is recognizing the interest of the husband and father in the life of the fetus. The rights of the father should not be nullified by a one-sided decision made by the mother. The idiosyncrasy of the statute allows the rights of the mother to preponderate, which results in the state not being able to protect the rights of the father. It is truly surprising that the majority opinion finds a rule in the Constitution that grants a pregnant woman absolute authority to cut off potential life by abortion while completely rejecting a father's decision to let the fetus live and mature. In describing a mother's interest in terminating a pregnancy, the Court, in *Roe vs. Wade*, stressed the obligation and sacrifices associated with postchildbirth, while at the same time rejecting the argument that a woman can do with her body as she pleases. Missouri has a law that prevents a woman from putting a child up for adoption if her husband objects. The law is valid, but no more so than section 3(3), now before us, resting on the same judgment.

Section 3(4) requires that an unmarried woman who is under 18 years of age obtain consent of a parent as a condition to an abortion. Once again the Court has invalidated a provision with one sentence. The parental-consent requirement was invalidated by the Court for the identical reason that section 3(3) was invalidated; the state does not have the authority to give a third party an absolute authority arbitrarily to veto a decision made by the physician and his patient.

The decision to terminate a pregnancy is one of the most important decisions a woman will ever make since the procedure is irreversible. It is for this reason that Missouri is entitled to protect unmarried adolescents from making a decision which may not be in their best interest. A popular method used to protect children from their own immaturity and ill-advised decisions is requiring parents to participate in providing guidance and consent.

Saline amniocentesis, an abortion procedure used in approximately 75 percent of all post–first-trimester abortions, was prohibited in the state of Missouri. In prohibiting the use of saline, the Missouri legislature viewed it as not as safe as prostaglandin infusion injection, even though the method was not in wide use in this country. The Court took testimony and evidence on the use of saline amniocentesis and summarized its findings. The trial record discloses that the use of saline exposes a woman to the dangers of severe complications, regardless of the skill of the physician or the amount of precaution taken. Saline use may cause one or more of the following conditions: (1) Disseminated intravascular coagulation or 'consumptive coagulapathy' (disruption of the blood clotting mechanism), which may lead to severe bleeding and possibly death. (2) Hypernatremia (an increase in the blood/sodium level), in some cases causing convulsions and death. (3) Water intoxication (accumulated water in the body tissue; a condition occurring at times when oxytocin is used with saline); this may result in damage to the central nervous system, leading to death. Saline amniocentesis has also been known to cause tissue destruction to the inside of the uterus.

When the district court outlawed the use of saline as a method for second-trimester (post–first-trimester) abortions, it suggested the use of a much safer method: prostaglandin injection. Doctor Anderson, chief of obstetrics at Yale University, recommended that physicians should be liable for malpractice if they chose saline over prostaglandin, after being informed on the facts of both methods.

The Court has decided (despite the facts presented) to reverse the decision of the district court on the saline issue, citing several reasons for reaching its decision: (1) saline was widely used before Missouri passed its statute banning the use, (2) the prostaglandin method of abortion was seldom used and not generally available in the state of Missouri, and (3) other techniques more dangerous than saline were not banned from use. The majority finding on this issue is based on a single fact that the prostaglandin method was unavailable to the women of Missouri. Justice Blackmun alluded to the fact that prostaglandin injection was not widely used in this country as an acceptable abortion procedure. Appellees also failed to produce evidence showing the method was available in the state of Missouri. The Court therefore concluded that the proscription of the saline method as an accepted method of abortion was unreasonable and arbitrary, and designed specifically to inhibit the vast majority of abortions after the first 12 weeks of pregnancy.

No evidence was presented that would substantiate the finding of the majority opinion that women in Missouri were unable to locate abortion facilities using the prostaglandin infusion injection method. Lower-court records showed that the method was second to the use of saline in abortions performed in this country. Prostaglandin infusion injection was used for a time as an experimental abortion procedure, but the method was available for public use in smaller facilities around the country during the time of this litigation. Dr. Anderson, chief of obstetrics at Yale University, testified that if saline was outlawed, hospitals would quickly switch to the prostaglandin method. The Court reached its majority opinion based on the testimony of one doctor, who noted that indeed prostaglandin had been available since early 1974. In what manner this evidence supports the assertion that the method was unavailable to the women of Missouri escapes me!

The legislative history of section 9 clearly shows that the statute was passed on June 14, 1974; that evidence to sustain the ban on saline was taken in July 1974; that action to overturn the ban was filed in January 1974; and that the Court judged the statute banning saline as unconstitutional in July 1976. However, in 1974, the Upjohn Company issued a statement regarding the distribution of prostaglandin injection: Sales would be restricted to larger facilities for a period of six months, afterwards sales would be unrestricted. There was never substantial evidence presented that would lead one to believe that prostaglandin injection was not available during the entire span of this investigation. The majority ruling held that women would not be able to have an abortion after the first 12 weeks of pregnancy if saline was banned. This ruling was unjustified.

Section 6(1) requires the physician to preserve the life of the fetus if it can survive independently outside the womb, regardless of the wishes of the mother. The statute requires the physician to exercise the care that would be expected of him if the circumstances were normal childbirth instead of abortion. The statute applies to abortions performed in the "gray" area of pregnancy, between the 24th and 27th week of pregnancy, the stage in which there is a possibility the fetus will be born live during an abortion attempt. The judgment of viability is made and certified by the woman's physician. It is incredible that the Court has interpreted the statute in a manner that requires the physician to preserve the life of the fetus, whatever the stage of pregnancy, thereby rendering a statute passed by the Missouri legislature incapable of surviving a constitutional challenge.

There is not the slightest reason to believe that the Missouri legislature would not require proper care for live births just because it cannot require physicians performing abortions to take care in preserving the life of the fetus. The attorney general of Missouri has argued that the only intent of the statute was in requiring physicians to support a live baby that resulted from an abortion.

The Court's Decision

On July 1, 1976, amid much dissension between jurists and an overriding split of opinions, a majority opinion was reached on Missouri's abortion statutes. Justices voted to affirm in part and to reverse in part the ruling of the lower court.

The opinion of the Court was read by Justice Blackmun and joined by Justices Brennan, Stewart, Marshall, Stevens, and Powell. Justice Stewart read an opinion agreeing with the majority, which was joined by Justice Powell. While Justice Stevens did join in the majority decision, he expressed objections to the Court's invalidation of the statute that banned saline amniocentesis as an abortion procedure and the statute requiring written consent by the woman's husband. Stevens read his opinion before the Court, concurring in part and dissenting in part.

Justice White wrote an opinion concurring in part and dissenting in part and was joined by Chief Justice Burger and Justice Rehnquist. Although the three did agree in part, they voted to dissent.

5: Massachusetts Abortion Statute [Sec. 12P] [Enacted 1974]

Part 1

If the mother is less than eighteen (18) years of age and has not married, the consent of both the pregnant adolescent and her parents are required. If one or both of the minor's parents refuse such consent, it may be obtained by order of a judge of the Superior Court, after good cause is shown; a hearing shall not require that a guardian be appointed for the pregnant adolescent.

If one of the parents has died or has deserted his or her family, consent by remaining parent is sufficient. If both parents have died or have deserted the family, consent of the guardian of the minor or other person having duties similar to a guardian or any person who has assumed care and custody of the minor is sufficient.

Part 2

The commissioner of public health shall prescribe a written consent form for such consent. Such form shall be signed by the proper person or persons and given to the physician performing the abortion who shall maintain it in his permanent files.

Nothing in this section shall be construed as abolishing or limiting any common law rights of any person or persons relative to consent to the performance of an abortion for the purposes of any civil action or any injunctive relief under [Sec. 12R].

Bellotti, Attorney General of Massachusetts vs. Baird

One of the primary concerns of this action was the question of abortions for adolescents versus the degree of legal jurisdiction parents may exercise over the wishes of their daughter in making the abortion decision. This was a 1974 case, but the issues were still hotly debated in the late 1980s.

Massachusetts enacted a statute regulating abortions in that state for adolescents. In 1974, the act was known as "An act to protect unborn children and maternal health within present constitutional limits." The act, more

47

commonly known as section 12P, will hereafter be referred to as such. The statute defined and governed the type of consent required prior to an abortion for an unmarried woman under the age of 18. Plaintiffs in this action were the Parents' Aid Society, Inc., a nonprofit corporation providing abortion services and counseling to women considering an abortive remedy. Its president and director, William Baird, along with four pregnant minors who wished to have an abortion without their parents' knowledge, brought this case before the court. The four claimed to be representing all others who were capable of giving mature, informed consent to an abortion without parental intervention. However, because section 12P required permission of both parents, plaintiffs brought a class-action suit against the defendants, the attorney general of Massachusetts and the district attorneys of all counties in the commonwealth. Plaintiffs asked for both injunctive and declaratory relief, claiming that the statute in question was a violation of their Fourteenth Amendment rights. The court allowed a third party as an intervenor in the proceedings — Jane Hunerwadel, a resident of Massachusetts and parent of an unmarried teenager of childbearing age. Hunerwadel, given the title of intervenor-appellant in the proceedings, represented all other parents similarly situated.

On October 31, 1974, a single-judge United States district court issued a restraining order, blocking the enforcement of section 12P while agreeing to have the conflict heard before a full court of three judges. Later, a three-judge district court panel ruled the statute unconstitutional. The court felt the statute added another "tier" to the abortion decision, thus allowing for a veto of a decision reached earlier by the physician and his adolescent patient.

Defendants, not satisfied with the ruling, appealed the decision of the lower court to the Supreme Court. The defendants became the appellants, and the plaintiffs took on the role of appellees as part of the process of appealing the case to the Court. After careful consideration of all issues pertaining to this complex case, a decision was reached on July 1, 1976. The Court was unanimous in vacating (nullifying) the decision of the lower court, thus reinstating the statute.

Parental Consent

Plaintiffs viewed section 12P as a form of parental veto. At some time in the future a court might inadvertently misinterpret the statute as requiring the consent of parents of a mature minor capable of giving informed consent for the abortion. A judicial error of this type could prove to be unduly burdensome for minors who are responsible citizens.

Defendants agreed that indeed the language of the statute was a bit vague and could be misconstrued as requiring consent of parents for all minors seeking an abortion. However, even though their preference would be to have a law requiring all minors to obtain permission for an abortion from their parents, they insisted that the language in the statute provided special consideration for minors who are mature by allowing them the option of obtaining a court-ordered abortion without consent of the parents if the teenager was able to show that an abortion would be in her best interest.

In *Planned Parenthood vs. Danford,* the Court invalidated a statute requiring parental consent, which it viewed as being a form of parental veto while upholding a law requiring written consent of a pregnant adult. However, this case differed in that the implied restrictions of the statute were aimed at persons unmarried and under 18 years of age. In the eyes of the law, people who fall into the above-mentioned age group and marital status are considered too immature to consent to an abortion. The problem with this statute and others that place a "blanket" restriction on minors by presuming that because they are unmarried or under 18, they possess very little maturity was that legislators place very little emphasis on a person's individuality. Assumptions like this lead to questions of constitutionality when they are considered inflexible by the public.

If this statute was upheld by the Court, it would be difficult to predict the ramifications that could arise in one particularly sensitive area — the patient-physician relationship.

Opinion of the Court:
Read by Justice Blackmun (Paraphrase)

Appellants made the following observations on section 12P: (1) The implication of the statute is that parents are entitled to more than just a simple requirement of communication between the adolescent and her physician. They commented that although the restrictive elements of this statute are not apparent now, in the future it could become a part of some state legislation. (2) The language of the statute fails to exclude mature adolescents who are capable of providing intelligent, informed consent; the only conclusion that may be made for now is that the restrictions of this statute include all minors. The statute does recognize consent of some minors to an abortion without parental approval; however, the recognition is somewhat limited in that if the approval does not come from parents, it must be by court order. (3) Supposedly, the statute does contain a provision for consent to an abortion by a mature minor; however, plaintiffs have argued that the way the statute is worded, it gives probable "veto" rights to parents that are independent of a minor's personal interest. Many view the statute as a layer of restriction for the abortion procedure because no matter what the circumstances, parents must be consulted.

Plaintiffs contended that the Fourteenth Amendment and the Bill of Rights were not drawn up for the sole protection of adults. They argued that a state does not have the authority of exercising more control over a first-trimester abortion of a minor than of a mature adult. They further argued that the statute was not written to protect minors, as defendants would have one believe, but to recognize the rights of parents. Essentially, the question raised by the statute is whether parents possess the authority, aside from counseling and providing guidance, to veto the abortion decision. Should they have rights to compete for something that is already theirs?

The defendants, of course, viewed the statute from a different perspective. They argued that in a situation where an abortion is desired by an adolescent, there should be no objection, constitutional or otherwise, to providing minors with an extra layer of protection in order to ensure that the decision for an abortion will be a correct one, even if it entails receiving guidance from parents or a judge. Furthermore, the statute allows both parents to become part of an important decision, each providing valuable input in assisting their pregnant daughter during a very stressful time in her life. If both parents, however, decide to abstain from making a decision, it is then left to the discretion of the court. If the court finds the adolescent to possess a high level of maturity, she will be granted the right to exercise her constitutional rights to terminate her pregnancy.

The 1974 statute will continually be vulnerable to constitutional scrutiny because of the almost "invisible" meaning behind its interpretation. The wording of the statute prefers parental consent and guidance, at the same time allowing mature minors to obtain a court order for the abortion without notifying parents. The statute, in addition, allows immature minors the option of a court-ordered abortion without parental intervention if the adolescent can show the court that the abortion would be in her best interest.

The Court's Decision

The Supreme Court first heard the case on March 23, 1976, and after much debate declared in essence that section 12P may appear to be inflexible but does provide options for minors desiring to terminate an unwanted pregnancy.

Justice Blackmun delivered the opinion of the Court, ruling that the judgment of the lower court was invalid, thus vacating (nullifying) that decision.

This was a rare occasion when the Court's decision was unanimous.

6: The Connecticut Welfare Department Abortion Regulation [Sec. 275] [Enacted 1975]

The department makes payments for abortions under the Medical Assistance (Title XIX) Program when the following conditions are met:

(1) In the opinion of the attending physician the abortion is medically necessary. The term *medically necessary* includes psychiatric necessity.
(2) The abortion is to be performed in an accredited hospital or licensed clinic when the patient is in the first trimester of pregnancy.
(3) The written request for the abortion is submitted by the patient and, in the case of a minor, the parent or guardian.
(4) Prior authorization for the abortion is secured from the Chief of Medical Services, Division of Health Services, Department of Social Services.

Maher, Commissioner of Social Services of Connecticut vs. Roe

The Equal Protection Clause of the Fourteenth Amendment does not require a state participating in the Medicaid program to pay for elective abortions for indigent women simply because it has a policy to pay for natural childbirth.

The Connecticut Welfare Department enacted a regulation restricting state Medicaid payments for first-trimester abortions to those that are "medically necessary." In order to obtain authorization for an abortion, a welfare recipient must procure from the facility where the abortion procedure is to be performed a certificate of approval by the attending physician stating that the abortion is medically necessary. This procedure applies to first-trimester abortions only.

The appellees in this court action were two indigent women who were denied a certificate of medical necessity. At the time of this litigation, Mary

Poe was 16 and had obtained an abortion at a Connecticut hospital but was unable to pay for the services. Because her abortion was not considered a medical necessity, the Department of Social Services refused to reimburse the abortion facility. Susan Roe was a mother of three children and unmarried at the time of this court action. Roe was unable to have an elective abortion because her physician refused to certify that the procedure was medically necessary. Both Poe and Roe brought an action attacking the constitutionality of the regulations as violating their Fourteenth Amendment rights of Due Process and Equal Protection before the federal District Court for the State of Connecticut.

A three-judge district court panel held the Connecticut regulation to be invalid, stating that the Equal Protection Clause of the Fourteenth Amendment forbids the exclusion of first-trimester nontherapeutic abortions from a state's welfare program that subsidizes medical expenses for pregnancy and childbirth.

The case was appealed to the Supreme Court for further evaluation. Arguments were presented on January 11, 1977. On June 20, 1977, the Court ruled that the decision of the lower court was in error and reversed its ruling, thus reinstating the original regulation.

Medicaid Payments for Abortions

The Constitution does not obligate states to pay pregnancy-related expenses to indigent women on welfare. However, a state that is compassionate to its citizens and interested in their welfare may decide to ease the hardships of its poverty-ridden residents by providing medical-care benefits to its indigents. The Constitution does limit the manner in which payments of federal funds are disbursed.

Medicaid Payments to Indigent Pregnant Women

A financial need does not specifically recognize a certain segment of society (the indigent) for the purpose of equal-protection analysis.

This case does not involve discrimination against a certain class of society. Guidelines expressed in the Constitution do not recognize an indigent pregnant woman in need of funds for an abortion as part of a disadvantaged class. In closely examining the Equal Protection Clause, the Court has never distinguished persons in need of welfare assistance (alone) as part of a separate class.

The question concerns the Connecticut regulation for abortion procedures, specifically in relationship to indigent women. The determination must be made whether the regulation represents government encroachment upon certain fundamental rights explicitly or implicitly protected by the Constitution. The Court established in *Roe vs. Wade* that women do have a fundamental right to an abortion, concluding that nothing less than a binding interest of the state in the abortion procedure would justify treating a termination-of-pregnancy procedure and natural childbirth differently.

Prohibiting Abortion for Indigent Women

The Medicaid regulation of abortion in Connecticut was not intended to violate a woman's fundamental right to terminate her pregnancy. An indigent woman's decision to have an abortion is not infringed upon by a state that chooses to fund childbirth and not elective abortions. The system appears to be fair in that it allows the pregnant woman to make a value judgment, as the state is allowed to do in choosing to prefer natural childbirth over abortions.

This case differs from other abortion cases argued before the Court. The Connecticut regulation of abortions does not in any way prohibit women from exercising their constitutional rights to have an abortion. Although it is understandable that state preference of natural childbirth over abortion makes childbirth an attractive option, no attempt is made to place an indigent woman who desires to have an abortion at a disadvantage. The state has not imposed any restrictions on a woman's access to the abortion procedure; she is virtually free to seek private sources for her desired services.

Connecticut lawmakers acknowledged the difficulty indigent women may experience in seeking an abortion, which she may not be able to afford; however, the Medicaid restriction cannot be held responsible for creating or effectuating the situation. It must therefore be concluded that the Connecticut Medicaid abortion restriction does not interfere with the definition of fundamental rights that the Court validated in earlier decisions. The Supreme Court found Connecticut's Medicaid program of preferring childbirth over abortion a rational approach in furthering the interests of the state.

Abortion for the Indigent: Obligations and Concerns

States have a vested interest in protecting the potential life of the fetus; the interest increases as the pregnancy advances to full term. States also have an interest in future population growth and increasing medical costs for natural childbirth, which already far exceed the cost of a first-trimester abortion. Funding childbirth makes it an attractive option for women to consider.

The Court acknowledged that the regulation does influence the decision of many women.

Lawmakers, though aware of the plight of indigent women who desire but cannot afford an abortion, commented that the Constitution was not intended to remedy every social and economic situation. The decision to provide public funds for nontherapeutic abortions is accompanied with judgments of policy and values, over which opinions are greatly divided. The Court concluded that the Connecticut regulation is not constitutionally defective. The decision is not based on the wisdom of the regulation or its social desirability. Laws are not subject to invalidation simply because they do not agree with a certain philosophical belief.

Upon ruling that the Connecticut Abortion Restriction was valid, the Court stipulated that the decision should not be misconstrued as a total ban of government funding for nontherapeutic abortions. The funding of a state's Medicaid program is not a function of the Court; it is the responsibility of Congress. Regardless of the outcome of this litigation, Connecticut is still free to choose whether to provide funds for elective abortions.

Opinion of the Court:
Read by Justice Powell (Paraphrase)

Title XIX of the Social Security Act does not require the funding of nontherapeutic abortions as conditional in participating in the joint federal-state Medicaid Program. Involved in this litigation is the question of whether providing public funds for natural childbirth is constitutional if they are denied for women desiring nontherapeutic first trimester "elective" abortions.

The Connecticut Welfare Department limits state Medicaid benefits for nontherapeutic abortions to those defined as medically or psychiatrically necessary. To qualify for public assistance for obtaining an abortion, it is necessary for the attending physician to submit a certificate attesting to the fact that the abortion is a medical necessity to the facility where the abortion is to be performed prior to executing the procedure. The appellants, both indigent women, were unable to obtain the necessary certification from their attending physicians. They challenged the constitutionality of the Connecticut Medicaid regulation in court on grounds the rules were in violation of the fundamental rights guaranteed in the Due Process Clause of the Fourteenth Amendment.

The Constitution does not require states to pay medical expenses of indigents. However, when a state decides to alleviate some of the adversity of poverty by providing medical-care benefits to some indigents while denying similar assistance to others, a question of constitutionality arises.

The question of constitutionality was entered into the Court record by appellees who contend that Connecticut must provide funding for abortion if it allows financial assistance for indigents who have a normal childbirth. Furthermore, adopting a philosophy that is one-sided by displaying preferential treatment for one group of women while denying equal consideration for others is unconstitutional.

The Court is certainly not unsympathetic to the plight of the indigent woman who desires an abortion, but the Constitution does not provide judicial remedies for every social and economic ill.

Viewpoint: Selected Concurring Views of Chief Justice Burger (Paraphrase)

I join the Court's opinion (reversing the lower-court opinion). I do not read any decision of this Court that requires a state to fund nontherapeutic abortions. We held in *Roe vs. Wade* and *Doe vs. Bolton* that a state should not create barriers for women who desire abortions over natural childbirth. Our previous rulings should not be misinterpreted as imposing an obligation on states to assist a woman in her decision to have an abortion.

A part of sound public policy is for lawmakers to provide citizens who are in need with certain health and social services. Encouragement of childbirth and childcare is not a novel undertaking in this regard. Many governments, both in this country and abroad, have encouraged childbirth and child care for centuries. The decision to provide or not to provide funding for medical or other needed services is not a requirement the Constitution imposes upon any state. In addition, the Constitution does not provide for equal funding of programs for the needy.

In conclusion, the Connecticut legislature has created no barriers for a woman desiring an abortion, nor does the regulation require the state to provide such services.

Viewpoint: Selected Dissenting Views of Justice Brennan (Paraphrase)

Justice Brennan wrote the dissenting opinion, in which Justice Blackmun joined.

The district court, in reversing the Connecticut restriction, held that Connecticut's refusal to fund elective abortions, while at the same time providing necessary funds for natural childbirth, child care, and therapeutic abortions, place a restriction on the pregnant woman in choosing to exercise her constitutionally protected rights to have an abortion which is elective. The woman's choice is affected by the obvious absence of public assistance for abortions and the availability of funds for natural childbirth. When a state infringes upon fundamental rights, it automatically asserts a compelling interest.

The majority decision is a misinterpretation of the basic issue involved in this litigation of fundamental rights that the Court upheld in *Roe vs. Wade.*

The Connecticut legislature's use of public funds for natural childbirth has made it an attractive alternative to abortion and has probably contributed to the decision of many women to forgo abortion. Indigent women may have difficulty in obtaining an abortion without the assistance of public funds, and, as regrettable as the situation may be, the full blame for the conditions that exist cannot be placed entirely on the Connecticut Welfare Regulation because the regulation neither created nor influenced the established restrictions. Nevertheless, there is evidence of massive insensitivity embodied within the language of the regulation, its primary target being women who are both pregnant and impoverished. The deplorable reality of the situation is that although a woman's access to the abortion procedure is not blocked, there are tiers of restrictions, denying her services of the best and most competent physicians available simply because she cannot afford the luxury. In weighing the choices available to her, a woman who is needy and financially unable to have an abortion will be "forced" into carrying her pregnancy to full term, giving birth to a child that she cannot afford to feed or care for; all this because Connecticut's Welfare agency will pay for medical expenses attributed to childbirth. Disbursing state funds is a useful maneuver in coercing indigent pregnant women to bear children that they would otherwise elect not to have. Using financial pressure can only be successful when employed against the "vulnerable," in this case the indigent pregnant woman.

In *Roe vs. Wade* and *Doe vs. Bolton,* the Court stipulated that any state that funds the costs of natural childbirth is obligated to provide funding for elective abortions. The Connecticut regulation is intended to intrude upon an area of privacy (in litigation that has followed *Roe vs. Wade* and *Doe vs. Bolton,* courts have generally held that there is an area of privacy protected against state encroachment, which surrounds the abortion decision), by placing financial pressure on the indigent woman. Although the intent of the imposed regulation may not have been to prohibit all indigent women from electing to have an abortion, the critical point here is that the state has interfered with a fundamental right of women in making a choice that is free of government influence. However, Connecticut is not alone; many states have at various times throughout history interfered with an individual's fundamental right of choice.

Finally, the reason why the Connecticut welfare regulation is unconstitutional is that it requires a prior written certification by the attending physician testifying to the fact that the abortion is a medical necessity in addition to requiring that the abortion facility submit a request for authorization of professional services, including a statement indicating the necessity for the abortion procedure.

The Court's Decision

The case of *Maher vs. Roe* was first heard by the Court on January 11, 1977, and decided on June 20, 1977. The majority opinion of the Court reversed the ruling of the lower court, stipulating that it was not unreasonable for states to insist upon a showing of medical necessity in order to be assured that Medicaid payments were made for legitimate reasons. The district court's invalidation of the requirement to obtain a written request by the pregnant woman and a Department of Social Services authorization prior to having an abortion was an error of judgment by the lower court, probably resulting from a misinterpretation of the regulation. The Court found that invalidating the regulation was not reasonable, even though there were no similar restrictions imposed on other surgical procedures, the primary reason being that other surgical procedures do not involve the termination of potential life.

Justice Powell read the opinion of the Court and was joined by Chief Justice Burger and Justices Stewart, White, Rehnquist, and Stevens. In addition to joining in the majority opinion, Chief Justice Burger wrote a concurring opinion.

Justice Brennan wrote the dissenting opinion. He criticized his colleagues for misinterpreting the primary issue involved in this litigation, the fundamental rights of an individual, which the Court held as the primary problem at issue with *Roe vs. Wade* and *Doe vs. Bolton*. Justice Blackmun joined in the dissenting opinion, and while Justice Stevens did not directly join in the opinion expressed by Justice Brennan, he did dissent from the majority opinion.

7: Massachusetts Abortion Statute [Sec. 12S(P)] [Enacted 1974(77)]

The state of Massachusetts originally enacted this statute (sec. 12S) in 1974, but during the entire litigation of *Bellotti vs. Baird* in 1976, the statute was referred to as section 12P. In 1977, the state officially changed the numerical designation of the statute to 12S. The only noteworthy change to the statute was in dropping the numbered subsections; otherwise, the language remains as originally stated in 1976.

The text of the statute may be found at the beginning of Chapter 5.

Bellotti, Attorney General of Massachusetts vs. Baird (II)

On July 1, 1976, the United States Supreme Court ruled unanimously in favor of section 12P, invalidating an earlier decision reached by a three-judge district court panel.

Almost three years later, on February 27, 1979, arguments began before the Supreme Court on Massachusetts abortion statute section 12S. The statute was the same as section 12P; however, the numerical designation was changed in 1977, and will henceforth be referred to as section 12S. Apparently the statute was never enforced during the years following the original litigation in 1976. This was primarily due to numerous delays and "stays" of enforcement issued by the Court, in order that a decision could be reached on all appeals associated with the merits of the statute.

Plaintiffs were William Baird, founder and director of Parents' Aid Society; Gerald Zupnick, M.D., who performed abortions at the Parents' Aid Clinic; and Mary Moe (pseudonym), who was pregnant, unmarried, and living with her parents at their home during this litigation. Plaintiff Moe desired an abortion, which was denied on grounds that she did not want to inform her parents of her decision. The court allowed Moe to represent other minors who were similarly situated in her class-action suit.

Defendants in this action were the same persons who participated in 1976; Bellotti, attorney general of Massachusetts, and the district attorneys of all counties in the state. Also returning to represent all parents of unmarried minor daughters of childbearing age was Jane Hunerwadel, as "intervenor-defendant."

Section 12S requires parental consent prior to an abortion on an unmarried woman who is under the age of 18. If one or both of the parents refuse to grant consent, the abortion may be obtained by order of a judge of the superior court if "good cause" can be shown by the minor. Because of the restrictive nature of this statute, Mary Moe and other interested parties filed a class action suit challenging the constitutionality of the law.

The United States district court, hearing the appeal, proposed questions to the Supreme Judicial Court of Massachusetts, two of which were: Does the statute permit minors, mature or immature, to obtain judicial consent for an abortion, without first consulting parents? and If the court finds the minor capable of giving mature informed consent, will it refuse to grant permission for an abortion on grounds that the minor's parents have made a better decision? In replying to the first question, the court stipulated that consent must be obtained for every nonemergency abortion unless the minor's parents for some reason are unavailable. However, parents who are available must be given proper notice of any court proceeding involving a minor who is seeking an abortion. To the second question, the court answered without lengthy comment in the affirmative.

As was the case in 1976, the district court held the statute to be unconstitutional. The United States Supreme Court again vacated the lower-court ruling, remanding it back to the supreme judicial court for further evaluation. Following a judgment of reversal by the supreme judicial court, a three-judge United States district court panel once again declared the statute to be unconstitutional. And again the case was appealed to the Supreme Court. Arguments began on February 27, 1979.

After all arguments were heard, the Supreme Court this time ruled to affirm the judgment of the lower court insofar as it invalidated this statute.

Constitutional Rights of Adolescents

There are three primary reasons why many lawmakers believe that rights of adolescents cannot be equal to that of adults: (1) their inability to make critical decisions, (2) their vulnerability, and (3) their need for special guidance that only parents can provide.

There are some instances, however, when the rights of a child are equal to those of adults. During juvenile court proceedings, the Fourteenth Amendment's guarantee of due process of law is applicable. Additionally, minors are entitled to have the assistance of an attorney and may confront their accusers if they wish. If the juvenile court finds the youthful offender guilty beyond a reasonable doubt, he or she is not protected or excused from being incarcerated. Minors may also assert Fifth Amendment (self-incrimination) protection.

Although juvenile offenders are afforded some equal-right guarantees, the juvenile court system treats them differently. In order to maintain and preserve the difference, the court allows juvenile hearings to proceed in a manner that does not entirely conform with every requirement of an adult criminal trial. For instance, the Constitution does not guarantee juveniles a trial by jury; however, this method allows the state to adjust the legal process to account for the "innocence" of a child.

In previous litigation, the Court had held that a state has a valid right in limiting freedoms for adolescents in making decisions that may have serious emotional and physical consequences. The Court had recognized that from childhood to adolescence, minors lack the experience and judgment to make certain choices that could prove to be troublesome to them.

Many lawmakers assume that when parents provide the proper guidance in raising their children, it justifies limiting constitutional freedoms for adolescents. Ideally, states and parents are partners in protecting youth from their immaturity. In order that this system function properly, states have the responsibility of requiring parental consent and involvement in important decision making while parents are responsible for the emotional development of their child. Thus, together, the state and parents have a major role in preparing the nation's youth for future obligations.

The Adolescent and the Abortion Decision

The abortion decision is much different from most others made by minors, and thus states are required to consider the sensitivity of the matter prior to legislating any laws that encourage parental involvement in the abortion decision.

Section 12S declared that Massachusetts has taken the responsibility in reconciling the rights of a woman in consultation with her physician to terminate her pregnancy and the advice of her parents if she is unmarried and under 18 years of age. The question to be decided by the Court was whether section 12S provided for parental consent and notice without becoming burdensome and adding a tier of restriction to the abortion decision.

Plaintiffs contended that in its current interpretation by the court, the statute does indeed constitute an undue burden for pregnant minors who are mature and capable of giving informed consent. The situation is different for immature minors. For them the state must consider imposing a parental-consent restriction prior to the abortion.

Although the Fourteenth Amendment's Equal Protection Clause does not specifically mention rights of pregnant minors, its language may be interpreted as including protection for the minor when a state requires consent of both parents prior to an abortion. It must balance the law with an alternative method of approval for the procedure. In addition, a well-balanced law will provide pregnant minors with every opportunity to prove that they are mature and can make a rational decision in consultation with their physicians, without parental involvement. Minors who are incapable of making an independent decision may also seek the security afforded by the Equal Rights Clause. However, in order to accomplish this, they must obtain a court-ordered abortion, which will be granted only after the minor convinces the court that terminating her pregnancy would be in her best interest. In any case, when a state enacts a parental-approval law, it cannot be overly restrictive or impose an absolute parental veto of the abortion decision.

One cannot compare the everyday problems minors face with the abortion decision. Solutions to problems other than abortion can, in most cases, be postponed; however, a decision to terminate an unwanted pregnancy cannot be delayed since time is of the utmost importance.

Legislators who add tiers of restriction to the abortion decision are worlds apart from the emotional trauma women face when making a difficult decision of whether to terminate an unwanted pregnancy. It is most unfortunate that laws do not reflect the human, sensitive, and emotional side of the abortion decision. Besides the task of overcoming legal difficulties, much of the abortion dilemma rests with making decisions over future education, employment, job skills, financial resources, and the stress associated with the responsibility of an unwanted motherhood. Adding to the distress is the concern that a proper decision was made. Since abortion is irreversible, an incorrect decision could lead to a lifetime of emotional scars and guilt.

Terminating a pregnancy may not be the right answer for all minors, and if this is the case, perhaps an alternative plan should be discussed; for instance, marrying the father of the child, arranging for an adoption, or assuming the role of motherhood.

The Court felt that because of the physical and emotional ramifications involved with the decision to have an abortion, it is almost imperative that the decision be made without the involvement of a third party. If the law requires it, however, then the third party must not have an absolute and arbitrary power of veto over the abortion decision. It is therefore concluded that if a state requires approval of both parents prior to an abortion being performed, it should also allow for a substitute method of consent.

The supreme judicial court had interpreted section 12S as creating an undue burden to minors who are mature and seek abortion. The statute was constitutionally defective in two areas: (1) It permitted withholding of judicial consent for an abortion of a minor who has proved to the court that she is mature and capable of making an independent, fully informed decision. (2) It required parental consultation for all minors, regardless of their best interest. The statute did not permit the minor to obtain independent court verification attesting to her level of maturity in consenting to an abortion or that the procedure would be in her best interest. When arguments over the Massachusetts abortion statute are presented before a superior court judge, he must immediately reject all pleadings that have no relevance to the primary issue of the minor's best interest.

Parents usually have strong feelings (mostly negative) toward abortion. Adolescents who live with their parents are usually pressured into conforming with the rules of the house, whether or not the policies of the parents are in their child's best interest. In households that are restrictive, abortion is not often a topic of discussion between adolescents and their parents, but even more difficult is gaining access to the courts so that a ruling can be made on the abortion decision, which may override parental authority without infuriating the parents.

A law such as that enacted by the state of Massachusetts must allow for every minor to have direct access to a judicial remedy of her abortion dilemma, without requiring direct participation of her parents in the decision-making process. If the court finds the minor to be competent in making an intelligent decision on her own, she must be allowed to proceed with the abortion procedure without the consent of or consultation with her parents.

Of noteworthy interest is the fact that Massachusetts generally prefers a family resolution of the abortion dilemma rather than a judicial one. The state is of the impression that a majority of parents do take an active interest in the well-being of their children, which is particularly evident in families with strong ties.

Opinion of the Court:
Read by Justice Powell (Paraphrase)

There is no doubt that a female's right to have a first-trimester abortion is not dependent on her calendar age. The Court found no justification for the parental-consent restriction placed on that right as defined in section 12S since it has been concluded that the statute was enacted not to protect the rights of minors but to protect the fundamental rights of parents.

During this litigation, the Court was shown that many adolescents 17 and under are capable of providing mature and informed consent to an abortion procedure. It would not be in the best interest of every minor, who is incapable of giving mature consent, to inform her parents of her intention to have an abortion. Also determined was the fact that Massachusetts did not have the authority to insist that parents be notified in situations where the court has been given the responsibility of absolute authority over the minor's decision to have an abortion. The important point of law to remember is that states do not have the authority to override the jurisdiction of the court.

In finding section 12S constitutionally defective, the district court stipulated that judges do not have the authority to deny abortions to minors who are capable of giving informed consent to the procedure. In its ruling, the court reasoned that restrictions, judicial or otherwise, can't be placed on an adolescent who has proven her maturity beyond a reasonable doubt. Therefore, Massachusetts went overboard in restricting abortion when it drafted the language of section 12S because it creates an undue burden for the "mature" pregnant minor. But in addition, the court found the law to be discriminatory in that it denies the targeted age group equal protection of the law.

The language of the statute was vague on one important issue. It failed to define clearly that the only issue parents should consider in granting permission for an abortion is whether it would be in the minor's best interest. The vagueness of the statute would inevitably lead to a misinterpretation of the statute's meaning by well-intentioned parents. The weakly defined statute would cause parents to veto the abortion decision for other than the primary reason, resulting in a wrongful denial of the abortion. All of this would force the pregnant teenager into seeking a court-ordered remedy to the situation, with the probability that the court would override the parents' veto of the abortion, which might cause an angry division between the parents and their pregnant adolescent. The character of the family unit in our society requires that laws be applied with a blend of sensitivity and flexibility.

The state requires consent of both parents for abortion approval, whereas other surgical procedures require the consent of one parent. Nothing about abortion requires the minor to be treated differently. As a general rule, the requirement of consent from both parents is not unconstitutional in the sense of placing additional burdens or tiers of restriction on a minor's decision to have an abortion. The abortion has far greater consequences than any other medical treatment. When both parents are together and the adolescent resides in her parents' home, at least one of the parents, statistically speaking, will be supportive of the minor's dilemma. As stated earlier, the primary concern of parents in assisting their daughter with the abortion decision is to center their emphasis of support on the issue of what would be in their daughter's best interest. If parental consent is denied, the minor must have the option of presenting her case to the court with a prompt judicial resolution of her situation.

The Massachusetts Supreme Judicial Court held that the role of the judge is not limited to ruling simply on the issue of adolescent maturity or if an abortion would be in her best interest; rather the judge, in making his final ruling, must take into account all of the relevant facts presented and base that finding on the preponderance of evidence.

The Court agrees with the finding of the district court when it held that the decision of the minor who has proven herself to be mentally competent and to possess a full understanding of the seriousness of the abortion procedure cannot be neglected by the court; to do so would be a violation of her constitutional rights.

Viewpoint: Selected Concurring Views of Justice Rehnquist (Paraphrase)

I join in the opinion and the judgment of this court affirming the ruling of the lower court invalidating section 12S. At such time as this Court is willing to reconsider its earlier decision in *Planned Parenthood vs. Danford,* in which I joined the opinion of Justice White, dissenting in part, I shall be more than willing to participate in that task. But unless and until that time comes, literally thousands of judges cannot be left with nothing more than the guidance offered by a truly fragmented holding of this Court.

Viewpoint: Selected Concurring Views of Justice Stevens (Paraphrase)

Justice Stevens read his concurring opinion to the Court and was joined in his opinion by Justices Blackmun, Marshall, and Brennan.

In *Roe vs. Wade,* the Court held that a woman's right to terminate her pregnancy was embodied in the Fourteenth Amendment's Due Process Clause. In *Planned Parenthood vs. Danford,* the Court ruled that an adolescent had the right to decide on abortion without the condition that she obtain approval from at least one parent.

The Massachusetts statute in question has no hidden meaning; it contains language that is to the point. Clearly stated is that every woman under the age of 18 and unmarried, must receive approval of both parents before she may consent to an abortion. If one or both parents refuse consent, she has the opportunity of seeking judicial assistance from the superior court if she can prove good reason for a court-approved abortion. Both parents will be informed by the court that their daughter has initiated a court action to be granted permission for an abortion. During the term of litigation, the court will determine whether the abortion would be in the minor's best interest. The superior court judge will make a final ruling based on the preponderance of evidence presented during the hearing, and though he may consider the maturity level of the minor as part of his final judgment, it will not necessarily influence his decision either way.

According to Massachusetts law, pregnant minors who are capable of providing mature and informed consent to an abortion have the same rights as immature minors who lack the understanding necessary to comprehend the seriousness of a wrong decision. One may interpret the Massachusetts statute as stipulating that maturity of minors is not a factor in requiring parental consent prior to an abortion, that all minors must obtain the approval of both parents; if they are unavailable, a judge of the superior court, acting as a third party, may choose to veto the abortion decision, regardless of the maturity of the adolescent.

In *Planned Parenthood vs. Danford,* Missouri had a law that in some respects "mirrored" Massachusetts law. The Missouri law however required the approval of one parent and had no provisions for a substitute or alternative abortion approval. Massachusetts, on the other hand, does allow a judge of the superior court to act as a substitute authority, with the power of granting or overriding the abortion decision of the minor. However, the basic similarities of the laws in both states are that they impose restrictions on the right of a minor to have an abortion, without taking into consideration the minor's level of maturity.

Allowing a judge to have an absolute and arbitrary veto over the abortion decision made by a minor can be problematic. Along with a woman's right to have an abortion is her right to privacy and a guarantee that her decision will not be scrutinized by a third party. Section 12S is defective by constitutional standards because if for some reason a minor is unable to obtain an approval from both of her parents, she must risk her right to privacy by seeking a court-ordered remedy, thus becoming the focal point of judicial scrutiny by a judge of the superior court, who becomes an "uninterested" third party and has the power to veto the entire procedure.

Finally, the Massachusetts statute is potentially more restrictive than the statute in Missouri in respect to limiting a woman's constitutional right to terminate an unwanted pregnancy.

Viewpoint: Selected Dissenting Views of Justice White (Paraphrase)

I dissented in *Planned Parenthood vs. Danford* on the validity of requiring the consent of a parent when an unmarried woman under 18 years of age seeks an abortion. The arguments presented in this court have not been convincing enough to warrant changing my views. During *Danford*, I agreed with much of what Justice Stevens had said in his dissenting opinion. I would therefore not be in favor of invalidating this Massachusetts law.

But even if a parental-consent requirement of the type involved in *Planned Parenthood vs. Danford* was ruled invalid, that decision should have little to do with denouncing the Massachusetts law, which provides for alternative consent by a third-party intervenor (judge) if both parents refuse to give consent. The third-party intervenor has the authority to override the objections of the young woman's parents in deciding whether the abortion would be in the minor's best interest. But "going beyond" *Danford*, the Court has held unconstitutional an effort of the state to inform parents of their daughter's intentions to have an abortion; this move by the Court also denies parents the right to participate in any judicial hearing that will determine if undergoing abortion will be in the minor's best interest.

Until now, I would have thought inconceivable a holding that the United States Constitution forbids even notice to parents when their minor child who seeks abortion objects to such notice and is able to convince a judge that her parents should be denied participation in the decision.

With all respect, I dissent.

The Court's Decision

After nearly three years of delays and court-ordered "stays" that prevented section 12S from being enforced, final arguments on its merits began on February 27, 1979. It was not until July 2, 1979, that a final ruling on the matter was presented by the Court. The Court, in reversing its original 1976 ruling, voted this time to affirm the decision of the United States district court insofar as it invalidated this statute.

Justice Powell read the opinion of the Court, which severely criticized section 12S as constitutionally defective in at least two critical areas: (1) It permitted the court to deny authorization of an abortion of a minor who was found to be mature and fully competent. (2) It required parental notification and consultation, regardless of the minor's maturity, without giving her the opportunity of obtaining an independent judicial remedy of her situation. Joining the opinion were Chief Justice Burger and Justices Stewart and Rehnquist.

Justice Rehnquist filed a concurring opinion with some reservations. Justice Stevens also filed an opinion concurring with the majority holding and was joined by Justices Marshall, Brennan, and Blackmun.

Justice White, the lone dissenter, read a brief opinion denouncing his colleagues for their apparent inconsistency in handing down decisions. Justice White compared the decision in *Planned Parenthood vs. Danford*, in which a Missouri law was struck down that required parental approval of a minor seeking an abortion, to the just completed litigation over a Massachusetts law that permitted intervention by a third party, a judge of the superior court, without receiving the slightest condemnation by the Court. White explained it this way: In one state a law is struck that requires participation of the youth's parents, yet in another state the court allows participation without comment from a third party to intervene in the abortion decision. The superior court judge possesses the power to overrule the wishes of the young woman's parents, in addition to denying parents of any participation in the abortion decision of their daughter if their daughter requested that she objected to her parents' intervention.

8: Pennsylvania Abortion Control Act [Enacted 1974]

Title 35, Section 6605(a)
Protection of the Life of the Fetus

Every person who performs or induces abortion shall prior thereto have made a determination based on his experience, judgment, or professional competence that the fetus is not viable, and if the determination is that the fetus is viable or if there is sufficient reason to believe that the fetus may be viable, shall exercise that degree of professional skill, care, and diligence to preserve the life and health of any fetus intended to be born and not aborted, and the abortion technique employed shall be that which would provide the best opportunity for the fetus to be aborted alive so long as a different technique would not be necessary in order to preserve the life and health of the mother.

Title 35, Section 6605(d)

Any person who fails to make the determination provided in section (a) of this section, or fails to exercise the degree of professional skill, care and diligence or to provide the abortion technique as provided for in section (a) shall be subject to such criminal or civil liability as would pertain to him had the fetus been a child who was intended to be born and not aborted.

Colautti, Secretary of Welfare of Pennsylvania vs. Franklin

Over the veto of the governor of Pennsylvania, the state legislature passed the Abortion Control Act of 1974. Only days before the act was to go into effect (October 10, 1974), a suit was filed in the United States District Court for the Eastern District of Pennsylvania by the plaintiffs, identified as John Franklin,

M.D., a licensed and board-certified obstetrician and gynecologist and director of Planned Parenthood of Southern Pennsylvania, a nonprofit corporation; Concern for Health Options, Information, Care and Education, Inc.
(CHOICE), a nonprofit corporation and clergy consultation service of north-
eastern Pennsylvania. The district court subsequently dismissed all plaintiffs
with the exception of Dr. Franklin and the obstetrician society. The defendant in the suit was Pennsylvania Welfare Secretary Aldo Colautti.

At issue was section 5(a), which required any person performing abortions in the state of Pennsylvania to make a determination based on his or
her best professional judgment and competence that a fetus born as a result
of an abortion was not viable. If the abortionist determines that the fetus is
viable, or if he suspects the fetus may be viable, immediate steps must be taken
to employ methods that would promote fetal survival and to exercise the care
that would be afforded to a fetus intended to be born alive. The abortionist
must use techniques that provide the best opportunity for the fetus to be born
alive so long as the method does not endanger the life of the mother. Section
5(d) imposes criminal liability on the physician without regard to assigning
guilt or determining fault.

Plaintiffs charged that many sections of the act contained language that
was vague. A three-judge district court panel agreed with the plaintiffs, thus
ruling the Abortion Control Act unconstitutional. The defendant, Colautti,
became the appellant and the plaintiff, Franklin, was now identified as the
appellee as the case graduated to the United States Supreme Court.

The Court began hearing arguments on the merits of the law on October 3, 1978, with a decision not being reached until January 9, 1979. Jurists
had widely differing opinions; however, the majority of the Court favored the
earlier judgment of the district court and moved to affirm the lower court's
decision. There were at least two provisions the Supreme Court found constitutionally defective: (1) standard of care and (2) determination of viability.

The Ambiguity of Viability

The Abortion Control Act requires the attending physician to conform
to a predetermined standard of care if he has determined that a fetus born
as a result of an abortion is viable or if he has sufficient reason to believe the
fetus may be viable. Plaintiffs charged that the phrase "sufficient reason" is
somewhat ambiguous in that it may be subject to broad interpretations, largely
depending on the acceptable philosophy, either skill, judgment, training of
the attending physician, or the opinion of a cross section of the medical community.

Plaintiffs felt that the definition of the phrases "is viable" and "may be viable"
was vague. Defendants countered with the argument that there are actually

no differences in the meanings of either phrase and that the words "may be viable" acknowledge a medical fact that a fetus is viable if statistically it has a chance of independent survival. The defendants pointed out, however, that the true purpose of the law was not intended to equate the words "may be viable" to the medical definition of viability.

The Court completely disregarded the theory that the phrase "may be viable" does mean "viable." Jurists of the district court speculated that "may be viable" is a newly created stage of pregnancy where there exists a slight possibility that the fetus may survive outside the womb but has not reached the stage where there is a reasonable chance of survival under normal circumstances.

The Court, still grappling over the exact definitions of the two phrases, suggested that perhaps the phrase "may be viable" corresponds to viability as defined by the medical community and "is viable" refers to a stage of pregnancy that is yet undetermined. The Court pointed out that both "is viable" and "may be viable" refer to a particular circumstance, with the definition of each differing in some uncertain way.

The inflexible Pennsylvania law does not allow the attending physician a broad area of discretion. The act is both unclear and ambiguous in that it creates a situation of potential criminal prosecution against the physician. If the law was strictly enforced, it would lead to unfair treatment and a denial of an individual's constitutional rights.

If the probability exists that the fetus may be viable and the physician fails in exercising the standard-of-care procedure outlined in the Abortion Control Act, he could be held liable for civil or criminal charges, as would be the normal procedure if the fetus was intended to be born alive and not aborted. Section 5(d) applies the charges of criminal homicide to the physician, with areas of "guilt" determined by a court in weighing the criminal intent of the physician. The state is obligated to prove by a preponderance of evidence the mental state of the physician at the time of the alleged criminal act. In addition, the state must prove that his action was intentional and/or reckless in carelessly causing the death of a human being. The criminal homicide law of Pennsylvania and the Abortion Control Act stipulate, however, that the physician will not be held to blame if he fails in finding sufficient reason that the fetus may be viable.

Determining viability of a fetus is a difficult task. One cannot make an exact determination because each pregnancy is different and there are many fragmented opinions that add to the enormous number of variables. When states enact laws that closely examine a physician's judgment of viability, they often increase the chances of charges of criminal negligence against the attending physician. There is, however, a standard operating procedure that most physicians follow when determining fetal viability. Estimating the gestation age of the fetus is accomplished by checking the menstrual history of the patient.

The approximate weight of the fetus is determined by the size and condition of the uterus. As part of his service, a competent physician will continually monitor the health of the mother and show concern for the quality of pre- and postnatal care his patient will be receiving at the medical facility.

To reach an amicable decision on the probability of fetal survival is not an easy task since each physician employs a different method for assessing the chances of survival. There are no set standards of practice in determining fetal survival; therefore, many physicians refuse to determine a likely date, fearing criminal prosecution should they misdiagnose the estimated stage of viability.

The continued disagreement over viability, together with an inflexible law that if enforced may impose criminal or civil charges against a physician who performs abortions, creates a situation in which many physicians will elect not to perform late–second-trimester abortions.

The Court had no choice but to invalidate the viability-determination section of the Pennsylvania Abortion Control Act, because determining viability is not an exact science; therefore, the decision must be left to the responsibility of the attending physician who will make a judgment free of any government scrutiny. The Court felt no obligation at this time to decide the issue of criminal intent should a physician erroneously determine the viability of a fetus. The Court further resolved the issue of regulation, which should not intrude into an area of medical judgment. The Court concluded that if a law is to be constitutional, it must allow the physician flexibility in making his best medical judgment.

Standard-of-Care Provision Concerning Abortions

The standard-of-care provision of the Abortion Control Act requires physicians to employ abortion methods that would be best in promoting fetal survival, provided that other techniques would not be beneficial in saving the life of the mother or that the lifesaving measures performed on the fetus would not prove life-threatening to the mother. Testimony from a number of physicians provided the court with evidence that saline-amnioinfusion was the most common method of choice for second-trimester abortions. This method, which involves removal of amniotic fluid and injection of a saline or other solution into the amniotic sac, is inexpensive and works well for most patients, but physicians do caution that this method lessens any chance of fetal survival. In order to protect themselves from criminal prosecution, many physicians agree that if the antisaline provision is enforced in Pennsylvania, they would discontinue its use.

During the term of this litigation there were other methods of abortion introduced to the court, which included (1) oxytocin induction, (2) hysterotomy and (3) prostaglandin infusion. Oxytocin induction, also known as dilation/

curettage or dilation/suction, is common for first-trimester abortions, but rarely used after the 13th week of pregnancy. Hysterotomy (cesarean section) is the method the medical community almost unanimously supports as the safest for promoting fetal survival. There are some negative aspects in using the hysterotomy, however. It is a surgical procedure that involves the use of anesthesia and an incision into human tissue. Latest data (1986) suggest that this method is still in use but is more common with most post–first-trimester abortions. Future childbirths for women who have had a hysterotomy will have to be accomplished by cesarean section (C-section) because of the danger of rupture of the scar area if other methods are used. Prostaglandin infusion is a method not in wide use in the United States. Its disuse is probably the result of some very unpleasant side effects, which include nausea, vomiting, headache, and diarrhea. This method also cannot be used on women who have asthma, glaucoma, hypertension, cardiovascular disease, or epilepsy. The prostaglan-din-infusion abortion method incorporates the use of drugs that stimulate contractions of the uterus by which the fetus is expelled from the womb. Though medical experts were in agreement over the safety of this method when compared to saline, they did stress the importance of some serious side effects associated with its use.

Participants representing the medical community who testified in this litigation acknowledged the conflict that exists over the safety of second-trimester abortion procedures.

The Court was overwhelmed with questions over the numerous uncertainties of the Pennsylvania law, including clarifying whether a physician is allowed to exercise his commitment to his patient rather than his "legal" duty in promoting fetal survival.

As a final gesture in solving the dilemma brought on by these statutes, the Court suggested that the state must attempt to rid the abortion laws of all inherent vagueness prior to leveling charges of criminal neglect against physicians who perform abortions.

Opinion of the Court:
Read by Justice Blackmun (Paraphrase)

In *Roe vs. Wade*, the Court did not take into consideration the various questions that have since been raised over the issue of viability. In the 1973 litigation of *Roe vs. Wade*, the Court acknowledged the medical and scientific communities' definition of viability: A fetus is considered to be viable if it is potentially able to live outside the mother's womb, without the assistance of artificial aid. The Court added to the definition of viability that the fetus must be capable of sustaining "potentially meaningful life," not just brief survival. The point of viability was placed at approximately the 7th month or 28th week of pregnancy, but may occur as early as the 24th week. The stage when viability is reached was purposely left flexible because of the presumed advancement in medical technology.

The Court has always been in favor of allowing the physician to determine whether his patient should have an abortion; the task is too important to allow someone without a medical background to decide the issue. Up to the point of state intervention, the abortion decision and determination of viability are primarily and essentially a medical judgment. The Court felt that when a physician fails to follow his medical code of ethics, judicial remedies are available.

It was during the litigation of *Doe vs. Bolton* that the Court stressed the importance of allowing the physician absolute control in exercising his best medical judgment, and the Court emphasized the fact that although women do have a right to have an abortion, the right is not absolute and is not extended to women who want an abortion upon demand.

In a later case, *Planned Parenthood vs. Danford* (1976), Missouri had an abortion law that attempted to move the point of viability forward to an earlier stage of pregnancy. The law was challenged and subsequently ruled invalid on grounds that determining viability is a medical concept, not a judicial one. It was during this same litigation that the Court was asked to rule on an attempt by the state to set the point of viability at a predetermined "fixed" stage of pregnancy; this was also rejected by the Court: Since every pregnancy is different, the point of viability must remain flexible.

Appellants argued that the law is vague in specifying whether the life of the mother would be sustained over that of the fetus. Concern for the life of the mother is not mentioned in the first part and barely addressed in the second part of the statute, and then only in regard to abortion methods.

It appears that the primary message the law is attempting to convey is that emphasis should be on the abortion method that would be most suitable in promoting fetal survival.

The obvious is that opinions over abortion methods are varied, which is a clear indication of how complex the issue is. The Court concludes that both the standard-of-care and viability-determination provisions of section 5(a) are vague and hence constitutionally defective.

Viewpoint: Selected Dissenting Views of Justice White (Paraphrase)

Justice White dissented from the majority opinion. He was joined by Justice Rehnquist and Chief Justice Burger.

The Court has withdrawn from the states power to protect fetal life that was granted in *Roe vs. Wade* and reaffirmed in *Planned Parenthood vs. Danford*. It is for this reason that I dissent.

In *Roe vs. Wade*, the Court determined that the point of viability is when the state should be allowed to have an interest in the abortion procedure as it pertains to safeguarding fetal life and the authority of prohibiting the abortion, with the exception that it would place the life of the mother in jeopardy. The Court defined viability not as a stage of fetal development when it is thought the fetus would have the best chances for survival outside the womb but by the potential ability of long-term survival.

The state of Missouri defined viability as that stage of fetal development when the life of the unborn child may be continued indefinitely outside the womb by natural or artificial life support systems. In 1976, the Court attacked Missouri's definition of viability as misconstruing facts. In its condemnation the Court pointed out that it had already established that viability in a true sense of the word means more than momentary survival.

The problem with the Pennsylvania law is that if the physician fails in making a correct judgment of viability as defined in section 5(a), he may face charges of criminal or civil liability as established in section 5(d). However, the criminal homicide law in the state of Pennsylvania states specifically that a finding of criminal negligence will be based solely on the preponderance of evidence. The state would have to prove that the physician willfully, intentionally, and recklessly caused the death of a human being. The law leaves room for some flexibility in that it would be highly unlikely for a physician to be prosecuted if he "innocently" erred in determining the viability of a fetus. Regardless of the assumed flexibility of the criminal negligence law, the Court still felt that the statute was vague on this particular issue, that there existed a possibility the physician could be prosecuted for criminal homicide without the state proving elements of criminal intent. The obvious absence of a definition of "guilty knowledge" in the statute made it necessary for the Court to invalidate the statute on grounds that the statute was too vague in establishing guidelines on an important issue.

I don't see how it can be seriously argued that a doctor who makes an honest mistake about viability could be prosecuted for criminal homicide. The Court found the standard-of-care provision of section 5(a) to be vague because of the absence of a 'criminal intent' clause, whereas the district court found fault with section 5(a) because of its vague definition of viability provisions. However, it did not invalidate the standard-of-care provision.

I cannot join the court in its determined attack on section 5(a). I agree with the state of Pennsylvania that there is not the slightest chance that any physician will be prosecuted on the basis of making an honest error of judgment. If the Court has sufficient doubt, it should abstain from judgment to permit the courts to act on the issues that they are so much more familiar with than is this Court or any other federal court.

The Court's Decision

In deciding the case on January 9, 1979, the Supreme Court voted to affirm the earlier decision reached by the lower court invalidating section 5(a). The Court stipulated that it reached a decision based on the fact that language embodied within the standard-of-care and viability-determination provisions was vague, thus leading to confusion within the medical community and creating more questions than answers.

Justice Blackmun read the opinion of the court, with Justices Brennan, Stewart, Marshall, Powell, and Stevens joining. There were no concurring opinions and only one dissenting opinion, read by Justice White, who felt that the standard-of-care provision was not vague and clearly defined its guidelines. White also felt that the viability-determination provision was fair and not vague as the court suggested. He was joined in his opinion by Chief Justice Burger and Justice Rehnquist.

9: State of Utah Annotated Code

Section 76-7-304

Considerations by physician: Notice to minor's parents or guardian or married woman's husband. To enable the physician to exercise his best medical judgment, he shall:

(1) Consider all factors relevant to the well being of the woman upon whom the abortion is to be performed, including but not limited to:
  (a) Her physical, emotional, and psychological health and safety;
  (b) Her age; and
  (c) Her family situation.

(2) Notify, if possible, the parents or guardian of the woman upon whom the abortion is to be performed if she is a minor, or the husband of the woman if she is married.

Section 76-7-305

Consent requirement for abortion.
(1) No abortion may be performed unless a voluntary and informed written consent is first obtained by the attending physician from the woman upon whom the abortion is to be performed.
(2) No consent obtained pursuant to the provisions of this section shall be considered voluntary and informed unless the attending physician has informed the woman upon whom the abortion is to be performed:
  (a) Of the names and addresses of the two licensed adoption agencies in the state of Utah and the services that can be performed by those agencies and nonagency adoption may be legally arranged; and
  (b) Of the details of development of unborn children and abortion procedures, including foreseeable complications and risks, and the nature of the post-operative recuperation period; and
  (c) Of any other factors he deems relevant to a voluntary and informed consent.

H.L. vs. Matheson, Governor of Utah

The plaintiff, H.L., was a 15-year-old Utah resident living with her parents who were contributing to her support. In the spring of 1978, she discovered she was pregnant. She enlisted the aid of a social worker and a physician, who recommended that abortion "would probably be in her best medical interest." But there was an obstacle between H.L. and her desired abortion. Utah had a strict law requiring physicians who perform abortion procedures on unmarried women under 18 years of age to inform parents of their daughter's intentions prior to performing the procedure.

H.L. decided to proceed with her plans to have an abortion, regardless of what the law stipulated. She informed her social worker of her plans but did not wish to inform her parents of her dilemma or decision. The social worker went along with H.L.'s decision to have an abortion. H.L. was in her first trimester when she filed a court action with the Third Judicial District Court of Utah, listing the defendants as the governor and the attorney general of Utah.

H.L. sought to have the court declare the law unconstitutional. In addition, she asked that an injunction be issued to prevent defendants from enforcing the abortion statute. The plaintiff also petitioned the court for permission to represent a class consisting of unmarried minor women who are suffering unwanted pregnancies and desire to terminate the pregnancies but may not do so because of their physicians' insistence on complying with section 76-7-304(2). The trial judge ruled against the plaintiff, refusing to issue a temporary restraining order or a preliminary injunction. The court felt that Utah's abortion statute does not unconstitutionally restrict the right of privacy of the minor in obtaining an abortion, or to enter into a doctor-patient relationship. In addition, the judge interpreted the statute as requiring parental notification only if it is physically possible. However, the judge did find the plaintiff to be well qualified to represent her class. But since he ruled against the plaintiff on the primary issues, the complaint was subsequently dismissed.

Still believing it to be her constitutional right to have an abortion without notification of her parents, the plaintiff next appealed her case before the Utah State Supreme Court. However, the state supreme court quickly rejected the appeal on grounds that the abortion law was constitutionally valid.

Even though two courts rejected her arguments on the merits, H.L. was determined to have the abortion she desired; she took her case to the final step in the appeals process, the United States Supreme Court. Beginning on October 6, 1980, the Court took into consideration all relevant matters pertaining to this case. A decision was reached on March 23, 1981. The Court ruled that section 76-7-304(2) was constitutionally valid, thus affirming the judgment of the lower courts.

Questions Concerning Mature Consent

The constitutionality of section 76-7-304 was challenged by the plaintiff because it failed to take into consideration the rights of unmarried adolescents who were mature and emancipated. The law required the attending physician to notify parents of a minor who desired an abortion if she resided in her parents' home and was dependent upon them for support, or if she was not married and not emancipated. The strict law also included minors who made no attempt to prove themselves capable of giving mature consent to an abortion.

In *Planned Parenthood vs. Danford,* the Court invalidated laws that required consent from the woman's spouse or from her parents if she was unmarried. In the 1976 Missouri litigation the Court ruled that a state does not have the authority to give a third party an absolute and possibly arbitrary veto over the decision of the physician and his patient in terminating her pregnancy, regardless of the reason for withholding consent. However, the Court did make it very clear that its ruling should not be misconstrued as advocating abortion for every minor, regardless of age or maturity.

In another decision of the Supreme Court, *Bellotti vs. Baird (II),* the Court invalidated a statute requiring either parental or judicial consent before the physician could proceed with the abortion procedure, regardless of the adolescent's level of maturity. The statute was construed as allowing the court to invalidate an abortion decision made by a minor even if it found the minor to be capable of giving mature, intelligent, and informed consent. The law was subsequently ruled unconstitutional by the Supreme Court on grounds that it failed to give separate consideration to minors who are mature. The Court gave a second reason for invalidating that law. By granting either parents or a judge the power to allow or veto an abortion decision, a third party was allowed to override a decision that had been made by the attending physician and his mature patient. This had been ruled unconstitutional.

In earlier litigation the Court had ruled that a state cannot make a blanket law that is inflexible; doing so would be unconstitutional. On the other hand, the Court found no constitutional defect in notifying parents of immature, dependent minors of a planned abortion. The Court felt that immature minors are incapable of providing informed and intelligent decisions on issues that may have serious long-term emotional and physical consequences. They deemed it more desirable in such situations for parents to be fully informed of their child's decision to have an abortion.

Clarifying the Law

Statutes that have been enacted to regulate abortions fall primarily into two categories: (1) requiring consent and (2) requiring information. A Missouri law that was challenged in *Planned Parenthood vs. Danford* required both parental and spousal approval. The difference in Utah's requirement was that the information acquired from the parents is for the personal and private use of the physician. Many psychologists have alluded to the fact that many adolescents under the age of 18 are more susceptible to feelings of physical and

emotional anxiety than are older people, which necessitates parental involvement in their daughter's dilemma by providing both psychological and medical
data to the minor's physician.

Plaintiffs contended that the statute was constitutionally defective because
it was not specific as to what information would be furnished the physician
and it failed to disclose or clarify a mandatory waiting period that a number
of states require after parents are notified. To this argument, the Court replied
that it felt Utah's law was fair in allowing ample time for parents to assist their
daughter in a decision that has probable traumatic consequences.

Opinion of the Court:
Read by Chief Justice Burger (Paraphrase)

In regard to section 76-7-304(2) the Utah Supreme Court stipulated that
the requirement of notifying parents of minors who seek abortion is logical
because parents usually are better informed on the medical and psychological
history of their daughter. The information provided to the minor's physician
is beneficial in furthering his knowledge of his patient so that he may exercise
his best medical judgment. Additionally, the statute did not interfere with the
minor's right to have an abortion, since nowhere does the statute imply "consent" or "veto power."

The appellant-plaintiff challenged the statute on grounds that it was arbitrary, in that it could be misconstrued to include minors who are unmarried,
mature, or emancipated. The Court felt no obligation to act upon the challenge
since the plaintiff was unmarried, resided at home, and was dependent on her
parents for support. Also, it was pointed out that the plaintiff at the time was
15 years of age. After considering all pertinent facts related to this case, there
were insufficient grounds for the appellant's claims.

The district court held that the Utah abortion statute did not apply to
emancipated minors since doing so would be unconstitutional. It seems inconceivable to assume that a minor in need of emergency medical treatment
would be turned away because she had not informed her parents of her
dilemma. Opponents of the statute have implied that a prerequisite of requiring parental notice prior to an abortion being performed unduly burdens the
minor's right to have an abortion. However, the opposition fails to acknowledge
that it is constitutionally permissible to impose a requirement of consent or
notification prior to a minor entering into any legal agreement or making any
important decisions, abortion or otherwise.

The basic structure of the American society recognizes parental authority. The relationship between parent and child is a protection afforded by the
Constitution. Of paramount concern is in maintaining the responsibility of
raising children both socially and morally as a task of parents and not the state.

The Constitution does not require states to enact laws that are constructed specifically to encourage abortions. Quite the opposite is true. States openly encourage childbirth, which is closer related to the idealism of governmental philosophy, protection of potential life.

The Court finds the statute to be valid in that it does not violate any constitutional guarantees.

Viewpoint: Selected Concurring Views of Justice Powell (Paraphrase)

Justice Powell read an opinion agreeing with the majority opinion. He was joined by Justice Stewart.

This litigation requires the Court to rule again on a law that requires parental participation in a minor's decision to have an abortion. I'm in total agreement with the finding of this court that section 76–7–304(2) does not in any way burden a minor's constitutional right to have an abortion.

The statute requires a physician to notify parents of a minor who desires an abortion prior to the performance of the procedure. Plaintiffs have based their challenge almost entirely on one issue, that sometime in the future it could be interpreted to include minors who are mature and emancipated. This particular case involved a young woman who testified that she did not wish to include her parents in her decision because she felt that "it would be in her best interest not to." The 15-year-old plaintiff also testified that she was fully knowledgeable of the seriousness surrounding abortion, including its long-term effects, but that her physician still refused to perform the procedure without first notifying her parents. Although she expressed her knowledge of the abortion procedure and the serious ramifications of its aftermath if an error was made in her decision, she never officially stated what her level of maturity was, nor did the plaintiff ever state if indeed her parents would object to the abortion if notified. The physician testified that he was willing to perform the abortion, and because he felt that parents of the plaintiff would not prohibit him from performing the procedure, he saw no problem with notifying them.

Adult women possess a constitutional right to have an abortion, but that right is not absolute. However, adolescents who desire an abortion also have rights, with some variation which includes consideration of some relevant matters such as (1) age and level of maturity, (2) soundness of family life and relationship with parents, (3) mental and physical condition, and (4) married or emancipated status. In previous cases the Court has never considered the opinion of one physician to override important concerns of parents and the state.

If a state requires parental notice regardless of the minor's level of maturity, it must in addition provide the minor access to an independent remedy in order that she may prove herself capable of giving intelligent and informed consent or that abortion would be in her best interest.

Viewpoint: Selected Concurring Views of Justice Stevens (Paraphrase)

Plaintiffs in this class-action suit represent all minors who are similarly situated, desiring to terminate an unwanted pregnancy but prohibited from doing so because physicians have chosen to conform to guidelines of section 76-7-304(2). Plaintiffs contend that they became concerned after the Utah Supreme Court mindfully implied that the regulation could at some time in the future apply to all minors regardless of individual situations.

The importance of the abortion decision justifies reasonable caution. Aside from consulting with a physician concerning the medical aspect of abortion, minors should in addition enlist the assistance of other forms of counseling, including the advice of parents, simply because the long-term emotional and physical stress and trauma associated with the post-abortion "depression" is not entirely medically related.

Just because a state enacts a law requiring parental notice prior to an abortion being performed, there is no guarantee that parents will react in a positive manner by counseling their daughter. Many families do not live under "ideal" conditions where compassion freely flows from one family member to the next, which makes the interchanging of ideas and thoughts concerning abortion a very difficult task. Some parents will inevitably react in a negative manner to their daughter's situation, while others who react with more compassion may innocently err in advising their daughter. However, these varied situations are not sufficient grounds to invalidate a statute that attempts to initiate methods that could prove beneficial in assisting an adolescent in making a correct abortion decision.

This situation is similar to what was argued in *Planned Parenthood vs. Danford:* A state is justified in protecting a young pregnant female from severe physical and emotional trauma that may result from an incorrect abortion decision by requiring parents to be notified prior to the physician performing an abortion. I therefore agree with the ruling of the Utah Supreme Court in affirming this statute.

Viewpoint: Selected Dissenting Views of Justice Marshall (Paraphrase)

Justice Marshall delivered an opinion that differed from the majority opinion and thus dissented. Justice Marshall was joined in his opinion by Justices Brennan and Blackmun.

The Court found defects in the appellant's (plaintiff's) arguments because she failed to establish her personal status of being mature or emancipated. In addition, it was never made clear why she wished her parents not be informed of her abortion decision. Based primarily on these facts, the Court has decided that the appellant lacks sufficient grounds in challenging the validity of this statute.

It is apparent that since the plaintiff has made no attempt to disclose her level of maturity or whether she is emancipated, she therefore has not established any basis for voicing her objection to the insensitivity of this statute. The Court, left with no other alternative, ruled that she is not a qualified member of adolescents who may fall into the category exempt from the requirements of this statute, and furthermore the Court has resolved that this particular plaintiff is not viewed as being a knowledgeable spokesperson for others similarly situated.

The fact of the matter is that after the plaintiff's consultation with her physician, social worker, and attorney, she felt fully knowledgeable of what was involved in her decision. In a pretrial hearing the plaintiff stated that she felt it would be difficult to discuss the abortion with her parents. The fact that the plaintiff has maintained a persistent attitude in her belief that notifying her parents would not be in her best interest is sufficient grounds to challenge this statute.

The true reason for the plaintiff's opposition to the statute is its restrictive and narrow definition of "no exception" to the requirement of notifying parents. Its construction may erroneously find the statute to include all minors who are similarly situated. But it is not necessary for the Court to evaluate the logic used in the plaintiff's opposition to the statute in order to find that perhaps there is some solid foundation to her standing on this issue.

The Court has set a dangerous precedent by denying the plaintiff her right to be a spokesperson for her adolescent class, because by doing so the Court has erroneously labeled all adolescents with similar problems who are living with parents and not married or emancipated as unqualified in representing the issue. But while going on record as denying the plaintiff the right to represent her class of adolescents, the Court did acknowledge the approval of the lower court of the plaintiff's excellent qualifications in representing other minors similarly situated. The class of minors the plaintiff asked to represent included all minor women who are pregnant and desire to terminate their pregnancies but were denied that right because physicians in Utah have refused to perform the procedure on minors unless they are in full compliance with the provisions of section 76-7-304(2). Though the minors were from varied backgrounds (dependent on their parents for support, independent and emancipated, mature and immature), they fell under the auspices of Utah's statute that denies women and their physicians the freedom to choose to terminate their pregnancy. If the Court has a doubt concerning the qualifications of the plaintiff as a spokesperson, it should follow the proper judicial course by remanding the case back to the trial courts for a rehearing on all relevant issues. By using the proper jurisprudence, the Court may be able to prove its theories and place its assumptions to rest. The remand would serve to protect members of the class of adolescents by allowing the lower court to determine if the plaintiff has a valid claim as being qualified to represent others that are not exempt from the restrictions of the statute and if her individual situation is indeed similar to those she desires to speak for. Trial courts are allowed considerable leeway in approving class action suits, which makes a remand in this litigation a necessity. Remember, the trial judge did find the appellant adequate in representing her class of adolescents directly affected by the guidelines of this statute. The expressed interest the plaintiff shows should be sufficient justification for qualifying her to challenge this statute.

During the early years of abortion litigation, certain fundamental rights were established, including a woman's right to choose whether to terminate her pregnancy, a right to privacy, and the right to get married, to bear children, and to use contraceptives. These rights are guaranteed by the Constitution against government encroachment. The Court also established that the Due Process Clause of the Fourteenth Amendment protects a woman's independence in making important decisions on certain matters and included is the right to choose not to disclose those matters in public.

In reviewing some previous abortion litigation, the Court ruled in *Roe vs. Wade* that in the first trimester of pregnancy a state could not override a woman's decision in consultation with her physician to terminate her pregnancy. In *Doe vs. Bolton,* the Court invalidated a Georgia law that imposed a level of restriction on a woman's private decision to have an abortion, by subjecting her case to be reviewed before a board of physicians, but in addition to her private physician. But that was not the final step in the procedure, for afterward the woman had to obtain a final approval by a hospital committee who had the power to grant or deny the abortion. In 1976, in *Planned Parenthood vs. Danford,* it was established that many of the rights that are guaranteed by the Constitution, including the right to privacy, protect adults and adolescents alike. Only a few problems faced by minors are considered to be serious, and one of the major problems is abortion. Prohibiting a minor from obtaining one could result in serious emotional problems for the youngster. The seriousness of the problem makes it imperative that government restriction of abortion should occur only when absolutely necessary in satisfying an important state interest.

The theory of idealism in American society supports the strong belief that the future of America lies with the strength of individual family units. Because this idealistic theory is so deeply instilled in the general populace, it seems almost contradictory to study restrictions imposed by law requiring parental notice of a daughter's decision to terminate her pregnancy. The idealism that surrounds the American family gains importance when put through the test during adverse and troubled times. Strength within the central core structure of the family unit can do much in providing support, understanding, and assistance. Within idealistic parameters, a minor facing a decision to terminate her pregnancy will find parental support and intelligent advice, in addition to comfort and wisdom. If pregnant minors confided in their parents, the necessity of state-imposed restrictions would be nullified.

What was described in the above paragraph is a very idealistic characterization of what family life should be, but unfortunately it is not representative of how things really are. For a moment, let's talk realism in American family life. Since most adolescents oppose both state and parental intervention in their problems, preferring the same guarantees of privacy as their adult contemporaries are afforded, family life in America could best be described as less than idealistic.

If parents become involved in problems that face their child, it nullifies their fundamental right of personal choice in revealing private matters. Whether it be an adult or adolescent, consultations between a doctor and his patient are considered privileged and not open to scrutiny by a third party. There are no set standards as to how parents will accept their daughter's abortion plans; reaction varies, with some reacting in a violent manner, possibly inflicting mental and physical abuse on their child, while others may interfere or obstruct the abortion. Fearing parental reaction is the main reason why adolescents choose not to inform their parents of their dilemma. Many will opt to delay a first-trimester abortion as long as possible, while others may attempt self-abortion or solicit illegal remedies. It is significant to note that minors who choose to carry their pregnancy to term are not affected by the Utah statute. The state-mandated law of notifying parents prior to an abortion amounts to nothing more than placing an obvious tier of obstruction on a minor who asks for no more than to have her right to privacy not violated.

During one of the Court's previous abortion cases (Planned Parenthood vs. Danford), it was established that no law would have a chance of survival if the law could not be justified by important state interest. The Court concluded in Roe vs. Wade that a first-trimester abortion does not necessitate state intervention.

Defendants pointed out that none of Utah's abortion statute applies to pregnant adult women, but were quick in citing two important reasons for enacting a law that regulates abortion for adolescents, the first being that parents are more knowledgeable of their daughter's medical history. The information they would provide could be invaluable to the physician in treating his minor patient. Secondly, this type of law may be beneficial in encouraging communication between parent and child.

The difficulty with the statute is that it never made clear the specific information the law required parents to pass on to their daughter's physician, nor were there any solid answers as to why parents would possess pertinent medical information about their daughter that she was not aware of. Questions have risen over the logic of withholding a person's medical records if she has already obtained both medical and psychological advice. A doctor who solicits consultation of the parents of his minor patient is not prohibited from freely doing so, which places the necessity of this statute in question.

Aside from the law's being unclear and confusing in some areas, it is ambiguous in that it does not require some of the restrictions that it seemingly imposes. On the surface the statute's strict guidelines require the physician to notify the parents of a minor desiring an abortion, giving them ample time to decide on the issue; however, in order that the regulation be satisfied, the physician does not have to have any direct communication with the parents. He may notify them by mail or telephone them only minutes before he is to perform the abortion. Exempted from the restrictions are minors who are married or decide to carry their pregnancy to full term. In addition, no parental approval is needed for pregnant minors who consent to surgical procedures that are related to natal care, with the exception of abortion.

The statute applies to all minors without exception but does not include the exempt class. Even after the physician judges the abortion to be in his patient's best interest, he is prohibited from performing the procedure unless he first complies with the restrictive nature of Utah's law. When Utah decided to reject the idea of rescinding the "no-exception" clause of its statute, it sent the message to all adolescents and physicians that they are forbidden from exercising their right to privacy. In *Bellotti vs. Baird II,* it was established that minors had the option of securing a judicial remedy to their dilemma, but such is not the case with Utah's law, allowing for no judicial recourse.

There is no doubt that the statute under attack in this litigation does violate a woman's constitutional right to privacy. None of the reasons cited by the state of Utah in justifying the enactment of this statute can be considered valid. The statute prevents a physician from exercising his professional medical judgment free of state-imposed restrictions. In addition, the statute fails in the area of transferring medical data from parents to the physician by requiring nothing more than a phone call minutes before performing the abortion.

Finally, the clear ambiguity of the statute's construction becomes apparent with appellee's (defendant's) contention that the statute's primary concern is promoting important state interests in maintaining strong family unity, which is traditionally and ideally rooted within American culture.

The Court's Decision

On March 23, 1981, the Supreme Court, finding no constitutional defect with section 76-7-304(2), voted to affirm the finding of the Supreme Court of Utah.

Chief Justice Burger read the opinion of the Court, stating the confidence of the Court in the fairness of Utah's abortion statute. The opinion was joined by Justices Stewart, White, Powell, and Rehnquist. Justice Powell wrote an opinion that agreed with the majority finding. In his summary opinion, Powell said that this litigation requires the Court to rule again on a law that requires parental participation in a minor's decision to have an abortion. Section 76-7-304(2) does not in any way burden a minor's constitutional right to have an abortion. The opinion was joined by Justice Stewart.

Justice Stevens also wrote an opinion in agreement with the judgment of the Court. The importance of the abortion decision justifies reasonable caution be taken that the decision be made wisely. This includes consultation with a physician, but perhaps of more importance is that because the long-term consequences are not medically related, it is necessary to seek other forms of counseling, including the advice of parents.

Justice Marshall delivered a dissenting opinion. He criticized the majority opinion for not finding Utah's statute in violation of an individual's right to privacy guaranteed in the Fourteenth Amendment, as established in *Roe vs. Wade, Doe vs. Bolton,* and *Planned Parenthood vs. Danford.* Marshall was joined in his opinion by Justices Brennan and Blackmun.

10: The City of Akron (Ohio) Ordinance No. 160-1978 [Enacted 1978]

1870.01(B) [Defines *Hospital*]

Hospital: a general hospital or special hospital devoted to gynecology or obstetrics which is accredited by the Joint Commission on Accreditation of Hospitals (JCAH) or by the American Osteopathic Association.

1870.02 [Defines *Abortion Facility*]

[Provides that first trimester abortions must be performed in a hospital or an abortion facility. Abortion facility is defined as a clinic, physician's office, or other place or facility where abortions are performed, other than a hospital.]

1870.03 Abortion in Hospital

No person shall perform or induce abortion upon a pregnant woman subsequent to the end of the first trimester of her pregnancy unless such abortion is performed in a hospital.

1870.05 Notice and Consent

No physician shall perform or induce abortion upon an unmarried pregnant woman under the age of 18 years without first having given at least 24-hour notice to one of the parents or the legal guardian of the minor pregnant woman as to the intention to perform such abortion, or if such parent or guardian cannot be reached after a reasonable effort to find him or her, without first having given at least 72 hours constructive notice to one of the parents or legal guardian of the minor pregnant woman by certified mail to the last known address of one of the parents or guardian, computed from the time of mailing, unless abortion is ordered by the court having jurisdiction over such minor pregnant woman.

1870.05(B)

No physician shall perform or induce abortion upon a minor pregnant woman under the age of 15 years without first having obtained the informed written consent of the minor pregnant woman in accordance with §1870.06 of this chapter, and;

1870.05(B)(1)

First having obtained the informed consent of one parent or legal guardian in accordance with §1870.06 of this chapter, or

1870.05(B)(2)

The minor pregnant woman first having obtained an order from a court having jurisdiction over her that the abortion be performed or induced.

1870.06(A) Informed Consent

An abortion otherwise permitted by law shall be performed or induced only with the informed written consent of the pregnant woman and one of her parents or her legal guardian whose consent is required in accordance with §1870.05(B) of this chapter, given freely and without coercion.

1870.06(B)

In order to insure that the consent for an abortion is truly informed consent, an abortion shall be performed or induced upon a pregnant woman only after she and one of her parents or legal guardian whose consent is required in accordance with §1870.05(B) of this chapter have been orally informed by her attending physician of the following facts and have a signed form acknowledging that she and the parent or legal guardian where applicable, have been informed as follows:

1870.06(B)(1)

That according to the best judgment of her attending physician she is pregnant.

1870.06(B)(2)

The number of weeks elapsed from the probable time of conception of her unborn child, based upon information provided by her as to the time of her last menstrual period or after a history and physical examination and appropriate tests.

1870.06(B)(3)

That the unborn child is a human life from the moment of conception and that there has been described in detail the anatomical and physiological characteristics of the particular unborn child at the gestation point of development at which time the abortion is to be performed, including but not limited to, appearance, mobility, tactile sensitivity, including pain, perception, or response, brain and heart function, the presence of internal organs and the presence of external members.

1870.06(B)(4)

That her unborn child may be viable and thus capable of surviving outside the womb if more than 22 weeks have elapsed from the time of conception, and that her attending physician has a legal obligation to take all reasonable steps to preserve the life and health of her viable unborn child during the abortion.

1870.06(B)(5)

That abortion is a major surgical procedure, which can result in serious complications, including hemorrhage, perforated uterus, infection, menstrual disturbances, sterility, and miscarriage and prematurity in subsequent pregnancies; and that abortion may leave or worsen any existing psychological problems she may have and can result in severe emotional disturbances.

1870.06(B)(6)

That numerous private and public agencies and services are available to provide her with birth control information and that her physician will provide her with a list of such agencies and the services available if she so requests.

1870.06(B)(7)

That numerous public and private agencies and services are available to assist during her pregnancy and after the birth of her child, if she chooses not to have an abortion, whether she wishes to keep her child or place him or her for adoption, and that her physician will provide her with a list of such agencies and the services if she so requests.

1870.06(C)

At the same time the attending physician provides the information required by paragraph B of this section, he shall at least orally inform the pregnant woman and one of her parents or her legal guardian, whose consent is required in accordance with §1870.05(B) of this chapter of the particular risks associated with her own pregnancy and the abortion method to be used, providing her with at least a general description of the medical instructions to be followed subsequent to the abortion in order to insure her safe recovery and shall in addition provide her with such other information which in his own medical judgment is relevant to her decision as to whether to have an abortion or carry her pregnancy to term.

1870.06(D)

The attending physician performing or inducing the abortion shall provide the pregnant woman or one of her parents or legal guardian signing the consent form where applicable with a duplicate copy of the consent form signed by her and one of her parents or her legal guardian where applicable in accordance with paragraph B of this section.

1870.07 Waiting Period

No physician shall perform or induce abortion upon a pregnant woman until twenty-four (24) hours have elapsed from the time the pregnant woman and one of her parents or her legal guardian whose consent is required in accordance with §1870.05(B) of this chapter have signed the consent form required by §1870.06 of this chapter and the physician so certifies in writing that such time has elapsed.

1870.16 Disposal of Remains

Any physician who shall perform or induce abortion upon a pregnant woman shall insure that the remains of the unborn child be disposed of in a humane and sanitary manner.

[A violation of any section of the ordinance is punishable as a criminal misdemeanor. If any provision is invalidated, it is to be severed from the remainder of the ordinance. The ordinance effective date: May 1, 1978.]

Sections 1870.05(B) Notice and Consent, 1870.06(B) Informed Consent, and 1870.16 Disposal of Remains, were invalidated by a U.S. district court in 1979. Sections 1870.06(C) Informed Consent and 1870.07 Waiting Period, were invalidated by the U.S. Circuit Court of Appeals (for the Sixth Circuit) in 1981. Section 1870.03 Abortion in a Hospital, was invalidated by the U.S. Supreme Court.

City of Akron vs. Akron
Center for Reproductive Health

The city of Akron (Ohio) enacted a number of ordinances that severely restricted abortions in that city. The ordinances were to go into effect on May 1, 1978, but on April 19, 1978, a class-action suit was filed in the federal District Court for the Northern District of Ohio, challenging all of the ordinances' provisions. The legal maneuver was important in order that implementation of the abortion ordinances be blocked until all relevant matters surrounding the facts were presented in court.

The plaintiffs were three abortion facilities located in the city of Akron and a physician who performed abortions at one of the facilities. The defendants included the city of Akron and three of the city's officials. The court also allowed two intervenor-defendants to participate. They represented all parents of unmarried minor children of childbearing age.

In August 1979, after several months of testimony, the district court ruled the following sections unconstitutional: 1870.06, requiring disclosure of facts relating to a minor's pregnancy to her parents; 1870.05, requiring parental notice and consent of their daughter's desire to have an abortion; and 1870.16, disposal of fetal remains. The court found the remainder of the ordinances to be constitutionally valid.

Neither side was totally satisfied with portions of the ruling, which led to an appeal with the Sixth Circuit Court of Appeals. After hearing arguments from both sides, the circuit court agreed with the decision of the district court in part, but added sections 1870.06(C) and 1870.07 to the invalidation list on grounds they were constitutionally defective.

After much dissatisfaction over the rulings of both lower courts and many appeals later, the case was finally approved for a hearing before the United States Supreme Court. Arguments began on November 30, 1982. A final ruling reversed in part and affirmed in part the decision of the lower court.

Limiting a State's Abortion Concern

Presumably a state should have no legal interest in the abortion procedure until at least the 13th week of pregnancy. However, the implied interest should remain within established guidelines of matters relating to maternal health only. If at any time during the second trimester, the interest of the state is either overly burdensome or restrictive, or departs from acceptable medical procedure, the Court may hold the state interest invalid.

The interest of the state in matters of maternal health during the second trimester of pregnancy is limited and may be expressed only if there is proof of "justification" for the concern. For instance, if the health of the pregnant woman does not appear to be in any immediate danger, there is no justification for state intervention in the abortion procedure. Additionally, there is seldom a need for the state continually to check the health of the woman or look into the abortion procedure throughout the second trimester. The state is obligated to use its power of regulation properly and to limit the restrictive effects of its expressed concern on the pregnant woman.

Hospitalization for Post–First-Trimester Abortions

One of Akron's abortion ordinances stipulates that no physician shall perform or induce an abortion upon a pregnant woman subsequent to the end of the first trimester of her pregnancy, unless such abortion is performed in a (full service) hospital. The restriction essentially places in jeopardy the existence of less expensive outpatient abortion facilities for women seeking a second-trimester dilation-and-evacuation procedure. Because of the restrictive overtones of this particular ordinance, the city of Akron has imposed an unnecessary burden on a pregnant woman's access to a conventional abortion procedure that could be construed as unreasonably infringing upon a woman's constitutional rights.

The strict requirement places an obvious barrier in the path of a woman desiring to terminate her pregnancy and severely limits the availability of the abortion procedure in Akron. Obviously full-service hospitals are more costly than smaller clinics that specialize in abortion. The difference in rates between the two may be so great that many women would not be able to afford abortion, thus being "forced" into bearing children they may not want. Aside from the cost factor, another area of concern is the number of available full-service hospitals that are properly equipped to accommodate abortion patients.

The city of Akron has contended that the enactment of the hospitalization ordinance was not intended to place a tier of restriction or to discourage women from having an abortion; rather, the city saw it as a reasonable way to protect maternal health.

In 1973, the Court argued the merits of Texas abortion statutes in *Roe vs. Wade*. At that time the Court established that hospitalization for second-trimester abortion patients was a reasonable request and highly recommended by the medical community. But almost 10 years later, the success record of second-trimester abortions had proven that dilation and evacuation, used in a majority of post–first-trimester procedures, was safe, thus eliminating the need for any hospitalization requirement. During the litigation of this case before the circuit court, evidence was presented that positively showed the "D & E" method to be the safest procedure for post-first-trimester abortions. Of noteworthy interest is the fact that in 1973, second-trimester abortions were not permitted between the 12th and 16th week of pregnancy, but 10 years later, due to the advancement in medical technology, abortion during this span of pregnancy was legalized.

Adolescent Maturity

One of the abortion ordinances enacted by Akron has presumably placed all minors 18 and under in the same "immature" category without allowing them to prove their maturity. The district court ruled the ordinance invalid on grounds that some minors are capable of making mature and informed decisions, regardless of their age. If a law of this type survives a challenge, it is usually because it provides for an option of allowing unwed pregnant minors to prove they are sufficiently mature in making the decision to have an abortion.

Informed Decision

If a state is serious in expressing its desires to protect maternal health, then it must be responsible for educating pregnant women on the options available to them for abortion or natural childbirth. The requirement does not imply that states have absolute authority in selecting the type of educational material women will receive; that is the responsibility of the attending physician. The perimeter of state concern should not go beyond assuring that the educational material is free of any leading or persuasive data and that the language is flexible and nonjudgmental.

An informed decision begins with the attending physician, who must give his patient an oral briefing of the status of her pregnancy. The briefing should include details of the development of the fetus as well as information concerning the physical and emotional trauma that may be felt after the abortion is performed. Additionally, the woman should be informed of the number of agencies that offer assistance in learning methods of birth control, adoption, and childbirth.

Akron also enacted an ordinance that required the physician to supply his patient with information describing the unborn fetus as a living human being; life begins at conception. The ordinance describes abortion as a major surgical procedure, placing emphasis on the physical and emotional trauma that may occur.

The ordinance was found to be inflexible in that it required the physician to provide information to his patient that may not have been relevant to her situation.

Twenty-Four-Hour Waiting Period

The Akron law requires a woman desiring an abortion to wait 24 hours after she signs the consent forms authorizing the procedure. The city reasoned that the 24-hour waiting period gave the woman time to change her mind if she was unsure of her decision. The court, however, disagreed with the implied intent of the ordinance. The judges viewed the ordinance as unnecessary in that it does not further the interest of the state in protection of the health and safety of the pregnant woman. Additionally, the court found that a 24-hour waiting period will not insure the state that a pregnant woman will receive proper guidance during that designated waiting period. The district court originally upheld the law on grounds that the state was exercising extra precautions in making sure that the pregnant woman was making a correct decision and that the only way the state could express its concern was by imposing a restriction of this type on the abortion procedure. When the case was appealed to the circuit court, however, the ruling of the district court was reversed because the law was found to be inflexible and had no medical significance. The circuit court found the prudent consideration of the state in the woman's decision to have an abortion "admirable" but beyond the limits of enforceable power entrusted to the state. The court further stipulated that the judgment of proceeding with an abortion decision is a medical one made by the physician in consultation with his patient, not a legislative one. The Code of Medical Ethics requires that a physician advise his patient to postpone the abortion if he feels it would be to her benefit. After a woman receives proper counseling and gives her written consent approving the procedure, the state is virtually powerless in delaying the abortion.

Disposing of Fetal Remains

The law in Akron stipulates that physicians who perform abortions within the city must be sure that remains of the unborn fetus are disposed of in a "humane" and "sanitary" manner. The court was troubled with the definition of the word "humane" as used in the ordinance. The court felt the word to be vague in defining the physician's anticipated conduct in the disposal of fetal remains. The court chose to invalidate the law, citing the vagueness of the word "humane" as its primary reason.

The city of Akron, in responding to the court ruling on this issue, argued that the sole purpose of the ordinance was to prevent the arbitrary dumping of fetal remains in dumpsters or onto trash piles. The court replied that the ordinance was unclear and that there existed a probability that more was involved in enacting the provision. In the manner in which the court construed the law, the words "humane" and "sanitary" suggest a later attempt by the state to broaden the language of the ordinance to allow for a proper "burial" of fetal remains. If this occurred, many doctors would be prosecuted for criminal acts. Additionally, the court found the ordinance to fail to give a physician proper notice that his anticipated conduct in the disposal of fetal remains may be unlawful. The Supreme Court invalidated the ordinance because it was in violation of the established meaning of the Fourteenth Amendment's Due Process Clause.

Opinion of the Court:
Read by Justice Powell (Paraphrase)

Ten years ago we handed down a landmark decision on abortion, changing many laws that had been in effect for nearly a century. In *Roe vs. Wade* we held that the right of privacy is contained in the concept of personal liberty guaranteed by the Constitution; the right is broad enough to include a woman's right to terminate her pregnancy. Several states have responded with challenges to our original findings. They contended that we made too many errors in judgment when we limited a state's authority in regulating the abortion procedure.

The right to privacy is found in the Fourteenth Amendment's Due Process Clause, and the concept of personal liberty includes the right to be free from government intrusion into matters of family life and marriage. The right is comprehensive enough to include a woman's right to terminate her pregnancy. Although the Constitution does not specifically mention a right to terminate a pregnancy, the liberty defined in the Due Process Clause represents a broad interpretation of the rights of an individual.

An individual's fundamental rights include the right of the woman's physician freely to treat and counsel his patient without government intrusion, so that he may at all times exercise his best medical judgment. But the state does have a right, and the Court does acknowledge that at some point during the term of pregnancy the interest of the state is profound enough to prohibit the abortion. The legitimate interest of the state in protecting potential life continues through the term of pregnancy but becomes more significant when the fetus becomes viable. Additionally, a state does have jurisdiction in overseeing the standard of health care at abortion facilities, so that the health and safety of the pregnant woman will be properly maintained. But a state cannot overstep its boundaries that were set by the Court. A state cannot block the abortion procedure without showing good cause, nor can the state be concerned about matters that do not involve maternal health.

A state's compelling interest is not necessary during the first 12 weeks of pregnancy, but the holding of the Court on this issue should not be misconstrued to imply that the first trimester of pregnancy is free from regulation.

Viewpoint: Selected Dissenting Views of Justice O'Connor (Paraphrase)

Historical Note: The United States Supreme Court was authorized by Article III of the Constitution. Its organization was first established by the Judiciary Act of 1789. In the 190 years that followed, the United States Supreme Court had all male justices until the selection of Sandra Day O'Connor in 1980 by President Ronald Reagan.

Justice O'Connor disagreed with the majority opinion of the Court and thus dissented. She was joined by Justices White and Rehnquist.

A regulation placed on legal abortion is not unconstitutional unless it interferes with the right in choosing to have an abortion. The burdensome guidelines should be applied to the challenged regulations during the entire term of pregnancy, without regard to a particular stage. Regardless of what we believe is wise or common sense in this area, the Constitution does not require of us to be "Platonic Guardians," nor does it impose upon the Court an absolute authority to invalidate laws simply because they do not meet our standards of social policy, wisdom, or prudence.

The trimester approach to regulating abortion enacted by the Court more than 10 years ago and used by the Court today in rationalizing the regulations in the cases before us cannot be considered as a legitimate framework for protecting women's rights or a state's interest. The decision of the Court today clearly demonstrates why a trimester approach is completely unworkable as a way of considering the conflict of personal rights and the binding interest of the state, which are involved in the abortion situation.

Over the last 10 years, 1973–1983, great strides have been made in upgrading medical technology, which the Court has acknowledged in commenting that a state's compelling interest in the abortion procedure must change to coincide with the improvements in medical technology. A prime example of the advancements in medicine is that in 1973, physicians recommended hospitalization for second-trimester abortion patients, but the method used today for second-trimester procedures is safe enough that there is no need for a law requiring hospitalization. The dilation-and-evacuation method being used today for post–first-trimester abortions is not new; in 1973 it was used for first-trimester abortions, but because of improved medical technology, the method can be used safely in second-trimester abortions until the 16th week of pregnancy in a nonhospital setting.

But regardless of the advancements in medical technology and the presumed safety of abortions, the Court has yet not made any strides of its own in changing what it established 10 years ago, by "clinging" onto the trimester approach it adopted a decade ago. A law enacted 10 years ago to regulate abortions cannot be relied on today. States must continually study medical literature in determining whether a particular regulation is constitutional, in accordance with acceptable medical practice, while taking into account the trimester approach to abortion procedures.

Medical knowledge will continually move forward, while technology will move the point of viability backward. In 1973, the accepted point of viability was 28 weeks; any earlier case was considered unusual. Recent research has indicated that earlier fetal development is a growing theory. The probability of first-trimester viability may not be unusual in the near future. The Court, realizing that medical science is constantly in a state of flux, has rightfully left the point of viability flexible since it has already been established that viability is a combination of medical judgment, skill, and technical ability.

The process is almost reciprocal in that as medical science advances, the risk in having an abortion continually declines. A state's interest in the abortion procedure as it relates to maternal health begins just prior to the end of the first trimester, approximately the 12th week of pregnancy. However, as medical technology advances, the probability increases of a state's becoming involved early, with the point of viability moved back to conception. The legal precedent of *Roe* is inherently tied to the condition of medical technology that exists at the time of the particular litigation. There is a consensus of opinion that legislatures are (now) better prepared in making judgments in this area. The Court tends to force state legislatures to weigh facts pertaining to acceptable medical standards prior to enacting laws. Courts do not have experts in this area and must assume scientific awareness in order to review legislative judgments.

Assuming that a woman does have a fundamental right to terminate her unwanted pregnancy, relying on the logic of the trimester system adopted 10 years ago, the question must be asked, Is it still applicable today? Furthermore, can the Court justify applying a possible outdated system on abortion litigation of today? The reasoning used by the Court for this practice is the basic foundation of common law; similar cases are decided employing the reasoning of previous litigations *(stare decisis)* unless there is a compelling reason for the Court to do otherwise.

The Court acknowledged in *Roe vs. Wade* that a state has important interests in the areas of patient health care, both preoperative and postoperative, and the medical standards of the hospital or health facility. In addition, the state is obligated by law to see that the abortion procedure is treated with concern for the health and safety of the patient, as would be required of other surgical procedures, as well as the protection of potential life. I agree completely that the state has these interests, but in my view the point at which these interests become compelling does not depend on the trimester of pregnancy.

The Constitution does not dictate that states have the power to legislate the safety of surgical procedures. The procedures and methods of diagnosis used in treating patients are not the decisions of judges. The guidelines of the trimester system do not require a state to have an intensive involvement in the area of maternal health until approximately the end of the first trimester, reasoning that abortions performed during the first trimester are relatively safe. In some medical circles a first-trimester procedure is thought to be safer than normal childbirth.

The Court-imposed trimester system prohibits a state from assuming an interest in the abortion procedure until the point in the pregnancy when abortion becomes more dangerous than childbirth. Lawmakers who oppose the trimester system have had difficulty in finding the logic of allowing a state to intervene only after the point when abortion is, statistically speaking, considered more dangerous than childbirth, while not allowing them to observe the situation during the "safe" period of abortion.

Ten years ago the Court established that a state may have legitimate interest in potential life when the fetus is viable, but even at this stage of pregnancy the decision for determining viability is made by the physician. However, the rationale is unclear because potential life is no more potential at viability than during the first weeks of pregnancy. A life can be considered potential at any time during a term of pregnancy. The Court abstained from resolving the question of when life begins but did choose the point of viability. I believe that a state's interest in protecting potential human life exists throughout pregnancy.

Referring to the Akron ordinance that requires hospitalization for second-trimester patients, the Court misinterpreted the meaning of the ordinance in finding that it was overly restrictive because it placed "obstacles" in the path of women desiring to terminate their unwanted pregnancy. The Court reasoned that full-service hospitals were more expensive and had fewer facilities for accommodating second-trimester abortion patients, whereas the smaller, less expensive abortion clinics had more facilities in the city of Akron. The Court's primary argument in opposing the ordinance focused (unjustifiably) on the increased costs and decreased availability of full-service hospitals, while at the same time the city continually denied that Akron's two full-service hospitals have ever refused admittance of a pregnant woman desiring a second-trimester abortion or that the hospitals involved have ever prohibited the use of the "D & E" method. Additionally, there was no evidence that would lead one to believe that hospitals outside the city limits of Akron would refuse to perform second-trimester abortions.

Perhaps the expressed concern over the issue of hospitalization for second-trimester patients is a bit exaggerated by the Court when there are other higher-priority issues for which the Court may wish to consider state interference. These matters are more closely related to a patient's well-being and include the woman's physical, emotional, and psychological condition, in addition to her age. The American College of Obstetricians and Gynecologists (ACOG) Technical Bulletin No. 56, section 4, states that regardless of the advances in abortion technology, mid-trimester terminations will likely remain more hazardous, expensive and emotionally disturbing for a woman than early (in pregnancy) abortions. The hospitalization requirement is rational in that it is based on a valid objective of insuring the health and safety of the pregnant woman will be maintained.

Section 1870.05(B)(2) of the Akron ordinance (providing that no physician shall perform an abortion on minors who are unwed and under 15 years of age unless the minor gives written consent and the physician obtains informed written permission from a parent or guardian) was held unconstitutional by the Court on grounds that it may be construed as being an opportunity to create a system of case evaluation of the level of maturity of the pregnant minor. I believe that the Court should have abstained from declaring the ordinance invalid.

The Court feels that any law which requires parental consent for mature minors would be ruled unconstitutional. There is no reason to believe that the Akron ordinance would be an encouragement to judges arbitrarily to inform parents if the notification was against the minor's best interest. The Court's lack of knowledge of the workings of the Akron consent ordinance displays a total disregard for the rightful independence of state government.

During the litigation of *Planned Parenthood vs. Danford,* the Court found no constitutional defect in allowing an adult pregnant woman desiring to terminate her pregnancy to consent to the procedure in writing. Justices felt a requirement of this nature to be beneficial and should be a compulsory part of an abortion decision, because a woman who must face a resolution of this magnitude is placed under a lot of stress and participating in the planning of the abortion is essential. Furthermore, justices did not find the requirement to be unduly burdensome or overly restrictive, because it in no way blocked her abortion decision. Akron enacted a similar law, which the Court has held to be unconstitutional. The sole purpose of Akron's law was to insure all interested parties that women desiring to terminate their pregnancies would be fully informed of the serious consequences of a wrong decision. The requirement does not violate an individual's right to privacy, guaranteed in the Fourteenth Amendment.

The 24-hour waiting period was invalidated by the Court because it created a change in first-trimester abortion decisions. The Court concurred with the lower court's resolution, but for different reasons. It found that the ordinance failed to prove that it would be of great importance in furthering a state's interest in the abortion decision. In addition, the requirement was found to be overbearing and inflexible. The Court accepted the argument of the Akron Center (plaintiff), regarding increased costs and extra trips to and from the hospital, plus the risks involved in delaying the abortion if the 24-hour waiting period was enforced. The Court felt that a decision to delay or proceed with the abortion is a medical judgment that should be made by a medical practitioner.

In 1982 the American College of Obstetricians and Gynecologists recommended that women should obtain specialized counseling, which would be beneficial in assisting in regulating the unwanted pregnancy and in analyzing the risks involved; the woman should have time to reflect on her decision before consenting to the procedure.

There is no logic behind the Court's decision to invalidate the 24-hour waiting period, when it was shown that during an emergency situation the edicts of the requirement would be waived. Emergencies would include the concerns of the attending physician if he felt that an additional waiting period would place the life of his patient in danger. A state's compelling interest in maternal health and protection of the fetus is enough to justify a waiting period of 24 hours. The waiting period is not a great consequence to impose when one considers that the procedure involves the purposeful termination of potential life.

Regarding the decision of the Court to invalidate a regulation requiring the "proper" disposal of fetal remains, the ordinance was invalidated on grounds that some of its language was vague. Earlier, the district court likewise invalidated the ordinance on grounds that there were strong implications that at some future time the requirement would result in expensive burials for the fetus, regardless of its stage of development. The city of Akron, however, made an unsuccessful attempt to convince the Court that there were no "hidden intents" in the ordinance that would require physicians to provide burials for the fetuses they abort.

The Court's Decision

On June 15, 1983, almost seven months after arguments began on all relevant matters pertaining to Akron's abortion ordinances, a decision was reached. The justices, in a split decision, voted to affirm the findings of the lower court, with the exception of one provision. In the opinion of the Court, section 1870.03 was unconstitutional. There can be no doubt that (imposing) hospitalization for second-trimester abortions places a significant obstacle in the path of women seeking an abortion.

Justice Powell read the majority opinion of the court and was joined by Chief Justice Burger and Justices Brennan, Marshall, Blackmun, and Stevens. Justice O'Connor read a lengthy dissenting opinion, disagreeing with the Court majority on most of the issues. O'Connor was joined by Justices White and Rehnquist.

11: Missouri (Kansas City) Statutes on Abortion

188.025: Every abortion performed subsequent to the first twelve weeks of pregnancy shall be performed in a hospital.

188.047: A representative sample of tissue removed at the time of the abortion shall be submitted to a board of eligible or certified pathologists, who shall file a copy of the tissue report with the State Division of Health and who shall provide a copy of the report to the abortion facility or hospital in which the abortion was performed or induced, and the pathologist's report shall be made a part of the patient's permanent record.

188.030.3: An abortion of a viable unborn child shall be performed or induced only when there is in attendance a physician other than the physician performing or inducing the abortion who shall take control of and provide immediate medical care for a child born as a result of the abortion. During the performance of the abortion, the physician performing it, and subsequent to the abortion the physician required by this section to be in attendance, shall take all reasonable steps in keeping with good medical practice consistent with the procedure used to preserve the life and health of the viable unborn child; provided that it does not pose an increased risk to the life or health of the woman.

188.028.1: No person shall knowingly perform an abortion upon a pregnant woman under the age of 18 years, unless:

188.028.1(1): The attending physician has secured the informed written consent of the minor and one parent or guardian; or,

188.028.1(2): The minor is emancipated and the attending physician has received the informed written consent of the minor; or,

188.028.1(3): The minor has been granted the right to self consent to the abortion by court order pursuant to (2) of this section and the attending physician has received the informed written consent of the minor; or,

188.028.1(4): The minor has been granted consent to the abortion by court order and the court has given its informed written consent in accordance with (2) of this section and the minor is having the abortion willingly in compliance with (3) of this section.

188.028.2: The right of a minor to self-consent to an abortion under 188.028.1(3) or court consent under 188.028.1(4) may be granted by a court pursuant to the following procedures:

188.028.2(1): The minor or next friend shall make an application to the juvenile court which shall assist the minor's next friend in preparing the petition and notices required pursuant to this section. The minor or next friend of the minor shall thereafter file a petition setting forth the initials of the minor, the age of the minor, the names and addresses of each parent, guardian, or, if the minor's parents are deceased and no guardian has been appointed, any other person representing the minor, that the minor has been fully informed of the risks involved and consequences of the abortion; that the minor is of sound mind and has sufficient intellectual capacity to consent to the abortion; that if the court does not grant the minor majority rights for the purpose of consent to the abortion, the court should find that the abortion is in the best interest of the minor and give judicial consent to the abortion; that the court appoint a guardian of the child if the minor does not have private counsel. The petition shall be signed by the minor or next friend.

188.028.2(3): A hearing on the merits of the petition, to be held on record, shall be held as soon as possible within five days of the filing of the petition. At the hearing, the court shall hear evidence relating to the emotional development, maturity, intellect, and understanding of the minor; the nature, possible consequences, and alternatives to the abortion and any other evidence that the court may find useful in determining whether the minor should be granted majority rights for the purpose of consenting to the abortion or whether the abortion is in the best interests of the minor.

188.028.2(4): In the decree the court shall for good cause;
(a) Grant the petition for majority rights for the purpose of consenting to the abortion; or
(b) Find the abortion to be in the best interest of the minor and give judicial consent to the abortion, setting forth the grounds for so finding; or
(c) Deny the petition, setting forth the grounds on which the petition is denied.

188.028.3: If a minor desires an abortion, she shall be orally informed of and if possible sign the written consent required by 188.039, in the same manner as an adult person. No abortion shall be performed on any minor against her will, except that an abortion may be performed against the will of a minor pursuant to a court order described in 188.028.1(4) that the abortion is necessary to preserve the life of the minor.

The federal district court invalidated all sections but 188.047: Requiring a Pathologist's Report. The United States court of appeals reversed in part and affirmed in part the findings of the district court.

It reversed section 188.028: Protection of Immature Minors (including all subsections) and section 188.047: Requiring a Pathologist's Report.

It affirmed and sustained section 188.030.3: Requiring a Second Physician and section 188.025: Requiring Hospitalization for Second Trimester Abortions.

The United States Supreme Court reversed in part and affirmed in part the judgment of the court of appeals.

Section 188.025: Requiring Hospitalization for Second Trimester Abortions was ruled unconstitutional by the United States Supreme Court.

Section 188.030.3: Requiring a Second Physician, Section 188.047: Requiring a Pathologist's Report, and Section 188.028: Requiring Protection of Immature Minors (including all subsections) were ruled constitutional.

Planned Parenthood of Kansas City vs. Ashcroft

Kansas City (Missouri) enacted a number of abortion laws that severely restricted abortion procedures in that city. A complaint was filed in the District Court for the Western District of Missouri. The plaintiffs in this action were Planned Parenthood of Kansas City, Missouri, Inc., an abortion clinic, and two Missouri physicians who perform abortions. In their suit against John Ashcroft, attorney general of Missouri, plaintiffs listed a number of sections they considered to be unconstitutional. They included: 188.025, requiring hospitalization for abortions performed after the 12th week of pregnancy (a similar law was struck down in the Akron litigation); 188.047, requiring a pathologist's report be filed after each abortion; 188.030.3, necessitating that a second physician be present for abortions performed after the stage of viability; and 188.028, requiring either parental or judicial (juvenile court) permission for minors who seek an abortion.

In 1981 the United States district court, after hearing testimony from both sides, invalidated all but one statute. Not entirely satisfied with the finding of the district court, the case was next appealed to the United States court of appeals, which reversed in part and affirmed in part the decision of the district court. The United States Supreme Court began hearing the case on November 30, 1982, reaching a decision on June 15, 1983.

Second Physician

The Court decided that the requirement of a second physician in attendance during a postviability abortion procedure is reasonable in furthering the interest of the state in protecting of a fetus that is "presumed" to be viable.

In the abortion cases of 1973, it was established that a state assumes a "binding" interest in the life of the fetus when it reaches viability. At this stage the state has the right to enforce its power to regulate the abortion or to prohibit it. The state of Missouri has completely prohibited abortion after the stage of viability unless it becomes necessary to preserve the life of the mother. That law states that if it is necessary to perform an abortion involving a live fetus, a second physician must be in attendance to assist in the procedure. The duty of the second physician is to take responsibility for preserving the life and health of the unborn child. The lifesaving methods must not present or create a hazard to the life and health of the female patient, however. The second physician is also required to provide immediate medical care for a child born during an abortion procedure.

The lower court invalidated the second-physician requirement because jurists felt that the idea misconstrues the traditional patient-doctor relationship, in addition to the fact that the state of Missouri does not require a second physician to assist in normal childbirths or for delivery of a premature infant. The other side argued, however, that third-trimester abortions are usually performed under emergency conditions, making the assistance of a second physician almost a necessity. The presumption is that one physician would employ his best medical skills in preserving the life of the pregnant woman, while the other physician would work to protect the life and health of the aborted fetus.

Pathologist's Report

The Court found the requirement of a pathologist's report necessary to further important health-related concerns of the state, which in no way interferes with the abortion decision or procedure. The benefits medical science receives from a pathologist's examination of vital tissue is of significant value and worth the small additional costs incurred.

Pathologist reports are required for all surgeries. Abortion is not singled out in this case, the only difference being that with abortion the pathologist is required to file a report with the state Division of Health.

While the court of appeals acknowledged a pathologist report essential in furthering the interest of a state in areas of maternal health and providing valuable information on the effects of future pregnancies, plaintiffs argued that the attending physician is as qualified as a pathologist in examining tissue. The defendants countered with the argument that in most surgeries it is customary to have a pathologist, not the physician, perform the postoperative procedure.

The Court found that the benefits medical science will receive in furthering the protection of maternal health outweigh the additional costs for the pathologist. Furthermore, the Court felt the requirement in no way added additional burdens to a woman's decision to have an abortion.

Hospitalization for Second-Trimester Abortions

The Court found this requirement to be unconstitutional because it required second-trimester abortions to be performed in a hospital with a JCAH accreditation. The law was similar in design to that of Akron, which was ruled unconstitutional by the Court because requiring second-trimester abortions to be performed in a full-service hospital exclusively is unconstitutional. In 1973, there was strong support in favor of hospitalization for second-trimester abortions, but advances in medical technology have made the requirement unnecessary. Abortions may now (in 1983) be performed in a nonhospital setting up to the 16th week of pregnancy, using the "D & E" abortion method. The Court found the regulation to be a violation of a woman's constitutional right to have an abortion and cited similar reasons used in the Akron litigation for invalidating Missouri's statute.

Substitute Consent

The Court acknowledged that a state has a vested interest in protecting immature minors who are pregnant and desire an abortion. For this reason the Court found the substitute-consent requirement to be constitutional, in that it allows for parental or judicial consent. The meritorious tone of this statute is that if parents are not agreeable to an abortion for their teenage daughter, she may seek the help of a juvenile court as a source of substitute consent; the court cannot refuse the consent application unless "good cause" is shown as to why the application should be denied. An example of "good cause" would be that a minor did not understand the serious physical and emotional trauma that can be the result of a wrong decision.

When a state enacts a law requiring consent, it must provide for alternative measures so that an adolescent who does not possess a high level of maturity will have every opportunity to establish her level of understanding in making an informed decision to have an abortion. The Missouri law exempts women who are under 18 years of age and either emancipated or married from the consent provision. The Court agreed with the interpretation of the statute.

Opinion of the Court:
Read by Justice Powell (Paraphrase)

The city of Akron had a similar law that allowed second-trimester abortions to be performed only in a full-service hospital that had a JCAH accreditation or was certified by the American Osteopathic Association. The Court invalidated that ordinance on grounds that it unreasonably infringed upon a woman's constitutional right to obtain an abortion. Action similar to the Akron litigation is taken here; Section 188.025 is invalidated.

Missouri prohibits all postviability abortions unless the health of the pregnant woman is in jeopardy. In addition, the state forbids any abortion method that would endanger the life of the unborn child, the exception being to save the life of the mother. Missouri enacted a law that requires a second physician to be present during abortions performed after the stage of viability is reached. The primary intent of the law is to insure that the second physician will use his best medical judgment to preserve the health and life of the unborn child. Accordingly the second physician is made responsible for providing immediate medical attention to the fetus if it is delivered during an abortion. This procedure fulfills a state's obligation to protect potential life. Preserving the life of a viable fetus is not 100 percent sure, but the state has a compelling interest in providing safeguards in case the unusual occurs. The Court therefore feels that a second physician requirement is reasonable and reverses the findings of the lower court.

The regulation of hospital services in the state of Missouri requires that all tissue removed during surgery shall be examined by a pathologist, either in a hospital facility or by arrangement at an outside medical laboratory. Missouri law clearly stipulates that the examination is to be done by a recognized pathologist, not the attending physician. The appellate court agreed with the theory that a pathologist examination of tissue is significant in furthering medical science. This examination can lead to discoveries not visible to the naked eye, including any abnormalities that could provide the attending physician with valuable advance warning of possible serious fetal disorders.

The importance of the medical data derived from a pathology examination far outweighs the additional costs of the abortion procedure. The Court views this type of postoperative service as an insignificant burden.

Missouri has a vested interest in the protection of immature minors who are pregnant and desire an abortion. A law enacted in Missouri provides for alternative consent, parental or judicial. The juvenile court, in its role as a source of alternative consent, will exercise its option on an application of consent of a pregnant minor only after it is made aware of pertinent data on the minor, including her emotional development, maturity, intellect, and limits of understanding. After reviewing all of the evidence, the court can deny the application only for "good cause." If the application is denied, it is usually because the court feels the adolescent lacks the necessary level of maturity to make the decision on her own. The court of appeals was correct in its interpretation of this regulation, which is void of constitutional defect.

Viewpoint: Selected Views of Justice Blackmun, Concurring in Part, Dissenting in Part (Paraphrase)

Justice Blackmun was joined in his opinion by Justices Brennan, Marshall, and Stevens.

I am in agreement with the opinion of the Court in its finding that second-trimester abortions must be performed only in a hospital setting as being

unconstitutional and with the ruling that a second physician in attendance during late-trimester abortions is not an unreasonable requirement. But I do not
agree with the requirement of a pathologist's report. The requirement applies
to first-trimester abortions as well as those performed later in the term of
pregnancy. Previous decisions of the Court have prohibited any state interference for first-trimester abortion procedures. As was noted in *Akron*, the
rule applied to first-trimester procedures does not mean that any regulation
has to be justifiably constitutional. Valid regulations regarding first-trimester
abortions must have no significant effect on a woman's fundamental right to
have an abortion, and motives of the state in protecting maternal health must
be important enough to justify constitutional regulation.

A pathologist's report does not justify a state's important commitment to
maternal health. This is not meant to imply that such a report is not helpful
in some cases. The law goes beyond a simple requirement. According to plaintiffs, the condition is a "demand" that the report be written by a select board
of recognized pathologists, rather than the woman's personal physician.

According to plaintiffs, it is not a "generally accepted medical practice"
to require a pathologist's report. The usual method is for the attending physician to perform a visual or gross examination of any tissue removed during
an abortion or any other surgery. The only justification for a pathologist's report
would be the physician's discovering abnormalities in the removed tissue. A
report issued by the American College of Obstetricians and Gynecologists
(ACOG), titled "ACOG Standards for Obstetric-Gynecologic Services" stated
that there is no real necessity for a pathologist report. Tissue removed should
be submitted to a pathologist for examination. An exception to the practice
may be in elective terminations of pregnancy in which definitive embryonic
or fetal parts can be identified. In such instances the physician should record
a description of the visual products. Unless definite embryonic or fetal parts
can be identified, the products of elective interruptions of pregnancy must be
submitted to a pathologist for gross and microscopic examination.

A group calling themselves the National Abortion Federation released
a statement on the issue of a pathologist's report. In it they stated that all tissue
must be examined visually at the time of the abortion by a physician or trained
assistant and the results recorded on a chart. In the absence of visible fetal
parts or placenta upon gross examination, obtained tissue must be examined
under a low power microscope for the detection of "villi" (a minute projection
arising from mucous membranes). If the examination is inconclusive, the tissue
should be sent to the nearest suitable pathology laboratory for microscopic
evaluation.

The court of appeals acknowledged that a medical practitioner other than
a pathologist is probably just as capable of performing a gross examination
on removed tissue. Though a pathologist may be more experienced in performing the procedure of microscopic examinations, Missouri does not require that

form of evaulation unless fetal parts are unidentifiable. In essence the appellate court found the requirement for a pathologist report unnecessary since the responsibility is usually that of the attending physician.

I must therefore conclude that the state did not prove that a requirement of a pathologist's report is important in furthering a state's concern relating to maternal health. Evidence during this litigation has shown that Missouri does not require the report of a pathologist for surgeries performed in a clinic or for "minor" surgeries performed in a hospital. I cannot say that the cost is equally insignificant for all women who seek abortion. Women on welfare or an unemployed teenager may not be able to afford the costs added to the abortion procedure.

In the state of Missouri, an abortion can be performed after the stage of viability only if the life of the mother is at risk. For this late procedure there must be a second physician in attendance who is responsible for providing immediate medical care for a child born as a result of the abortion. The Court ruled the second physician requirement to be valid, because jurists felt that it furthered the interest of the state in protecting the life of the fetus. I agree with the concept of requiring a second physician to preserve the life of a fetus born alive. However, this type of assistance is possible only when the abortion method used is one that may result in a live birth. Although Missouri ordinarily requires a physician performing a postviability abortion to use the abortion method most likely to preserve fetal life, this restriction does not apply when this method would present a greater risk to the life and health of the woman.

At times it may be necessary to use the "D & E" method because the technique is considered to be the safest method for late-trimester abortion procedures. But, while the D & E method provides the most protection for saving the life of the pregnant woman, it offers very little hope for fetal survival. Even though this is a known fact, the method is still preferred by many physicians for late procedures. This leads to the reasoning that a second physician's participation is not necessary. His presence would only create more stress for the pregnant woman.

As part of planning an abortion, physicians choose the method well in advance of performing the procedure. Missouri requires physicians to select the abortion method that will best promote fetal survival, but also to take into consideration the health of the pregnant woman by selecting a method that would not jeopardize her life. If a late abortion is scheduled for the period following viability of the fetus, Missouri requires a mandatory certification by the physician in writing stating his choice of abortion method. If he selects the D & E method, there is no need for a second physician.

The Court found the law to be constitutionally defective because it failed to provide for exceptions in the event of an emergency situation. Justice Powell, in his opinion, commented that an emergency may arise in which delay could be dangerous to the life of the pregnant woman. Since the state of Missouri requires a second physician for all postviability abortions, the inflexibility could eventually lead to a second physician's not being available when needed, and thus a problem results. However, not only is the law inflexible, but it is also vague in that it fails to provide definite instructions for physicians to follow in the event a second physician is unavailable for an emergency postviability abortion. This type of situation is very delicate since the life of the pregnant woman may lie in the balance.

A Missouri law requires either parental or court-ordered consent for minors who are not emancipated and desire an abortion. In previous litigations, the Court has invalidated all substitute-consent requirements. The reasoning the Court used to invalidate similar legislation was that a state is powerless to grant a third party absolute authority in vetoing an abortion decision.

Because Missouri law allows for a parental or judicial veto of a minor's abortion decision, I believe it to be unconstitutional.

Viewpoint: Selected Views of Justice O'Connor, Concurring in Part, Dissenting in Part (Paraphrase)

Justice O'Connor made some brief comments on various issues involved in this Court action, agreeing with some of the majority holdings and disagreeing with others. She was joined in her comments by Justices White and Rehnquist.

For reasons stated in my dissent in *Akron vs. Akron Center for Reproductive Health,* I believe that a law requiring hospitalization for second-trimester abortion procedures is not unduly burdensome. Assuming the requirement was indeed burdensome, it would nevertheless be considered a reasonable effort in protecting maternal health. I therefore dissent from the Court's ruling to invalidate the statute.

I agree with the Court in finding the law (requiring two physicians in attendance) constitutional because the state has a binding interest in protecting and preserving prenatal life. However, I believe that this interest exists throughout the term of pregnancy. I therefore concur with the finding of the Court regarding the need for two physicians during abortion procedures performed after the viability of the fetus.

I feel that the pathology-report requirement imposes no burden on the limited right to undergo an abortion. I am therefore in agreement with the ruling. I do not believe the legality of this law is conditional to the particular trimester of pregnancy in which it is imposed. I concur with the findings of the Court.

Missouri law imposes no unjustified obligation on any right a minor may have in arranging for an abortion. I concur with the judgment of the Court on the substitute-consent requirement being constitutional.

The Court's Decision

On June 15, 1983, the United States Supreme Court, after lengthy debates that resulted in a widely split court, voted by a bare-minimum majority to reverse in part and to affirm in part the decision of the lower court.

Justice Powell read the opinion of the Court in respect to Missouri statutes sections 188.025, Requiring Hospitalization for Second Trimester Abortions; 188.047, Requiring a Pathologist's Report; 188.030.3, Requiring a Second Physician; and 188.028, Protection of Immature Minors. Chief Justice Burger joined in the majority opinion on all issues with the exception of section 188.025. Burger did not support the majority opinion with respect to hospitalization for second-trimester abortions.

Justices Brennan, Marshall, and Stevens joined in the opinion of Justice Blackmun, who dissented on some issues and concurred with the majority on one issue, section 188.025, Requiring Hospitalization for Second Trimester Abortions. Among the issues that Justice Blackmun dissented were Requiring a Pathologist's Report, Requiring a Second Physician for Late Trimester Abortions, and Protection of Immature Minors.

Justices White and Rehnquist joined in the opinion of Justice O'Connor, who agreed in part with the majority opinion. Justice O'Connor concurred on Missouri statutes sections 188.030.3, 188.047 and 188.028, but expressed disagreement with the Court majority on section 188.025, which required hospitalization for post–first-trimester abortion procedures.

12: The State of Virginia
Abortion Ordinance Sec. 18.2–71

Producing Abortion or Miscarriage

Except as provided in other sections of Article IX, if any person administer to or cause to be taken by a woman any drug or other thing, or use means with intent to destroy her unborn child or to produce abortion or miscarriage and thereby destroy such child or produce such abortion or miscarriage, he shall be guilty of a class 4 felony.

There are four exceptions to this law of criminal liability:
   (1) The abortion is performed within the first trimester.
   (2) Second-trimester abortions are performed in a state-licensed hospital.
   (3) Third-trimester abortions are performed under state-mandated regulations.
   (4) Abortion is necessary to save the mother's life.

Simopoulos vs. The State of Virginia

The plaintiff-appellant in this action was an obstetrician-gynecologist who was convicted for violating a Virginia law that made it unlawful to perform second-trimester abortions at any facility the state did not consider a licensed hospital. The word *hospital*, as defined by the Virginia State Department of Health, is a facility that performs surgical procedures on outpatients. The definition also includes clinics that perform abortions among other minor surgeries. Charges were filed against the appellant after it was learned that he performed a second-trimester procedure on an unmarried minor, using the saline method at his private "unlicensed" clinic. A misunderstanding between physician and patient resulted in the minor aborting her fetus in a motel room approximately 48 hours after the saline-infusion method was used.

As a result of the physician's actions, he was indicted and subsequently convicted by the Fairfax County Circuit Court. During his testimony, the appellant stated that he was a practicing obstetrician-gynecologist who was certified by the American Board of Obstetrics and Gynecology. In November

1979, he was in private practice in the city of Woodbridge, Virginia, as well as being on staff at four local hospitals and his clinic in Falls Church, Virginia. The appellant had performed first-trimester abortions at his clinic even though it was not licensed by the state. There was no evidence presented that showed that the appellant had made an effort to license his facility.

In November 1979, an unmarried pregnant minor who was under 18 years of age went to the unlicensed clinic operated by the appellant for an abortion. The minor was 22 weeks pregnant and desired to terminate her pregnancy without informing her parents. The appellant testified that he had talked to her about including her parents in the abortion decision and discussed alternatives to abortion, including the possibility of carrying her pregnancy to term. The minor, however, was determined to have an abortion without involving her parents.

The appellant performed the abortion, using the saline-infusion method. Afterward the minor informed the appellant that she intended to deliver her fetus in a motel room, assuming that he agreed with her wishes. After providing his patient with a prescription for a pain killer and instructions on what to do when labor began, things began to go awry. A presumed miscommunication occurred when the minor understood the appellant to agree with her plan to deliver the fetus in a motel and did not recall being advised to go to a hospital when labor began. Later in the day, police discovered the fetus in the motel room wastebasket, along with the pain killer medication and written instructions provided by the appellant.

The physician-appellant was later indicted for unlawfully performing an abortion during the second trimester of pregnancy outside a licensed hospital. He was subsequently convicted by the Circuit Court of Fairfax County, Virginia. The indictment and later conviction were based on appellant's violation of Virginia Code, Section 18.2-71. The state of Virginia describes a class 4 felony as a violation that subjects a physician's license to practice to a mandatory revocation and an automatic prison term of 2 to 10 years. The Virginia Supreme Court affirmed the conviction of the lower court.

Regulating Second-Trimester Abortion Procedures

The state of Virginia enacted a law that required all second-trimester abortions to be performed in a hospital facility licensed by the state and certified by the Virginia Department of Health. The law strictly prohibited second-trimester abortions from being performed in any facility that was not certified by the state as a facility that performs surgical procedures. State lawmakers felt the law to be in total compliance with federal guidelines with respect to a state's interest in matters of maternal health.

The court found the law to be restrictive, but with more flexibility than the hospitalization requirements imposed by the city of Akron, which required second-trimester procedures to be performed in a full-service hospital approved by the state. The Virginia restriction did not require hospitalization for second-trimester procedures, nor did it insist that the abortion be performed in a full-service hospital. The law defined a *hospital* as an outpatient clinic that specializes in performing surgical procedures and is licensed by the state.

The Virginia law appeared to be in compliance with acceptable medical standards, even though the method of choice for second-trimester abortions up to the 16th week of pregnancy is dilation and evacuation, which can be used in a nonhospital setting. The American Public Health Association (APHA) recommends the procedure be performed in a state-approved surgical facility, however.

Opinion of the Court:
Read by Justice Powell (Paraphrase)

Justice Powell read the opinion of the Court and was joined by Justices Brennan, Marshall, Blackmun, and Chief Justice Burger.

Appellant's argument is narrowly based on his assumption that a state does not have the authority to require second-trimester abortions be performed in full-service hospitals. However, it is conceivable that appellant has misconstrued Virginia's statute as restricting second-trimester abortions to full-service hospitals when in actuality the statute merely requires that the procedure be performed in a state-approved hospital that performs outpatient surgeries.

The Virginia law is clearly stated; there are no hidden meanings. There is little reason to believe that a properly certified state-approved clinic would have difficulty in performing second-trimester abortion procedures. The Court has therefore concluded that Virginia's requirement is not unreasonable in satisfying a state's mandated interest in protecting matters relating to maternal health. A decade ago (1973) in *Roe vs. Wade,* the Court made a stipulation that state laws regulate all surgical procedures in a like manner, that abortion should be treated no differently, because the major concern should be to insure maximum protection of a patient's health and safety. Another major point leading to the strong validity of the statute is that it did not impose the restriction that second-trimester procedures be performed only in acute-care facilities of a full-service hospital.

Virginia's abortion statute is in compliance with acceptable medical practice and is flexible in leaving the abortion decision as a medical judgment made by the physician and his patient.

Viewpoint: Selected Concurring Views of Justice O'Connor (Paraphrase)

Justice O'Connor read an opinion that was in agreement with the Court majority. She was joined by Justices White and Rehnquist.

I concur with the judgment of the Court insofar as it affirms the finding of the lower court. Virginia's mandatory abortion requirement is not dependent on the trimester. The statute does not impose additional burdens on the abortion decision.

Viewpoint: Selected Dissenting Views of Justice Stevens (Paraphrase)

Prior to the 1973 court decision of *Roe vs. Wade,* it was a felony to perform an abortion in the state of Virginia, the exception being that it was performed in a hospital accredited by the Joint Committee on Accreditation of Hospitals and licensed by the State Department of Health. The procedure had to be approved by a hospital committee consisting of three physicians. After meeting the state-mandated requirements, a pregnant woman found an additional tier of restrictions that prohibited abortion if (1) her health was not in jeopardy, (2) her pregnancy was not a result of rape or incest, and (3) the possibility existed that the fetus would not be born with some irreversible mental or physical defect. In 1975 Virginia expanded abortion laws that required second-trimester procedures be performed only in state-approved facilities.

The statute in question may be interpreted in two ways; it may be construed as permitting second-trimester abortions to be performed only in a full-service hospital, acute-care facility, or, as the Court has chosen to define the word *hospital,* a state-licensed and certified outpatient surgical clinic. The possibility exists that the misinterpretation of the statute belongs to the Court. When the statute was first written, it made no reference to a hospital as an outpatient clinic. In 1977 the state of Virginia reported that out of the 26 hospitals in the state that were licensed to perform abortions, none were referred to as outpatient clinics; all were full-service hospitals with acute-care facilities.

The probability exists, however, that indeed the Court has interpreted the statute correctly. In any event, this Court does not include interpreting state laws as one of its functions, nor should it decide an issue based on the definition of a word it never endorsed. The Virginia Supreme Court defined the statute as implying that the state could require all second-trimester abortions be performed in full-service hospitals. The proper judicial remedy would be to vacate the ruling of the lower court and to remand the case back to that court so that all relevant issues could be reconsidered.

The Court's Decision

On June 15, 1983, the Supreme Court affirmed the decision of the Supreme Court of Virginia.

The opinion of the Court was read by Justice Powell. The Virginia abortion statute was not unconstitutionally applied to appellant on the asserted ground that the state failed to allege in the indictment and to prove the lack of medical necessity for the abortion. Under the authoritative construction of the statute by the Virginia Supreme Court, the prosecution was not obligated to prove lack of medical necessity beyond a reasonable doubt until appellant invoked medical necessity as a defense. In addition, appellant's contention that the prosecution failed to prove that his acts in fact caused the fetus's death is meritless in view of the undisputed facts proved at the trial. Concerning second-trimester abortions, Virginia's requirement that second-trimester abortions be performed in licensed outpatient clinics is not an unreasonable means of furthering the state's important and legitimate interest in protecting the woman's health, which interest becomes compelling at the end of the first trimester. In previous cases the Court had upheld challenges to laws that required abortions to be performed only in acute-care facilities of full-service hospitals, but Virginia does not require that second-trimester abortions be performed in such facilities, allowing them to be performed in outpatient clinics.

Although a state's discretion in determining standards for licensing of medical facilities does not permit it to adopt abortion regulations that depart from accepted medical practice, the Virginia regulations on their face are compatible with accepted medical standards governing outpatient second-trimester abortions. The opinion was joined by Chief Justice Burger and Justices Brennan, Marshall, and Blackmun.

Justice O'Connor agreed with the majority opinion, filing a separate concurring opinion in which Justices White and Rehnquist joined. Justice Stevens was the lone dissenter in this case. Stevens felt that because there was no mention of *hospital* being defined as outpatient clinics when the law was first written, it was possible the Court may have misinterpreted the meaning of the word *hospital*, while on the other hand according to Stevens, the possibility exists that the Court did indeed interpret the word correctly. In any event, interpreting state laws is not a function of the Court. Justice Stevens thought that it would be best to vacate (invalidate) the finding of the Virginia Supreme Court and to send the case back to that court so that all relevant matters could be reevaluated.

13: Pennsylvania Abortion Control Act [Enacted 1982]

3202: LEGISLATIVE INTENT

(a) RIGHTS AND INTERESTS: It is the intention of the General Assembly of the Commonwealth of Pennsylvania to protect the life and health of the woman subject to abortion and to protect the life and health of the child subject to abortion. It is the further intention of the General Assembly to foster the development of standards of professional conduct in a critical area of medical practice, to provide for development of statistical data, and to protect the right of the minor woman voluntarily to decide to submit to abortion or to carry her child to term. The General Assembly finds as fact that the rights and interests furthered by this chapter are not secure in the context in which abortion is presently performed.

(b) CONCLUSIONS: Reliable and convincing evidence has compelled the General Assembly to conclude and the General Assembly does hereby solemnly declare and find that:

(1) Many women now seek or are encouraged to undergo abortions without full knowledge of the development of the unborn child or of alternatives to abortion.

(2) The gestation age at which viability of an unborn child occurs has been lowering substantially and steadily as advances in neonatal medical care continue to be made.

(3) A significant number of late-term abortions result in live births or in delivery of children who could survive if measures were taken to bring about breathing. Some physicians have been allowing these children to die or have been failing to induce breathing.

(4) Because the Commonwealth places a supreme value upon protecting human life, it is necessary that those physicians which it permits to practice medicine be held to precise standards of care in cases where their actions do or may result in the death of an unborn child.

(5) A reasonable waiting period, as contained in this chapter, is critical to the assurance that a woman elect to undergo an abortion procedure only after having the fullest opportunity to give her informed consent thereto.

(c) CONSTRUCTION: In every relevant civil or criminal proceeding in

115

which it is possible to do so without violating the federal Constitution, the common and statutory law of Pennsylvania shall be construed so as to extend to the unborn the equal protection of the laws and to further the public policy of this Commonwealth encouraging childbirth over abortion.

(d) RIGHT OF CONSCIENCE: It is the further public policy of the Commonwealth of Pennsylvania to respect and protect the right of conscience of all persons who refuse to obtain, receive, subsidize, accept, or provide abortions, including those persons who are engaged in the delivery of medical services and medical care, whether acting individually, corporately, or in association with other persons; and to prohibit all forms of discrimination, disqualification, coercion, disability, or imposition of liability or financial burden upon such persons or entities by reason of their refusing to act contrary to their conscience or conscientious convictions in refusing to obtain, receive, subsidize, accept, or provide abortions.

3203: DEFINITIONS

The following words and phrases when used in this chapter shall have, unless the context clearly indicates otherwise, the meanings given to them in this section:

"ABORTION." The use of any means to terminate the clinically diagnosable pregnancy of a woman with knowledge that the termination by those means will, with reasonable likelihood, cause the death of the unborn child, except that, for the purposes of this chapter, abortion shall not mean the use of an intrauterine device or birth-control pill to inhibit or prevent ovulation, fertilization, or the implantation of a fertilized ovum within the uterus.

"BORN ALIVE." When used with regard to a human being, means that the human being was completely expelled or extracted from her or his mother and after such separation breathed or showed evidence of any of the following: beating of the heart, pulsation of the umbilical cord, definite movement of the voluntary muscles, or any brain-wave activity.

"FACILITY OR MEDICAL FACILITY." Any public or private hospital, clinic, center, medical school, medical-training institution, health-care facility, physician's office, infirmary, dispensary, ambulatory surgical-treatment center, or other institution or location wherein medical care is provided to any person.

"FIRST TRIMESTER." The first twelve weeks of gestation.

"HOSPITAL." An institution licensed pursuant to the provisions of the law of this Commonwealth.

"MEDICAL EMERGENCY." That condition which, on the basis of the physician's best clinical judgment, so complicates a pregnancy as to necessitate the immediate abortion of the same to avert the death of the mother or for which a 24-hour delay will create peril of immediate and irreversible loss of major bodily function.

"MEDICAL PERSONNEL." Any nurse, nurse's aide, medical school student, professional, or any other person who furnishes, or assists in the furnishing of, medical care.

"PHYSICIAN." Any person licensed to practice medicine in this Commonwealth.

"PROBABLE GESTATIONAL AGE OF THE UNBORN CHILD." What, in the judgment of the attending physician, will with reasonable probability be the gestational age of the unborn child at the time the abortion is planned to be performed.

"UNBORN CHILD." A human being from fertilization until birth; includes a fetus.

"VIABILITY." That stage of fetal development when, in the judgment of the physician based on the particular facts of the case before him and in light of the most advanced medical technology and information available to him, there is reasonable likelihood of sustained survival of the unborn child outside the body of his or her mother, with or without artificial support.

3205: INFORMED CONSENT

(a) GENERAL RULE: No abortion shall be performed or induced except with the voluntary and informed consent of the woman upon whom the abortion is to be performed or induced. Except in the case of a medical emergency, consent to an abortion is voluntary and informed if and only if:

(1) The woman is provided, at least 24 hours before the abortion, with the following information by the physician but not by the agent or representative of either.

(a) The name of the physician who will perform the abortion.

(b) The fact that there may be detrimental physical and psychological effects which are not accurately foreseeable.

(c) The particular medical risks associated with the particular abortion procedure to be employed, including, when medically accurate, the risks of infection, hemorrhage, danger to subsequent pregnancies, and infertility.

(d) The probable gestational age of the unborn child at the time the abortion is to be performed.

(e) The medical risks associated with carrying her child to term.

(2) The woman is informed, by the physician or his agent, at least 24 hours before the abortion:

(a) That medical assistance benefits may be available for prenatal care, childbirth and neonatal care.

(b) That the father is liable to assist in support of her child, even in instances where the father has offered to pay for the abortion.

(c) That she has the right to review the printed materials described in 3208 (relating to printed information). The physician or his agent shall orally inform the woman that the materials describe the unborn child and list agencies which offer alternatives to abortion. If the woman chooses to view the materials, copies of them will be furnished to her. If the woman is unable to read the materials furnished her, the materials shall be read to her. If the woman seeks answers to questions concerning any of the information or materials, answers shall be provided her in her own language.

(3) The woman certifies in writing, prior to the abortion, that the information described in paragraphs (1) and (2) has been furnished her and that she has been informed of her opportunity to review the information referred to in paragraph (2).

(4) Prior to the performance of the abortion, the physician who is to perform or induce the abortion or his agent receives a copy of the written certification prescribed by paragraph (3).

(b) EMERGENCY: Where a medical emergency compels the performance of an abortion, the physician shall inform the woman, prior to the abortion if possible, of the medical indications supporting his judgment that an abortion is necessary to avert her death.

(c) PENALTY: Any physician who violates the provisions of this section is guilty of unprofessional conduct and his license for the practice of medicine and surgery shall be subject to suspension or revocation in accordance with the procedures as outlined in the Medical Practice Act of 1974. Any other person obligated under this chapter to give information relating to informed consent to a woman before an abortion is performed and who fails to give such information, shall, for the first offense, be guilty of a summary offense and for each subsequent offense, be guilty of a misdemeanor of the third degree.

(d) LIMITATION ON CIVIL LIBERTY: Any physician who complies with the provisions of this section may not be held civilly liable to his patient for failure to obtain informed consent to the abortion within the meaning of that term as defined by the act known as the Health Care Services Malpractice Act.

3207: ABORTION FACILITIES

(a) REPORTS: Within 30 days after the effective date of this chapter, every facility at which abortions are performed shall file and update immediately upon any change, a report with the department, which shall be open to public inspection and copying, containing the following information:
   (1) NAME AND ADDRESS OF FACILITY.
   (2) NAME AND ADDRESS OF ANY PARENT, SUBSIDIARY, OR AFFILIATED ORGANIZATIONS, CORPORATIONS, OR ASSOCIATIONS.
   (3) NAME AND ADDRESS OF ANY PARENT, SUBSIDIARY OR AFFILIATED ORGANIZATIONS, CORPORATIONS, OR ASSOCIATIONS HAVING CONTEMPORANEOUS COMMONALITY OF OWNERSHIP, BENEFICIAL INTEREST, DIRECTORSHIP, OR OFFICERSHIP WITH ANY OTHER FACILITY. Any facility failing to comply with the provisions of this subsection shall be assessed by the department a fine of $500 for each day it is in violation hereof.

3208: PRINTED INFORMATION

(a) GENERAL RULE: The department shall cause to be published in English, Spanish, and Vietnamese, within 60 days after this chapter becomes law, the following easily comprehensible materials:
   (1) Geographically indexed materials designed to inform the woman of public and private agencies and services available to assist a woman through pregnancy, upon childbirth and while a child is dependent, including adoption agencies, which include a comprehensive list of agencies available, a description of the services they offer, and a description of the manner, including the telephone number, in which they might be contacted, or, at the option of the department, printed materials including a toll-free 24-hour-a-day telephone number which may be called to obtain orally such a list and description of agencies in the locality of the caller and of the services they offer. The materials shall include the following statement: "There are many public and private agencies willing and able to help you to carry your child

to term, and to assist you and your child after your child is born, whether you choose to keep your child or to place him or her for adoption. The Commonwealth of Pennsylvania strongly urges you to contact them before making a final decision about abortion. The law requires that your physician or his agent give you the opportunity to call agencies like these before you undergo an abortion."

(2) Materials designed to inform the woman of the probable anatomical and psychological characteristics of the unborn child at two-week gestational increments from fertilization to full term, including any relevant information on the possibility of the unborn child's survival. The materials shall be objective, nonjudgmental, and designed to convey only accurate scientific information about the unborn child at the various gestational ages.

3209: ABORTION AFTER FIRST TRIMESTER

All abortions subsequent to the first trimester of pregnancy shall be performed, induced, and completed in a hospital. Except in cases of good faith judgment that a medical emergency exists, any physician who performs such an abortion in a place other than a hospital is guilty of "unprofessional conduct," and his license for the practice of medicine and surgery shall be subject to suspension or revocation in accordance with procedures provided under the Medical Practice Act of 1974.

3210: ABORTION AFTER VIABILITY

(a) PROHIBITION: Any person who intentionally, knowingly, or recklessly performs or induces abortion when the fetus is viable commits a felony of the third degree. It shall be a complete defense to any charge brought against a physician for violating the requirements of this section that he had concluded in good faith, in his best medical judgment, that the unborn child was not viable at the time the abortion was performed or induced or that the abortion was necessary to preserve maternal life or health.

(b) DEGREE OF CARE: Every person who performs or induces abortion after an unborn child has been determined to be viable shall exercise that degree of professional skill, care and diligence which some person would be required to preserve the health and life of any unborn child intended to be born and not aborted and the abortion technique employed shall be that which would provide the best opportunity for the unborn child to be aborted alive unless that method or technique would present a significantly greater medical risk to the life or health of the pregnant woman than would another available technique or method and the physician reports his basis for his judgment. The potential psychological or emotional impact on the mother of the unborn child's survival shall not be deemed a medical risk to the mother. Any person who intentionally, knowingly, or recklessly violates the provisions of this subsection commits a felony of the third degree.

(c) SECOND PHYSICIAN: Any person who intends to perform an abortion the method chosen for which, in good faith judgment, does not preclude the possibility of the child surviving the abortion, shall arrange for the attendance, in the same room in which the abortion is to be completed, of a second physician. Immediately after the complete expulsion or extraction of the child, the second physician shall take control of the child and shall provide immediate

medical care for the child, taking all reasonable steps necessary, in his judgment, to preserve the child's life and health. Any person who intentionally,
knowingly, or recklessly violates the provisions of this subsection commits
a felony of the third degree.

3211: VIABILITY

(a) DETERMINATION OF VIABILITY: Prior to performing any abortion
upon a woman subsequent to her first trimester of pregnancy, the physician
shall determine whether, in his good faith judgment, the child is viable. When
a physician has determined that a child is viable, he shall report the basis
for his determination that the abortion is necessary to preserve maternal life
or health. When a physician has determined that a child is not viable, he shall
report the basis for such determination.

(b) UNPROFESSIONAL CONDUCT: Failure of any physician to conform
to any requirement of this section constitutes "unprofessional conduct" within
the meaning of the Medical Practice Act of 1974. Upon a finding by a state
board of Medical Education and Licensure that any physician has failed to
conform to any requirement of this section, the board shall not fail to suspend that physician's license for a period of at least three months. Intentional
knowing or reckless falsification of any report required under this section is
a misdemeanor of the third degree.

3214: REPORTING

(a) GENERAL RULE: A report of each abortion performed shall be made
to the department on forms prescribed by it. The report forms shall not identify the individual patient by name and shall include the following information:
   (1) Identification of the physician who performed the abortion and the facility
where the abortion was performed and of the referring physician, agency,
or service, if any.
   (2) The political subdivision and state in which the woman resides.
   (3) The woman's age, race, and marital status.
   (4) The number of prior pregnancies.
   (5) The date of the woman's last menstrual period and the probable gestational age of the unborn child.
   (6) The type of procedure performed or prescribed and the date of the
abortion.
   (7) Complications, if any, including but not limited to rubella disease,
hydatid mole, endocervical polyp, and malignancies.
   (8) The information required to be reported under 3211(a) (relating to
viability).
   (9) The length and weight of the aborted unborn child when measurable.
   (10) Basis for any medical judgment that a medical emergency existed as
required by any part of this chapter.
   (11) The date of the medical consultation relating to medical consultation
and judgment requirements.
   (12) The date on which any determination of pregnancy was made.
   (13) The information required to be reported under 3210(b) (relating to
abortion after viability).

(14) Whether the abortion was paid for by the patient, by medical assistance, or medical insurance coverage.

(b) COMPLETION OF THE REPORT: The reports shall be completed by the hospital or other licensed facility, signed by the physician who performed the abortion and transmitted to the department within 15 days after each reporting month.

(c) PATHOLOGICAL EXAMINATIONS: When there is an abortion performed during the first trimester of pregnancy, the tissue that is removed shall be subjected to a gross or microscopic examination as needed, by the physician or a qualified person designated by the physician to determine if a pregnancy existed and was terminated. If the examination indicates no fetal remains, that information shall immediately be made known to the physician and sent to the department within 15 days of the analysis. When there is an abortion performed after the first trimester of pregnancy where the physician has certified the unborn child is not viable, the dead unborn child and all tissue removed at the time of the abortion shall be submitted for tissue analysis to a board eligible or certified pathologists. If the report reveals evidence of viability or live birth, the pathologist shall report such findings to the department within 15 days and a copy of the report shall also be sent to the physician performing the abortion. Intentional, knowing, reckless, or negligent failure of the physician to submit such an unborn child or such tissue remains to such a pathologist for such a purpose, or intentional knowing or reckless failure of the pathologist to report any evidence of live birth or viability to the department in the manner and within the time prescribed, is a misdemeanor of the third degree.

(d) FORM: The department shall prescribe a form on which pathologists may report any evidence of absence of pregnancy, live birth, or viability.

(e) STATISTICAL REPORTS: Public availability of reports:

(1) The department shall prepare an annual statistical report for the General Assembly based on the data gathered under subsection (a) Such report shall not lead to the disclosure of the identity of any person filing a report or about whom a report is filed, and shall be available for public inspection and copying.

(2) Reports filed pursuant to subsection (a) shall not be deemed public records, but shall be made available for public inspection and copying within 15 days of receipt in a form which will not lead to the disclosure of the identity of any person filing the report. On those reports available for public inspection and copying, the department shall substitute for the name of any physician which appears on the report, a unique identifying number. The identity of the physician shall constitute a confidential record of the department. The department may set a reasonable per copy fee to cover the costs of making any copies authorized hereunder.

(3) Original copies of all reports filed under subsection (a) shall be made available to the State Board of Medical Education and Licensure and to law enforcement officials, for the use in the performance of their official duties.

(4) Any person who willfully discloses any information obtained from the reports filed pursuant to subsection (a), other than that disclosure authorized in paragraph (1), (2), or (3) hereof or as otherwise authorized by law, shall commit a misdemeanor of the third degree.

(f) REPORT BY FACILITY: Every facility in which an abortion is performed within this Commonwealth during any quarter year shall file with the department a report showing the total number of abortions performed within the hospital or other facility during that quarter year. The report shall also show the total abortions performed in each trimester of pregnancy. These reports shall be available for public inspection and copying.

(g) REPORT OF MATERNAL DEATH: After 30 days' public notice, the department shall henceforth require that all reports of maternal deaths occurring within the Commonwealth arising from pregnancy, childbirth or intentional abortion in every case of death, the duration of the woman's pregnancy when her death occurred and whether or not the woman was under the care of a physician during her pregnancy prior to her death and shall issue such regulations as are necessary to insure such information is reported, conducting its own investigation if necessary in order to ascertain such data. A woman shall be deemed to have been under the care of a physician prior to her death for the purpose of this chapter when she had either been examined or treated by a physician, not including any examination or treatment in connection with emergency care for complications of her pregnancy or complications of her abortion, preceding the woman's death at any time which is both 21 or more days after the time she became pregnant and within 60 days prior to her death. Known incidents of maternal mortality of nonresident women arising from induced abortion performed in this Commonwealth shall be included as incidents of maternal mortality arising from induced abortions. Incidents of maternal mortality arising from continued pregnancy or childbirth and occurring after induced abortion has been attempted but not completed as a result of ectopic pregnancy shall not be included as incidents of maternal mortality arising from induced abortion. The department shall annually compile a statistical report for the General Assembly based upon the data gathered under this subsection and all such statistical reports shall be available for public inspection and copying.

(h) REPORT OF COMPLICATIONS: Every physician who is called upon to provide medical care or treatment to a woman who is in need of medical care because of a complication or complications resulting in the good faith judgment of the physician, from having undergone an abortion or attempted abortion, shall prepare a report thereof and file the report with the department within 30 days of the date of his first examination of the woman, which report shall be open to public inspection and copying and shall be on forms prescribed by the department, which forms shall contain the following information, as received, and such other information, except the name of the patient, as the department may from time to time require:
   (1) Age of patient.
   (2) Number of pregnancies prior to the abortion.
   (3) Number and type of abortions prior to this abortion.
   (4) Name and address of the facility where the abortion was performed.
   (5) Gestational age of the unborn child at the time of the abortion, if known.
   (6) Type of abortion performed, if known.
   (7) Nature of complication or complications.
   (8) Medical treatment given.

(9) The nature and extent, if known, of any permanent condition caused by the complication.

(i) PENALTIES: Any person required under this section to file a report, keep any records, or supply any information who willfully fails to file such report, keep such records, or supply such information at the time or times required by law or regulation is guilty of "unprofessional conduct," and his license for the practice of medicine and surgery shall be subject to suspension or revocation.

(1) Any person who willfully delivers or discloses to the department any report, record, or information known by him to be false commits a misdemeanor of the first degree.

(2) In addition to the above penalties, any person, organization, or facility who willfully violates any of the provisions of this section requiring reporting shall upon conviction thereof: (1) for the first time, have its license suspended for a period of six months, (2) for the second time, have its license suspended for a period of one year and (3) for the third time, have its license revoked.

Sections 3205, 3208, 3214(a), (h), 3211(a), 3210(b), and 3210(c) were first invalidated by the Third Circuit Court of Appeals, and the invalidation was affirmed by the United States Supreme Court.

Thornburgh, Governor of Pennsylvania vs. American College of Obstetricians and Gynecologists

It had been nearly three years since the last abortion case was reviewed by the Supreme Court. During that time it became apparent that the political structure of the Court was slowly drifting from a "moderate" majority to the "new" conservative ideology that reflected the Reagan White House. Between the years 1983 and 1985, the Court experienced a "dry spell" in hearing abortion appeals, but the issue was far from dead. During those years, most of the abortion cases were being handled by the state courts, and, if appealed, they would not go beyond the circuit courts of appeals. In the meantime it was a well-known fact within judicial circles that the Supreme Court was searching for a test abortion case so that the new conservatism could be put to the test. Rumors began surfacing that the lull in abortion cases appealed before the Court was a direct result of the conservative swing of the Court, frightening off many appeals. Thus, when this case was appealed to the Court for judicial review in 1985, it became the test case that many felt would lead to the overturning of *Roe vs. Wade.*

Action was brought by a number of physicians, the American College of Obstetricians and Gynecologists, clinics performing first-trimester abortions in the state of Pennsylvania, and members of the clergy. The class-action suit challenged many of Pennsylvania's strict abortion statutes, known collectively as the Abortion Control Act. Action was filed in the federal District Court for the Eastern District of Pennsylvania. After taking into consideration testimony from both sides, the court granted in part but denied in part the plaintiff's motion for a preliminary injunction. Dissatisfied with the judgment, the case was next appealed to the Third Circuit Court of Appeals. Arguments began on March 11, 1983, a decision not being reached until May 31, 1984, over one year later. The appellate court invalidated many of Pennsylvania's abortion statutes including section 3205, requiring physicians to counsel women on the risks of the abortion procedure; section 3208, requiring distribution of printed materials designed to inform women of the consequences of the abortion decision and other options; section 3210(b), (c), requiring that the method of abortion used when the possibility existed that the fetus was viable must be one that would most likely result in the fetus being aborted alive unless that procedure would result in a significantly greater risk to the mother (it also required the presence of a second physician when the abortion was being performed by a method that did not preclude the possibility of the child surviving the abortion); section 3211(a), requiring the physician to report the basis for determining that the child was not viable, to make a report of the rationale he used in determining that the abortion was necessary to preserve maternal life and health; section 3214(a), (h), requiring a detailed report by the physician with regard to each abortion performed, regardless of the stage of pregnancy. This report would have a significant influence on the abortion decision by the nature of the complex reporting requirement. The above-mentioned statutes were invalidated by the circuit court on grounds that they interfered with a woman's fundamental right to have an abortion. In addition, section 3210(b), (c) was invalidated because it failed in preventing a trade-off of maternal health for the possibility of fetal survival.

Governor Thornburgh, not satisfied with the judgment of the lower court, took his appeal to the United States Supreme Court. What resulted was one of the most angrily and hotly debated Supreme Court sessions in history. The Court was not immune from verbal assaults as tempers flared over previous abortion decisions made by the jurists.

Influencing Informed Consent

The "informed consent" section of the Pennsylvania Abortion Control Act of 1982 requires that women give both voluntary and informed consent prior to having an abortion. The woman's physician is charged with the responsibility of securing the necessary information from his patient. In the event he fails to observe the guidelines of section 3205, the state may suspend or revoke his license to practice medicine in the state of Pennsylvania. The concept of requiring women to give consent to an abortion procedure is not viewed as unconstitutional; however, when a state requires that certain information be given to a pregnant woman containing wording that is specifically designed to influence her decision, questions of constitutional impropriety arise.

The Abortion Control Act requires that every woman seeking to terminate her pregnancy be given state-mandated information at least 24 hours prior to the abortion procedure. The information is issued by the state to ensure that the woman will be fully informed and can give intelligent consent to the abortion. The specific areas of information include (1) the physician's name, (2) a "warning" that serious emotional and physical trauma may result, which is not foreseeable prior to the procedure, (3) the "normal" risk associated with any surgical procedure including abortion, (4) the probable gestation age of the fetus at the time of the abortion, and (5) the medical dangers of carrying the pregnancy to term. There are two additional areas of information that are non-medical: (1) information of medical assistance available for prenatal and neonatal care and childbirth; (2) information that the father of the child may be liable for contributing to the support of the child even if he had insisted on paying for the abortion. In addition, section 3208(a)(1) requires that all printed material contain the following information: "There are many public and private agencies willing and able to help you carry your child to term, and to assist you and your child after your child is born, whether you choose to keep your child or place her or him for adoption. . . . The law requires that your physician or his agent give you the opportunity to call agencies like these before you undergo an abortion." And finally, section 3208(a)(2) mandates that material describe the likely anatomical and psychological features of the fetus at two-week (gestational) increments from fertilization to full term, including a prediction of the probability of the unborn fetus's chances of survival. Pertaining to this section, the stipulation is made that all materials be objective and non-judgmental, designed to relate only accurate information on the gestational stage of the unborn at various times during the term of pregnancy.

Postviability Abortions and the Second-Physician Requirement

A section of Pennsylvania's Abortion Control Act requires the physician who performs a postviability abortion to "exercise that degree of care" that he would normally use performing a normal childbirth to preserve the life and health of the unborn child. The state also requires the physician to use the method that would be most beneficial in promoting fetal survival as long as that method would not become a significant medical risk to the life of the pregnant woman. The Court ruled this section unconstitutional because it failed to make the life of the pregnant woman a significantly higher degree of concern for the physician.

The Abortion Control Act requires that a second physician be in attendance during late-trimester abortions when circumstances make it probable that the fetus is viable. The second physician will take charge of the born-alive fetus, providing it with all of the medical care that in his judgment will best preserve the life of the child. In *Planned Parenthood vs. Ashcroft,* the Court ruled that having a second physician available for late-trimester abortions is constitutional. However, Pennsylvania differs slightly in that it does not provide for an emergency situation in the event the mother's pregnancy becomes life-threatening. The wording of the Pennsylvania abortion law did not allow for flexibility during a crisis situation and was therefore ruled unconstitutional.

Maintaining Records on Abortion

In previous cases, record keeping on abortions was determined to be constitutional because it furthered medical knowledge, thus further protecting the health of the pregnant woman by increasing the procedure's safety. The requirement of Pennsylvania law, however, makes no guarantee of privacy. A woman's abortion records are available for copying by the public. There is no limit or restraints placed on the use and copying of these confidential files. The Court felt that a decision to terminate a pregnancy is private and deserves to be protected from scrutiny by the public. Justice Stevens, in *Bellotti vs. Baird* (1979), stated that it is inherent in the right to make the abortion decision that the right may be exercised without public scrutiny and in defiance of the contrary opinion of the sovereign or other third parties.

It was the feeling of the Court that the law impedes a woman's decision to have an abortion if she feels that her actions will be open to scrutiny by the public.

Opinion of the Court:
Read by Justice Blackmun (Paraphrase)

It seems clear that the judgment of the court of appeals was not a final judgment in the ordinary meaning of the term. The court did not hold the entire act unconstitutional, but ruled instead that some provisions were invalid and that the validity of other provisions might depend on evidence adduced at the trial.

This case, as it comes to us, concerns the constitutionality of six provisions of the Pennsylvania Act that the court of appeals struck down as invalid: section 3205, Informed Consent; section 3208, Printed Information; section 3214(a), (h), Reporting Requirements; section 3211, Determination of Viability; section 3210(b), Degree of Care Required in Postviability Abortions; and section

3210(c) Second Physician Requirement. We have no reason at this time to address the validity of the other sections of the act challenged in district court.

Plaintiffs challenged the constitutionality of sections 3205, 3208, and 3205(a) because they were enacted to discourage women from having an abortion. Essentially these sections require the pregnant woman to give "voluntary and informed" consent prior to an abortion procedure. The type of mandated information the state is soliciting is a contradiction of what is considered "informed consent." The commonwealth of Pennsylvania does not impose the same requirements for disclosing every possible "gory" and "horrible" element of other necessary surgeries or simple vaccinations. That abortion is singled out clearly reveals the antiabortion character of these provisions and their real intentions. In legislating these requirements, it is obvious that Pennsylvania has gone overboard in the subject matter it requires of informed consent. In addition, the commonwealth has mandated that the physician recite to his patient the edicts of the provisions, whether or not the information is relevant to his patient's abortion decision. Therefore the Court has found the informational requirements of section 3205 unconstitutional.

We next turn to the provisions that required an extensive report on the abortion and the determination of viability, sections 3241(a), (h), 3214(a)(8), and 3211(a). Section 3214(a)(8) required under section 3211(a) that the attending physician fully report his basis for determining that a fetus is not viable at the time of the abortion. This requirement applies only after the first trimester. Section 3214(a), (h) requires a detailed report that contains nonmedical information. The report must identify the attending physician and the facility where the abortion is to be performed, the woman's political affiliation, state of residence, age, race, marital status, and number of pregnancies. In addition, the report must include the date of the woman's last menstrual period, the probable gestational age of the fetus at the time of the abortion, and if a medical emergency occurred during the abortion, what basis the attending physician used in determining that fact or that the fetus would be nonviable. The report concludes with a required disclosure of the method of payment for the abortion.

Despite the guarantees stated by section 3214(e)(2) that such reports "shall not be deemed public records," within the definition of Pennsylvania's "Right to Know Law," the implied safeguards are ambiguous in that the law states that each report shall be made available for public inspection and copying within 15 days of receipt in a form which will not lead to the disclosure of any person filing a report. On a similar basis the "Report of Complication," required by section 3214(h), shall be open to the public for scrutiny and copying. If the attending physician fails to file a report as required under section 3214, the commonwealth would consider his actions "unprofessional conduct" and subject him to suspension or revocation of his license to practice medicine. The Court feels that the scope of required information, which is considered to be confidential but nonetheless is open for public scrutiny and copying, has caused the state to misrepresent its assertion that it is merely complying with its legitimate interest. In *Planned Parenthood vs. Danford,* we recognized that record-keeping and reporting provisions that are reasonably directed to the preservation of maternal health and that properly respect a patient's confidentiality and privacy are permissible.

It is apparent that the reports before the Court today are clearly different than what we have become familiar with in earlier cases. The Pennsylvania act goes beyond requiring health-related information by asking women to divulge their personal history as a basis for medical judgment. These provisions may deter the exercise of a constitutionally guaranteed right.

The intention of the state is clear; by requiring a stringent reporting law and then going a step further by making confidential personal information public, women will be more reluctant to choose abortion. Though the provision does not directly require that the woman's name be known, the amount of personal information she must give, including reasons for the abortion, makes it almost a certainty that her identity will be discovered.

The Court has consistently refused to allow government to chill the exercise of constitutional rights by requiring disclosure of protected but sometimes unpopular activities.

Finally, we take issue with section 3210(b) Degree of Care for postviability Abortions, and section 3210(c) Second-Physician Requirement when there is a possibility that the fetus may be viable.

Section 3210(b) requires the physician to exercise the same degree of care that he would normally if the fetus was intended to be born alive and not aborted. It states that he should choose the abortion method that would be best in promoting fetal survival, unless, in the good faith judgment of the physician that the method or technique would present a "significantly greater" medical risk to the life or health of the pregnant woman than another available method or technique and the physician reports the basis for his judgment. The law was ruled unconstitutional by the circuit court of appeals on grounds that its wording was faulty. The law as written failed to emphasize the importance of maternal health as the predominant medical concern of the attending physician. The district court made an attempt to save the statute by reconstructing its wording from "significantly greater" to "medically cognizable." The law now seemed to imply: "If the abortion technique that would save the fetus involves an increased risk to the mother, then the procedure safest for the mother must be used." The district court felt that restructuring the statute would render it constitutionally acceptable; however, the circuit court of appeals rejected this maneuver by the lower court, citing that changing the wording of a legislated statute is not a function of the court and reconstructing law so that it can be viewed as being constitutional completely alters its true legislative intent. The circuit court of appeals invalidated this section.

Our attention next focuses on section 3210(c), which requires that a second physician be in attendance during late-trimester abortions, when the probability is greatest that the aborted fetus will be viable. The second physician is charged with providing immediate medical care in preserving the life and health of the "born alive" fetus. The Pennsylvania law clearly made no exceptions in the event a life-threatening medical emergency occurred. The manner in which the law was written strictly prohibited late-trimester abortions from being performed without a second physician in attendance. There were no exceptions; the law was imprudently inflexible.

The circuit court of appeals concluded that as with section 3210(b), it could not rewrite the statute enacted by the legislature and thus held section 3210(c) similarly invalid. (The Supreme Court affirmed the invalidation of this statute, agreeing with the finding of the lower court.)

Constitutional rights do not always have easily ascertainable boundaries, and controversy over the meaning of our nation's most majestic guarantees frequently has been turbulent. As judges, however, we are sworn to uphold the law, even when its content gives rise to bitter dispute. We recognized at the very beginning of our opinion in *Roe vs. Wade* that abortion raises moral and spiritual questions over which honorable persons can disagree sincerely and profoundly. But those disagreements did not then and do not now relieve us of our duty to apply the Constitution faithfully.

Our cases long have recognized that the Constitution embodies a promise that a certain private sphere of individual liberty will be kept largely beyond the reach of government. That promise extends to women as well as men. Few decisions are more personal and intimate, more properly private, or more basic to an individual's dignity and autonomy than a woman's decision, with the guidance of her physician and within the limits specified in *Roe vs. Wade*, to end her pregnancy. A woman's right to make that choice freely is fundamental. Any other result, in our view, would protect inadequately a central part of the sphere of liberty that our law guarantees equally to all.

Viewpoint: Selected Concurring Views of Justice Stevens (Paraphrase)

Justice Stevens argued his concurring opinion by first interjecting several statements made by his colleague Justice White.

The scope of the individual interest in liberty that is given protection by the Due Process Clause of the Fourteenth Amendment is a matter about which conscientious judges have long disagreed. Although I believe that interest is significantly broader than Justice White does, I have always had the highest respect for his views on this subject. In this case, although our ultimate

conclusions differ, it may be useful to emphasize some of our areas of agreement in order to ensure that the clarity of certain fundamental propositions
not be obscured by his forceful rhetoric.

In *Griswold vs. Connecticut* (1962), which concerned a state's forbidding the
use of birth-control devices, the Court's opinion relied on a "right of marital
privacy" within the shadow of the Bill of Rights. Justice White's concurring
opinion went right to the heart of the issue: It would be unduly repetitious
and belaboring the obvious to expound on the impact of this statute on the
liberty guaranteed by the Fourteenth Amendment against arbitrary or
capricious denials or on the nature of this liberty. Suffice it to say that this
is not the first time this Court has had occasion to articulate that the liberty
entitled to protection under the Fourteenth Amendment includes the right to
marry, establish a home, and bring up children, and the liberty to direct the
upbringing and education of children, and that these are among the "basic
civil rights of man." These decisions affirm that there is a realm of family life
which the state cannot enter without substantial justification. Surely the right
invoked in this case, to be free of regulation of the intimacies of the marriage
relationship comes to this Court with a momentum for respect lacking when
appeal is made to liberties which derive merely from shifting economic ar-
rangements. Justice White found nothing in the record justifying the sweep-
ing scope of this statute, with its telling effect on the freedoms of married persons, and therefore concluded that it deprives such persons of liberty without
due process of law.

Thus, the liberty at stake in this case is the freedom from unwarranted
governmental intrusion into individual decisions in matters of childbearing.
Like the birth-control statutes involved in *Griswold,* the abortion statutes involved in *Roe vs. Wade* and in the case before us today apply equally to decisions made by married persons and by unmarried persons. Justice White was
consistent with his views in those cases, in which he agreed that a woman's
ability to choose an abortion is a species of "liberty" that is subject to the general
protections of the Due Process Clause.

Up to this point in Justice White's analysis, his opinion is consistent with
the accepted teachings of the Court and with the major premises of *Roe vs.
Wade.* However, for reasons that are not clear, Justice White abruptly announces
that the interest in "liberty" that is implicated by a decision not to bear children
that is made a few days after conception is less fundamental than a comparable
decision made before conception. I fail to see how a decision on childbearing
becomes less important the day after conception than the day before.

Indeed, if one decision is more "fundamental" to the individual's freedom
than the other, surely it is the postconception decision that is more serious.
Thus, it is difficult for me to understand how Justice White reaches the conclusion that restraints upon this aspect of a woman's liberty do not call into
play anything more than the most minimal judicial scrutiny.

If Justice White were correct in regarding the postconception decision whether to bear a child as a relatively unimportant, second-class sort of interest, I might agree with his view that the individual should be required to conform her decision to the will of the majority. In speaking of "sensitive areas of liberty" which are protected by the Constitution, Justice White characterized "reproductive decisions" in *Griswold:* No individual should be compelled to surrender the freedom to make that decision simply because her "value preferences" are not shared by the majority. In a sense, the basic question is whether the "abortion decision" should be made by the individual or by the majority.

Justice White is also surely wrong in suggesting that the governmental interest in protecting fetal life is equally compelling during the entire period from the moment of conception until the moment of birth. Again, I recognize that a powerful theological argument can be made for that position, but I believe our jurisdiction is limited to the evaluation of secular state interests. The state is constitutionally bound not to interfere with conception or the fostering of a newborn; the responsibility rests with individuals. No matter how important a traditional religious sacrament may be, the state may not punish a parent for not having a child baptized.

I should think it obvious that the state's interest in the protection of an embryo, even if that interest is defined as "protecting those who will be citizens," increases progressively and dramatically as the organism's capacity to feel pain, to experience pleasure, to survive, and to react to its surroundings increases day by day. The development of the fetus and pregnancy itself are not static conditions, and the assertion that the government's interest is static simply ignores this reality.

Life is not a static condition; there are some very obvious differences between a fetus, a child, and an adult, and until the law adopts the religious theory that a fetus is a person, we can only understand the knowledge that is before us. But, assume that a difference did not exist between a fetus and a human being. Would it then be logical to leave a decision of terminating the life of a fetus to the graces of a state legislature? However, just for the record, no member of the Supreme Court has ever even slightly hinted that a fetus is a "person."

If distinctions may be drawn between a fetus and a human being in terms of the state interest in their protection, even though the fetus represents one of those who will be citizens, it seems to me quite odd to argue that distinctions may not also be drawn between the state interest in protecting the freshly fertilized egg and the state interest in protecting the nine-month gestated, fully sentient fetus on the eve of birth. Recognition of this distinction is supported not only by logic, but also by history and our shared experiences.

In the final analysis, the holding in *Roe vs. Wade* presumes that it is far better to permit some individuals to make incorrect decisions than to deny all individuals the right to make decisions that have a profound effect on their destiny. Arguably, a very primitive society would have been protected from evil by a rule against eating apples; a majority familiar with Adam's experience might favor such a rule. But the lawmakers who placed a special premium on the protection of individuals' liberty have recognized that certain values are more important than the will of a transient majority.

Viewpoint: Selected Dissenting Views of Chief Justice Burger (Paraphrase)

I agree with much of Justice White's and Justice O'Connor's dissents. (Chief Justice Burger continued by recalling his statements in previous cases):

In *Doe vs. Bolton* (1973):

> I do not read the Court's holdings today as having the sweeping conse-quences attributed them by dissenting justices; the dissenting views discount the reality that the vast majority of physicians observe the standards of their profession and act only on the basis of carefully deliberated medical judgments relating to life and health. Plainly the Court today rejects any claim that the Constitution requires abortion on demand.

In *Maher vs. Roe* (1977):

> The Court's holding in *Roe vs. Wade* and *Doe vs. Bolton* simply requires that a state not create an absolute barrier to a woman's decision to have an abortion.

The right to an abortion is not unqualified and must be considered against state interests in regulation. Not one Supreme Court justice involved in the *Roe vs. Wade* decision thought that women should have the right to an abor-tion on demand. The Court's opinion today, however, plainly undermines that important principle, and I regretfully conclude that some of the concerns of the dissenting justices in *Roe vs. Wade*, as well as the concerns I expressed in my separate opinion, have now been realized.

The extent to which the Court has departed from the limitations expressed in *Roe vs. Wade* is readily apparent. In *Roe* the court emphasized that the state does have an important and legitimate interest in preserving and protecting the health of the pregnant woman.

The Court today has overruled a Pennsylvania law requiring women who are contemplating abortion to receive information that accurately characterizes the medical risk associated with the abortion procedure. The Court also pro-hibited women from obtaining information designed to alert them to the many state-funded agencies that provide alternatives to abortion. The question is: Would the state not provide similar information on the risks of any surgical procedure? Abortion is certainly not being singled out for special handling by the state since it is a known fact that physicians often will, as a matter of routine, inform their patients of the normal hazards involved with any surgery.

The information benefits both the patient and physician. The patient is made aware of probable dangers, and the physician protects himself from malpractice suits. But even if abortion was treated differently, perhaps the justification would be substantiated by the fact that it is irreversible and is one of the few surgical procedures that does not involve the saving of a life.

Yet the Court concludes that the state cannot impose this simple information-dispensing requirement in the abortion context where the decision is fraught with serious physical, psychological, and moral concerns of the highest order. Can it possibly be that the Court is saying that the Constitution forbids the communication of such critical information to a woman? We have already passed the point at which abortion is available on demand. If the statute at issue here is to be invalidated, the "demand" will not even have to be the result of an informed choice. The Court has chosen to invalidate the abortion information requirement on grounds that "such information may discourage women from having an abortion." It is puzzling why the Court thinks of abortion as something that is "advocated and encouraged."

The Court in *Roe* further recognized that the state has still another important and legitimate interest that is "separate and distinct" from the interest in protecting maternal health, that being an interest in "protecting the potentiality of human life." The point at which these interests become compelling under *Roe* is at viability of the fetus.

(Chief Justice Burger continues with his dissenting opinion by attacking the invalidation by the Court of Pennsylvania's abortion law that required a second physician be present during a postviability abortion procedure. The second physician was charged with the responsibility of providing immediate medical care to a fetus which is born alive, using his best medical judgment in preserving its life and health.)

The invalidation of a law that requires nothing more than the preservation of life for a viable fetus makes absolutely no sense. No governmental power exists to say that a viable fetus should not have every protection required to preserve its life. The commonwealth of Pennsylvania construed holding in *Roe* concerning the binding interest of a state in potential life after viability as its reasoning for legislating a second-physician requirement.

The Court has widened the gap between its holdings in *Roe vs. Wade* and its "astonishing" judgments in this litigation. Perhaps the first indication of a "deterioration" in rational judgment by the Court was realized during the litigation of *Planned Parenthood of Central Missouri vs. Danford* (1976). In that case the Court held that a state does not have the right to require that minors seeking abortion first obtain consent from their parents. Parents, not judges or social workers, have the inherent right and responsibility to advise their children in matters of this sensitivity and consequence. Can one imagine a surgeon performing an amputation or even an appendectomy on a 14-year-old girl without the consent of a parent or guardian except in an emergency situation?

In discovering constitutional infirmities in state regulations of abortion that are in accord with our history and tradition, we may have lured judges into roaming at large in a constitutional field. The soundness of our holdings must be tested by the decisions that purport to follow them. If *Danford* and today's holding really mean what they seem to say, I agree we should reexamine *Roe vs. Wade.*

Viewpoint: Selected Dissenting Views of Justice White (Paraphrase)

Today the Court carries forward the "difficult and continuing venture in substantive due process." I was in dissent in *Roe vs. Wade* and am in dissent today.

In *Roe vs. Wade* the Court held that a woman has a fundamental right to terminate her pregnancy but that that right is not absolute and may be barred if it is determined that having an abortion would prove to be more hazardous to the woman's health than carrying her pregnancy to term. In addition, the abortion procedure can be proscribed if the life of the fetus is placed in jeopardy during a late-trimester abortion, when it is certain that the fetus will be viable. A reader of the Constitution might be surprised to find that it encompassed these detailed rules, for the text obviously contains no reference to abortion nor indeed to pregnancy or reproduction generally; and, of course it is highly doubtful that the authors of any of the provisions of the Constitution believed that they were giving protection to abortion. However, even if that is the case, the framers did leave the wording of the Constitution "purposely" open to broad interpretation. The Constitution is not a deed setting forth the precise limits and bounds of its subject matter; rather, it is a document announcing fundamental principles in value-laden terms that leave ample scope for the exercise of normative judgment by those charged with interpreting and applying it. In particular, the Due Process Clause of the Fourteenth Amendment, which forbids the deprivation of "life, liberty, or property without due process of law," has been read by a majority of the Court to be broad enough to provide substantive protection against state infringement of a broad range of individual interests.

I can certainly agree with the proposition — which I deem indisputable — that a woman's ability to choose abortion is a species of "liberty" that is subject to the general protections of the Due Process Clause. I cannot agree, however, that this liberty is so "fundamental" that restrictions upon it call into play anything more than the most minimal judicial scrutiny. Only "fundamental" rights should have "added protection" of strict scrutiny by the Court in order that women be assured that state legislators will not encroach upon their rights when enacting laws.

As the Court appropriately recognized in *Roe vs. Wade,* the pregnant woman cannot be isolated in her privacy. The termination of pregnancy typically involves the destruction of another entity: the fetus. However one answers the metaphysical or theological question whether the fetus is a "person" as the term is used in the Constitution or a "human being," one must at least recognize first that the fetus is an entity that bears in its cells all the genetic information that characterizes a member of the species homo sapiens and distinguishes an individual member of that species from all others, and second, that there is no nonarbitrary line separating a fetus from a child or, indeed an adult human being.

If women have the fundamental right to have an abortion, it can in no way be linked to any of the previous Court actions but perhaps can be traced back to our implied idea of liberty "deeply rooted in this nation's history and tradition." Women were not given this fundamental right. The Court's opinion in *Roe vs. Wade* itself convincingly refutes the notion that the abortion liberty is deeply rooted in the history or tradition of our people, as does the continuing and deep division of the people themselves over the question of abortion. And as for the idea that abortion is an implied liberty of choice, it seems apparent to me that a free, democratic society that believes in equality does not presuppose any particular rule or set of rules with respect to abortion.

And again, the fact that many men and women of good will and high commitment to constitutional government place themselves on both sides of the abortion controversy strengthens my own conviction that the values that inspire the Constitution do not compel recognition of the abortion liberty as fundamental.

The Court erred in judgment in *Roe vs. Wade* when it limited a state's abortion concern to viability, thus prohibiting a state from interfering with the abortion decision, even though the concern of the state was expressed only in protecting the life, or as the Court described it, "potential life" of the fetus. The ruling led to many misconceptions, including one that women construed as giving them a "fundamental" right to abortion. As Justice O'Connor pointed out in 1983, in *Akron vs. Akron Center for Reproductive Health,* the Court's choice of viability as the point at which the state's interest becomes compelling is entirely arbitrary.

Because the Court has continually adhered to the assumption that the fetus is not capable of meaningful life until it is able to sustain independent survival outside of the mother's womb, it has held that a state does not have the authority of interceding in a woman's decision to have an abortion until the stage of viability is reached. During this stage of pregnancy the state may either restrict the abortion procedure to emergencies or prohibit it.

The primary legislative concern is over those who will be citizens if their lives are not ended in the womb. The objective is not in predicting the probability of whether the fetus will survive outside the womb. More rationally, the chance of fetal survival is based on the state of medical technology at the time; these are factors that are in essence morally and constitutionally irrelevant. The state's interest is in the fetus as an "individual" in itself, and the character of this individual does not change at the point of viability under conventional medical wisdom. Accordingly, the state's interest, if compelling after viability, is equally compelling before viability.

Both the characterization of the abortion liberty as fundamental and the "maligning" of the states' interest in preserving the life of the nonviable fetus are essential to the detailed set of constitutional rules devised by the Court to limit the states' power to regulate abortion. If either or both of these facets of *Roe vs. Wade* were rejected, a broad range of limitations on abortion (including outright prohibition) that are now unavailable to the states would again become constitutional possibilities.

In my view, such a state of affairs would be highly desirable from the standpoint of the Constitution. Abortion is a hotly contested moral and political issue. Such issues in our society are to be resolved by the will of the people, either as expressed through legislation or through the general principles they have already incorporated into the Constitution they have adopted. The holding in *Roe vs. Wade* would lead many to believe inaccurately that the people have spoken and resolved the arguments over abortion by "interpreting" that the Fourteenth Amendment contains the values and principles that answer the issue. As I have argued, I believe it is clear that the people have never — not in 1787, 1791, 1868, or at any time since — done any such thing. I would return the issue to the people by overruling *Roe vs. Wade*.

The holding of the Court in *Roe vs. Wade* was not based on the logic that the abortion procedure is either desirable as an integral part of the Constitution or socially acceptable. States neither fund nor encourage abortion, but they do advocate natural childbirth for pregnant women. The persuasiveness of the state is limited and must not intimidate women who have already decided on abortion. The provision before the Court today quite obviously represents the state's effort to implement such a policy.

The Court has invalidated a Pennsylvania law that was specifically designed to insure that the woman's choice of an abortion is fully informed. The Pennsylvania law went beyond requiring general information be passed to the pregnant woman; it alerted her as to the medical risks associated with the abortion procedure, as well as providing her with a wealth of information on the many state agencies that provide both medical and financial assistance for natural childbirth, thus creating an "attractive" alternative to abortion.

The *Roe vs. Wade* decision first made women aware that they do have the freedom of choice in the abortion decision, and when legislators enact laws that will provide women with all the pertinent information on abortion, it is to ensure that when a woman expresses her "freedom of choice," it will be a fully informed decision.

One searches the majority's opinion in vain for a convincing reason why the apparently laudable policy of promoting informed consent becomes unconstitutional when the subject is abortion. The majority opinion on this issue was based on the finding of a similar law in *Akron vs. Akron Center for Reproductive Health*. In that case Akron required the physician to provide his patients with information on "when life begins," including a speculation of the "anatomical features of the fetus carried by the woman seeking the abortion." The physician was also required specifically to emphasize all of the horrifying aspects of abortion, including the statement that it is "a particularly dangerous procedure." (Although Justice White had "no quarrel" with the *Akron* ordinance in general, he did express dissatisfaction with *Akron* because a campaign of state-promulgated disinformation cannot be justified in the name of "informed consent" or "freedom of choice.") The Pennsylvania law differs, as the majority concedes, in that it does not require that the woman be given any information that represents a false characterization of abortion or data that cannot be substantiated.

Why, then, is the statute unconstitutional? Three probable reasons support the majority argument: First, the information that must be provided will in some cases be irrelevant to the woman's decision. Its pertinence to the question of the statute's constitutionality, however, is beyond me. A broad scope of generalization of a particular subject matter is used when legislators enact laws. If a portion of the enacted legislation becomes "nonfunctional" in a legislative sense or if it is "counterproductive," it is not necessarily considered constitutionally defective. However, if the law encroaches upon an individual's fundamental rights, it could then be put under judicial scrutiny for evaluation. The statute requiring informed consent does not directly infringe the allegedly fundamental right to choose abortion. Indeed, I fail to see how providing a woman with accurate information, whether relevant or irrelevant, could ever be deemed to impair any constitutionally protected interest. The majority has suggested that the implied negativity of such information on abortion could have an upsetting effect on women who are contemplating abortion. Though that may be the case, it should not be used as a determining factor in preventing the flow of "vital" information. Thus, the majority's observation that the statute may require the provision of irrelevant information in some cases is itself an irrelevancy.

Second, the majority appears to reason that the informed-consent provisions are invalid because the information they require may increase the woman's "anxiety" about the procedure and even influence her choice. Again, both observations are undoubtedly true; but they by no means cast the constitutionality of the provisions into question. Understanding the pros and cons of an issue helps ensure an educated decision, and as long as the information remains accurate and nonmisleading, there should be no problem of interference with a woman's fundamental right of choice. If information may reasonably affect the patient's choice, the patient should have that information; and, as one authority has observed, the greater the likelihood that particular information will influence the patient's decision, the more essential the information arguably becomes for securing her informed consent. A provision of this type should not be considered unconstitutional simply because it may change her mind about abortion. The whole idea behind the litigation of *Roe vs. Wade* was not to increase the number of abortions through encouragement, but rather to increase a woman's awareness of her choices. Moreover, in some of our previous litigation, the indication was made that the state may encourage women to make their choice in favor of childbirth rather than abortion, and the provision of accurate information regarding abortion and its alternatives is a reasonable and fair means of achieving that objective.

Third, the majority concludes that the informed-consent provisions are invalid because they intrude upon the discretion of the pregnant woman's physician, violate the privacy of informed-consent dialogue between the woman and her physician, as well as officially structuring their dialogue. The provisions thus constitute "state medicine" that infringes upon the physician's professional responsibilities. This is nonsensical. I can concede that the Constitution extends its protection to certain zones of personal autonomy and privacy, and I can understand, if not share, the notion that the protection may extend to a woman's decision regarding abortion. But I cannot concede the possibility that the Constitution provides more than minimal protection for the manner in which a physician practices his or her profession or for the "dialogues" in which he or she chooses to participate in the course of treating patients. I had thought it clear that regulation of the practice of medicine, like regulation of other professions and economic affairs generally, was a matter peculiarly within the competence of legislatures, and that such regulation was subject to review only for rationality.

The majority's decision to strike down the reporting requirement of the statute is equally extraordinary. The requirements obviously serve legitimate purposes. The information contained in the reports is highly relevant to the state's efforts to enforce section 3210(a) of the statute, which forbids abortion of viable fetuses except when necessary to the mother's health. The information concerning the complications plainly serves the legitimate goal of advancing the state of medical knowledge concerning maternal and fetal health. Whenever the subject of abortion is mentioned, there usually follows an avalanche of opinion. There is strong interest in the general public, and that makes the distribution of information on abortion to the public ever more important. Although the required reports reveal some very personal information on the patient seeking an abortion, it should not interfere with either her decision or the medical judgment of her physician. In *Planned Parenthood vs. Ashcroft* (1983), a similar statute was approved by the Court.

Nonetheless, the majority strikes down the reporting requirements because it finds, notwithstanding the explicit statutory command, that the reports be made public only in a manner ensuring anonymity. The district court found that the requirements of confidentiality in section 3214(e) regarding the identity of both patient and physician prevent any invasion of privacy which could present a legally significant burden on the abortion decision. Rather than pointing to anything in the record that demonstrates that the district court's conclusion is erroneous, the majority resorts to the handy, but mistaken, solution of substituting its own view of the facts and strikes down the statute.

Finally, in addition to being procedurally flawed, the majority's holding is substantively suspect. The information contained in the reports identifies the patient on the basis of age, race, marital status, and "political subdivision" of residence. The remainder of the information included in the reports concerns the medical aspects of the abortion. It is implausible that a patient could be identified on the basis of the combination of the general identifying information and the specific medical information in these reports by anyone who did not already know (at a minimum) that the woman had been pregnant and obtained an abortion. Accordingly, the provisions pose little or no threat to the woman's privacy.

Linguistic nit-picking is the method used by the Court in striking down the provision that required the attending physician during late-trimester abortions to use the method of abortion that would best promote fetal survival, unless the method would pose a significantly greater medical risk to the life or health of the pregnant woman than other available methods. The majority opinion determined that the provision's use of the word *significantly* implies a trade-off between the health of the woman and the survival of the fetus. Not only is this conclusion based on a wholly unreasonable interpretation of the statute, but the statute would be constitutional even if it meant what the majority says it means.

In adopting the finding of the court of appeals, the majority rejected the context in which the term *significantly* was used in the wording of the statute. The statute requires only that the risk be a real and identifiable one. Surely if the state's interest in preserving the life of a viable fetus is, as *Roe* purported to recognize, a compelling one, the state is at the very least entitled to demand that the interest not be subordinated to a purported maternal health risk that is in fact wholly insubstantial. The statute, on its face, demands no more than this of a doctor performing an abortion of a viable fetus.

Even if the majority opinion of the Court were correct in its interpretation of the Pennsylvania law requiring a pregnant woman seeking abortion of a viable fetus to endure a method of abortion chosen to protect the health of the fetus despite the existence of an alternative that in some substantial degree is more protective of her own health, it still is not convincing that the statute is unconstitutional. Nothing in previous Court rulings of similar statutes had made the Court adopt a "trade-off" rule.

The Court's ruling in this respect is not even consistent with its decision in *Roe vs. Wade*. In *Roe vs. Wade* the Court ruled that the state has a compelling interest in any abortion procedure that occurs after viability of the fetus; the "binding" interest primarily focuses on preserving the life of the fetus. The Court has never backed down from this finding, until now. Apparently the Court has changed its mind on what constitutes a "binding state interest" with its stipulation in this case that the interest of the state in regulating postviability abortions is justified (in most cases); however, that justification is not a guarantee, especially in cases where the pregnant woman who desires to abort her viable fetus must be allowed to sacrifice its life if her own life is placed in jeopardy because of lifesaving attempts on the fetus. The holding directly contradicts the usual definition of the term *compelling interest*, which in the past was usually defined as a government interest that is so weighty it justifies substantial and ordinarily impermissible impositions on individuals; impositions that, I thought, could include the infliction of some degree of risk or physical harm. A good example of this would be military service.

As is evident, this holding itself involves a trade-off between maternal health and protection of the fetus, for it plainly permits the state to forbid a postviability abortion even when such an abortion may be statistically safer than carrying the pregnancy to term, provided that the abortion is not medically necessary. The so-called trade-off provision of the Pennsylvania act, even as interpreted by the majority, is in reality no different than our usual definition of the term. The requirement is simple in that during a medically necessary abortion it requires the physician to use his best medical judgment to save the life of the fetus unless the chosen method would place the life of the woman in jeopardy. The physician would then be required to use an abortion method with a lesser degree of success in preserving fetal life.

In 1973, *Roe vs. Wade* helped establish the rule that a state's interest in the abortion procedure becomes binding during the postviability stage of pregnancy. During this stage the state has the authority to prohibit the procedure or severely restrict it to life-threatening situations; for instance, if carrying the pregnancy to term would jeopardize the life of the woman. Also established in *Roe* was that "the state may require that post-viability abortions be conducted using the method most protective of the fetus unless a less protective method is necessary to protect the life or health of the pregnant woman." When comparing the precedents set in *Roe vs. Wade* with the Pennsylvania law, "which does not require women to accept any significant health risk to protect the fetus," it should be ruled as constitutionally valid.

The Court strikes down the statute's second-physician requirement because, in its view, the existence of a medical emergency requiring an immediate abortion to save the life of the pregnant woman would not be a defense to a prosecution under the statute. The Court does not question the proposition, established in the *Ashcroft* case, that a second-physician requirement accompanied by an exception for emergencies is a permissible means of vindicating the compelling state interest in protecting the lives of viable fetuses. Accordingly, the majority's ruling on this issue does not on its face involve a substantial departure from the Court's previous decisions.

The Court has decided to ignore a section of the statute that pertains to the second-physician requirement providing that it shall be a complete defense to any charge brought against a physician for violating the requirements of this section, that he concluded in good faith in his best medical judgment that the abortion was necessary to preserve maternal life or health.

The language of the Pennsylvania law may be "faulty" in construction, and if this is the case, it could be vulnerable to broad interpretations. The commonwealth, however, defines the statute as a defense for violating the second-physician requirement while in the process of performing a postviability abortion without a second physician in attendance, because in using his best medical judgment, the physician has determined that performing the abortion was necessary to save the health and life of the mother. The Court, on the other hand, chose to reject the commonwealth's definition of the statute; the majority felt that the wording of the law did not relate to the second-physician requirement because there was no mention made of "emergency situations." This reasoning eludes me. The explanation that an abortion was "medically necessary" should be a clear message for the defense of the physician who because of his conscientious dedication to his duty of saving a life, has managed to violate a statute law requiring a second physician. Could the Court's rejection of this law be another case of linguistic nit-picking? Invalidating an entire statute because the word *necessity* was used in place of *emergency* makes very little sense when a dictionary defines *emergency* as "a critical or crucial time or state of affairs" and the word *necessity* is defined by the same dictionary as "a very great need; something that is necessary." Surely by looking at both definitions, one can see that there is not much difference between the two.

Why this should make a difference is unclear; a defense of medically necessary is fully as the protective of the interests of the pregnant woman as a defense of emergency. The Court has obviously "retracted" to the idea that the legislature knows how to provide a medical-emergency exception when it chooses to do so. But the legislature obviously also "knows how" to provide a medical-necessity exception, and it has done so. Why this exception is insufficient is unexplained and inexplicable.

The Court's reading is obviously based on the principle that in cases involving abortion, a permissible reading of the statute is to be avoided at all costs. Not sharing this viewpoint, I cannot accept the majority's conclusion that the statute does not provide for the equivalent of a defense of emergency.

The decision today appears symptomatic of the Court's own insecurity over its handiwork in *Roe vs. Wade* and the cases that follow that decision. Aware that in *Roe* it essentially created something out of nothing and that there are many in this country who hold the decision to be basically illegitimate, the Court responds defensively. Perceiving in a statute implementing the state's legitimate policy of preferring childbirth to abortion a threat to or criticism of the decision in *Roe vs. Wade,* the majority indiscriminately strikes down statutory provisions that in no way contravene the right recognized in *Roe.* I do not share the warped point of view of the majority, nor can I follow the tortuous path the majority treads in proceeding to strike down the statute before us. I dissent.

Viewpoint: Selected Dissenting Views of Justice O'Connor (Paraphrase)

Justice O'Connor dissented. Joining O'Connor in her dissenting opinion was Justice Rehnquist.

The Court's abortion decisions have already worked a major distortion in the Court's constitutional jurisprudence. Today's decision goes further and makes it painfully clear that no legal rule or doctrine is safe from ad-hoc nullification by this Court when an occasion for its application arises in a case involving state regulation of abortion. The permissible scope of abortion is not the only constitutional issue on which this Court is divided, but, except when it comes to abortion, the Court has generally refused to let such disagreements, however long-standing or deeply felt, prevent it from evenhandedly applying uncontroversial legal doctrines to cases that come before it.

(Justice O'Connor states that she still adheres to the principles outlined in her dissenting opinion in *Akron vs. Akron Center for Reproductive Health* in 1983.)

The state has compelling interests in ensuring maternal health and in protecting potential human life, and these interests exist throughout pregnancy. Under the Court's fundamental-rights jurisprudence, judicial scrutiny of state regulation of abortion should be limited to whether the state law bears a rational relationship to legitimate purposes such as advancement of these compelling interests, with heightened scrutiny reserved for instances in which the state has imposed an undue burden on the abortion decision. An undue burden will generally be found in situations involving absolute obstacles or severe limitations on the abortion decision, not wherever a state regulation may inhibit abortions to some degree. And if a state law does interfere with the abortion decision to an extent that is unduly burdensome so that it becomes necessary to apply an exacting standard of review, the possibility remains that the statute will withstand the stricter scrutiny.

The Court today goes well beyond mere distortion of the unduly-burdensome standard. By holding that each of the challenged provisions is (on its face) unconstitutional as a matter of law, any new items of evidence that may change a current holding of the Court, precisely those that may interfere with a woman's exercised right to have an abortion, are immediately invalidated. Furthermore, sufficient grounds for invalidating an abortion law would come about if the Court had the slightest inclination that the law would have the effect of discouraging abortions. Simultaneously, the Court strains to discover the anti-abortion character of the statute, and as Justice White pointed out, invents an unprecedented canon of construction under which in cases of abortion, a permissible reading of the statute is to be avoided at all costs. Some critics view the Court's "dual approach" as "dangerous" and hopefully a temporary demonstration by the Court rather than a permanent method of deciding constitutional law. Suffice it to say that I dispute not only the wisdom but also the legitimacy of the Court's attempt to discredit and preempt state abortion regulation regardless of the interests it serves and the impact it has.

The Court's invalidating section 3205, the informed-consent requirement, was a blanket condemnation of the law on grounds that it was both irrelevant and caused some women to experience pain and suffering, as well as interfering with the "sacred" physician-patient relationship. In his argument on the informed-consent requirement, Justice White felt that the Court's criticism of this particular provision was inappropriate since the information it requires is relevant in most situations and was designed primarily to inform and not to intimidate women. Understandably, compliance with this type of regulation will often involve a moderate interference with the medical prudence of the physician as the sole adviser in his patient's abortion decision. But the nature of informed-consent statutes does tend to be somewhat intrusive.

The "parade of horribles" the Court invalidated in *Akron* is missing here. For example section 3205(a) requires that women be informed of the risks associated with a particular abortion procedure, and section 3205(a), (v) require the physician to inform the woman of the medical risks associated with carrying her child to term. This is the kind of information I would have thought all could agree is relevant to a woman's informed consent.

I do not dismiss the possibility that requiring the physician or counselor to read aloud the state's printed materials if the woman wishes access to them but cannot read raises First Amendment concerns. Even the requirement that women who can read be informed of the availability of those materials and furnished them on request may create some possibility that the physician is being required to communicate (the state's) ideology.

In the ruling on the informed-consent requirement, the Court criticized the provision that required the pregnant woman to receive information on the development of the fetus she was carrying every two weeks for the duration of her pregnancy. However, when it criticized the statute it apparently forgot to take into consideration that women had a choice of whether to view the information. If materials were sufficiently inflammatory and inaccurate, the fact that women must ask to see them would not necessarily preclude finding an undue burden, but there is no indication that this is true of the description of fetal characteristics the statute contemplates. Accordingly, I think it unlikely that appellees could succeed in making the threshold showing of an undue burden at this point, and the information is certainly not rationally related to the state's interests in ensuring informed consent and in protecting potential human life.

There is little chance for appellees to establish the defense that section 3205 will make the abortion decision unduly burdensome. The provision required that pregnant women be given information on agencies that provide medical benefits and assistance to women who choose natural childbirth over abortion, in addition to alerting women to the legal responsibilities of the father of the fetus. Although this provision is not medically relevant, it is important to many women who are undecided about having an abortion. To presume that the information will "place a severe limitation" on a woman's abortion decision is not a fair assumption.

The Court's rationale for striking down the reporting requirements of section 3214, as Justice White shows, rests on an unsupported finding of fact by this Court to the effect that identification is the obvious purpose of these extreme reporting requirements. The Court's finding, which is contrary to the preliminary finding of the district court judge that the statute's confidentiality requirements protected against any invasion of privacy that could burden the abortion decision, is simply another consequence of the Court's determination to prevent the parties from developing the facts. I do not know whether Justice White is correct in stating that the provisions pose little or no threat to the woman's privacy, and I would leave that determination for the district court, which can hear evidence on this point before making its findings. There is no threat to a woman's anonymity because the statute did not publicly disclose her identity in any way.

I am in full agreement with Justice White's stand on section 3210(b), the provision that required the attending physician to employ the abortion method that would be best in promoting fetal survival, unless the chosen method would place the life of the pregnant woman in greater danger. Since section 3210(b) can be read to require only the risk be a real identifiable one (Justice White), there is little possibility that a woman's abortion decision will be unduly burdened by risks falling below that threshold.

Section 3210(c), the second-physician requirement, is constitutional because it provides for an exception during an emergency. A similar law was ruled valid by the Court in *Planned Parenthood of Kansas City vs. Ashcroft.*

In my view, today's decision makes bad constitutional law and bad procedural law. The undesired and uncomfortable straightjacket in this case, is not the one the Court purports to discover in Pennsylvania's statute; it is the one the Court has tailored for the 50 states. I respectfully dissent.

The Court's Decision

The case was argued beginning on November 5, 1985, and decided more than seven months later on June 11, 1986.

In the years since this Court's decision in *Roe,* states and municipalities have adopted a number of measures seemingly designed to prevent a woman, with the advice of her physician, from exercising her freedom of choice. But the constitutional principles that led this Court to its decisions in 1973 still provide the compelling reason for recognizing the constitutional dimensions of a woman's right to decide whether to end her pregnancy. It should go without saying that the vitality of these constitutional principles cannot be allowed to yield simply because of disagreement with them. The states are not free under the guise of protecting maternal health or potential life to intimidate women into continuing pregnancies. This was the Court's opinion by Justice Blackmun.

This case seemed to draw more criticism from justices, and more disdain for the previous abortion decisions made by the Court as expressed by members of the bench who had been opposed to abortion, than any other. It appeared to be the end result of a three-year lull in abortion cases heard by the Court. During that period frustration and pressures grew to an explosive level, and the result was a case that had justices attacking one another and the Court itself.

Amid all the hostility, however, a decision was reached on June 11, 1986. Justice Blackmun read the opinion of the Court, in which Justices Brennan, Marshall, Powell, and Stevens joined. Justice Stevens filed the lone concurring opinion, attacking the opinion of Justice White. Chief Justice Burger filed a dissenting opinion. Justices White and O'Connor filed dissenting opinions severely criticizing the "opposition" and the Court for its rulings on abortion since *Roe vs. Wade.* Both of those opinions were joined by Justice Rehnquist.

The majority opinion voted to affirm the decision of the lower court invalidating many of Pennsylvania's abortion statutes.

The end to this case brought an end to a great era in American judicial history as the final curtain came down on the Burger Court. Warren Earl Burger, a staple on the bench of the Supreme Court for over 27 years, hung up his robe for the last time in June 1986. He had served his country well, leaving behind an indelible judicial record as a champion of civil-rights causes even though he was a political conservative appointed to the position of chief justice by President Richard Nixon.

If there was any doubt about the direction of the Supreme Court after Burger's retirement, it was quickly laid to rest with the appointment of Justice Rehnquist to the position of chief justice by President Ronald Reagan. To fill the vacancy left by Justice Rehnquist, Reagan appointed another conservative, Antonin Scalia. Shortly afterward, another Supreme Court "moderate" retired from the bench. In 1987, Lewis F. Powell, Jr., after serving 15 years, decided to retire, primarily due to "failing health." President Reagan nominated

Judge Robert Bork to the bench. Bork failed to pass the "test" during his confirmation hearings before the Senate judicial committee, touching off one of the most controversial and hotly debated Senate hearings in history. Angered by the Senate decision, President Reagan selected Judge Douglas Ginsberg to fill the vacancy on the bench. All went well until the "honest" Judge Ginsberg admitted that during his college days he had smoked marijuana, after which he abruptly left Washington, D.C., for home. Next on the Senate "hot seat" was a California law school professor with an almost impeccable record. Judge Anthony Kennedy was carefully screened by the Reagan administration before facing the Senate judicial panel. He passed the hearings with more ease than his two predecessors as there were no negative comments made during the Senate session. Kennedy is a very private person, but close associates label him as a political conservative and an independent thinker. He replaced Justice Powell in early 1988.

The shape of the Supreme Court in the early 1990s is as follows: conservatives: Chief Justice Rehnquist, Justices O'Connor, White, Scalia, and Kennedy; moderates: Justices Stevens, Marshall, Blackmun, and Brennan. The count is five conservatives and four moderates, which may be crucial when abortion cases are appealed in the future.

There is one final interesting fact concerning one of the litigants in this abortion case. Pennsylvania Governor Richard Thornburgh is now serving in the Bush administration as attorney general. The former governor was recently quoted as saying, "I will continue to press the high Court to overturn the *Roe* decision."

14: Conservatism: Ushering In a New Era in Jurisprudence

The Supreme Court has shifted from a majority of moderates to a majority of conservatives. This shift in ideology caused many to speculate that the years of legalized abortion would soon be coming to an end. Supporters of pro-life were overjoyed, and followers of pro-choice were worried.

Interest in the pros and cons of abortion was renewed, but opinions between factions were more divided than ever before. The renewed interest and increased public opinion were a result of the Reagan administration's efforts to pressure lawmakers to overturn *Roe vs. Wade*. The efforts failed, however, and *Roe vs. Wade* was still in effect when George Bush took office.

Between 1987 and 1989, many changes in political philosophy occurred. Opinions of medical experts, politicians, social workers, and psychologists also changed during this period. This chapter is designed to reflect these changes and includes all of the current statistics on abortion.

Shortly after Judge Anthony Kennedy was impaneled on the bench of the Court in February 1988, the Reagan administration experienced a new surge of confidence. The Supreme Court was composed of a conservative majority for the first time. The administration felt that the time and circumstances were perfect to begin work on overturning *Roe vs. Wade*.

One of the first challenges that many thought would eventually lead to a reversal of *Roe* was a Minnesota case that restricted abortions for minors. The case was first heard by the federal district court in November 1986 and appealed to the Eighth Circuit Court of Appeals in August 1987, where a three-judge panel ruled that two of Minnesota's provisions were unconstitutional on grounds that they required minors to obtain consent of both parents prior to an abortion even if the parents were separated, divorced, or not locatable. The law required a 48-hour waiting period after parents were notified. The case was once again appealed in August 1988. This time a federal appeals court upheld the tough Minnesota law by a 7–3 vote. The reversal was a reminder of the Reagan influence on the federal courts, as six of the seven judges voting in favor of the Minnesota law were Reagan appointees. During his term in office Reagan appointed nearly half of the federal judges, which number 370.

The American Civil Liberties Union attorney Rachael Pine, who argued the case, said that she did not feel that this case would be reviewed by the high Court, even though she was "a little worried about the current Supreme Court," not knowing what Justice Kennedy's feelings were on abortion because he had never ruled on an abortion case. Pine further stated, "If Kennedy were to vote with the four other justices who had called for narrowing or abandoning judicial protection of abortion, the Court might use the case to 'chip away' at abortion rights for minors and perhaps for adult women as well."

In summing up her opinion, Pine stated: "Twenty-five states have laws that require minors seeking abortion to notify or to obtain consent from at least one parent. Most of these laws, including Minnesota's, allow minors to seek special [court-approved abortion] to circumvent the notification or consent requirement."

In September 1988 one of the authors of the 1973 *Roe vs. Wade* decision spoke to a class of first-year law students at the University of Arkansas in Little Rock. Justice Harry Blackmun warned the law students that there was a good possibility that *Roe vs. Wade* would be overturned during the Court's 1988 session.

Justice Blackmun felt that the future of the freedoms women gained from the judgment in *Roe* would depend largely on the vote of one man, Justice Kennedy. Blackmun said no one knew how faithful Justice Kennedy is to the judicial doctrine of *stare decisis,* which states that courts should not disturb a settled point of law.

Blackmun admitted that he had been criticized for his majority opinion in *Roe vs. Wade* and that the condemnation had been worldwide, but said that he would probably not alter his feelings on the issue. His personal reasoning for his decision in *Roe* was based on his interpretation of the Constitution that women have a right to do with their body whatever they wish.

Justice Blackmun concurred with the opinion that abortion is a very controversial, emotional, distressful kind of litigation that has been politicized in the last few years. In parting, Blackmun said he was aware of the opposition and that he respected their opinions.

Again in September 1988, the Reagan administration applied pressure on the United States Senate to remove an abortion clause from a major medical-funding bill or face a complete veto. The abortion provision was part of a $140 billion health bill that would provide funding for AIDS research and cancer research. The abortion provision of the bill would have provided Medicaid funding for indigent women who were raped or were victims of incest and wished to terminate their unwanted pregnancy. The Senate instead voted by a 47 to 43 margin to maintain current federal abortion laws that permitted abortion only if the woman's life was in jeopardy.

Due primarily to President Reagan's threats to veto the bill, the House of Representatives bowed to the pressure and voted 216 to 166 to reject the Senate abortion provision. Senator James Exon (D–Nebraska) explained that Congress lacked the support to override the president's veto and that to jeopardize the chances of the passage of a crucial bill because of one objection would have been "foolhardy" because the bill also provided funds for job training, the homeless problem, the war on drugs and alcohol abuse, plus a long list of educational programs. Senator Alan Cranston (D–California) admitted that for him "the defeat of the Exon Amendment was painful, but we had no alternative." However, Pete Wilson (R–California) voted to keep the abortion provision in the bill.

Supporters of the Exon Amendment commented that their reasoning for supporting the provision "was a matter of conscience." They felt that the restrictive bylaws of Medicaid effectively, but unfairly, punished poor indigent women, who under normal circumstances could not afford an abortion. Senator Lowell Weicker, Jr. (R–Connecticut) said: "It's stand-up-and-be-counted time," in referring to the Exon bill. He continued, "None of us can imagine the horrors of rape or incest, certainly not the male members of this body. We're not talking about some isolated principle. We're talking about the rights of poor women to enjoy the same legal protection as anyone else." Weicker added that he did not feel that passage of the bill would have led to an "avalanche of new abortions."

Senator Barbara Mikulski (D–Maryland) told the story of a retarded 13-year-old girl who suffered from cerebral palsy. She was raped and became pregnant as a result. She carried her child to term, but the baby died shortly after birth. Mikulski stated, "A young mother should never have been put through such trauma. The lives of the poor are brutal enough, how can we deny them such justice?" The opponents countered with the fact that "violent sexual crimes against women or minors do not justify abortion," which pro-lifers equate with murder. Senator Don Nickles (R–Oklahoma) asked his colleagues, "Is a child conceived through rape or incest any less of a human being? Nobody is denying that these are terrible crimes, but that does not justify taking a life, which is what abortion is."

Senator Gordon Humphrey (R–New Hampshire) commented: "A vote against Exon's amendment would not overturn the nation's existing abortion laws." He felt that the issue was that taxpayers should not have to pay for such procedures.

The abortion issue entered the 1988 presidential race when the candidates (George Bush and Michael Dukakis) met in their first debate. Governor Dukakis said, "I don't favor abortion or think it's a good thing. In the last analysis it's up to the woman in the exercise of her own conscience and religious beliefs to make that decision. We should not brand women as criminals for making that decision. I think that's what most Americans believe." President Bush opposes legalized abortion but believes "the choice should be left to the woman." Bush said that he feels abortion should be permitted only for women who are victims of rape or incest, or to save their lives. He stated, "I oppose abortion and I favor adoption . . . let these children come to birth and then put them in a family where they'll be loved."

Carol Downer, founder of the Feminist Women's Health Center located in Los Angeles, in replying to George Bush's comments on abortion, said: "If George Bush were willing to make a society where a woman could assure her child of what it needed without having to be dependent on a man, or without having to interfere with her education or without having to destroy her career, he and I wouldn't have much disagreement. And, believe me, we would reduce abortion considerably." But right-to-life advocates have continually argued that abortion for any reason is murder, "and a society that condones killing a fetus is sick." Susan Carpenter-McMillan, president of Southern California's chapter of Right to Life League and of the National Feminists for Life, states, "You might as well go into all of the old folks homes, all the hospitals where people are unwanted, all the prisons and take a gun and shoot them."

Surveys conducted in 1987 found that the largest group of nonwhite women having abortions were black women between the ages of 15 and 44; they averaged nearly 5.3 abortions per 100 women. Non-Latino white women averaged approximately 2.3 abortions per 100. Statistics released in 1989 for the 15 to 44 age group showed little change (23.0 white compared to 52.6 nonwhite). Unchanged is the 3 of 100 women who had abortions. In the years from 1977 to 1987, nearly 3 of every 100 women between the ages of 15 and 44 had an abortion. The most often stated reason was that a child would interfere with their career or education. Some said they could not afford to care for a child.

Most experts agree that unwanted children face a future of uncertainty. They are often abused or neglected. Many would be adopted, but what about those who for one reason or another are "unadoptable"? They would probably require public funding for support. Many advocates of abortion cite the fact that opponents of abortion are usually conservatives who normally oppose spending public funds to correct social ills, including assisting indigent women who are single mothers.

Because the Hyde Amendment became law in 1978, federal Medicaid funding for (elective) abortions is prohibited; however, that is not the case for natural childbirth where federal funding is used as an incentive. California is one of the states that allows abortions from state funds as part of their medical program. Recent statistics revealed that in Los Angeles County alone, Medical provided funding for over 25,000 medically induced abortions at a cost of nearly $9.5 million. Comparatively Medical funds paid for over 40,000 natural childbirths in Los Angeles County, at a cost of over $75 million. If the issue concerns the saving of public funds, comparing the cost reveals that abortion is the less expensive of the two.

According to Dr. Ellen Alcon, medical director and deputy director of Los Angeles County's public-health programs, the assumption that women will carry an unwanted baby to term if abortion is outlawed is not a valid one, because prior to the legalization of abortion, many women placed their lives and health in jeopardy by attempting a "self"-abortion or going to a "back-alley" abortion clinic.

Kate Michelman is executive director of the National Abortion Rights Action League and holds a master's degree in developmental psychology. She said, "There's no question you will see an increase in child abuse, family dysfunction and the deepening of poverty if legal abortion is overturned. There is an unbelievable effect on the psychological development of a child who is unwanted. Michelman also believed that abortion is less expensive to taxpayers than supporting a family on welfare.

In November 1988, in *Conn vs. Conn*, the United States Supreme Court handed down an opinion in which the husband of a pregnant woman wished to block his wife's decision to have an abortion. Jennifer Conn, age 19, resided in the state of Indiana and discovered she was pregnant with her second child. She had a five-month-old daughter and was separated from her husband, with plans for a divorce. Because of her situation, she decided to have an abortion, but did not inform her husband of her decision. When Erin Conn learned of his wife's plans, he filed a suit in a Shelby, Indiana, court seeking an injunction to prevent his wife from going through with her plans. The judge compared it to a divorce case with a dispute over child custody. The judge issued a temporary injunction that prohibited Jennifer from having an abortion. The stay lasted for seven weeks.

The injunction was lifted when the Indiana State Appellate Court invalidated the injunction on grounds the Supreme Court, in *Planned Parenthood vs. Danford* (1976), struck down a law that a woman had to have spousal consent prior to having an abortion. The Court said: "The abortion decision is the woman's alone. When the wife and the husband disagree on this decision, the view of only one of two marriage partners can prevail. Inasmuch as it is the woman who physically bears the child and who is more directly and immediately affected by the pregnancy, the balance weighs in her favor." The Indiana Supreme Court affirmed the ruling by a 4 to 1 vote.

A last-ditch appeal was presented before the United States Supreme Court on behalf of Erin Conn by his attorneys, but both Chief Justice Rehnquist and Justice Stevens refused (without comment) to keep the injunction intact. Jennifer Conn had the abortion.

Erin Conn's attorney said: "The father has fundamental rights and interests in his unborn child, which should be judicially considered, on the facts of this case, along with the rights and interests of his wife in aborting their child." Jennifer Conn's attorney also commented on the case: "Every appellate court to consider the issue has held that a man does not have the right to a court order enjoining a woman from exercising her abortion right. This has been true (in previous litigations) where the man seeking the court order was the woman's husband."

Between March and November of 1988, there were 16 similar suits filed in nine states. This case represents only one of a growing number that involve fathers who feel that they are victims of discrimination. The appellate courts have refused to rule against a woman's abortion decision, and the decision by the Supreme Court in *Conn vs. Conn* solidifies the feeling.

Antiabortionists, joyful over the election of George Bush to the presidency, issued the following statement: "The election is just one sign that the movement is picking up momentum in a drive that will culminate in the reversal of the Supreme Court decision establishing a constitutional right to abortion."

The day after he was elected, George Bush said that he will be looking for conservatives to fill future vacancies on the bench of the Supreme Court, but more specifically he will be looking at candidates that will not use the Court as a forum to legislate new laws.

In November 1988, United States Solicitor General Charles Fried, acting as "friend of the court," filed a brief on behalf of the Reagan administration, urging justices of the Court to consider for review the Missouri case of *Webster vs. Reproductive Health Services* because the issues involved raised some substantial federal questions with the possibility that its resolution could lead to a reversal of the *Roe* decision.

On the day prior to the filing of *Webster vs. Reproductive Health Services* before the Supreme Court, C. Everett Koop, United States surgeon general, aired his views on abortion: "I'm still opposed to abortion, I know lots of people who've been troubled with abortion." In his report to President Reagan, the surgeon general explained, "At this time, the available scientific evidence about the psychological effects of abortion simply cannot support either the preconceived beliefs of those pro-choice or of those of pro-life."

When reviewing the statistics, Koop concluded that the information is not sufficient to make any conclusive opinion of the psychological impact of abortion on women. He stated, however, "It has been documented that after abortion there can be (increased risk) of infertility, a damaged cervix, miscarriage, premature birth, or low birth-weight babies. But such problems occur among women who have carried to term and to women who had never before been pregnant. And a lack of comprehensive data makes it impossible to judge whether the problems are more frequent or serious among those who have undergone abortions."

Although the surgeon general refused to enter into any debate on the issue of abortion, he did feel that sooner or later the Court would have no alternative but to overturn the *Roe vs. Wade* decision because of some profound and serious problems that are inherent with the procedure.

Among the inherent problems the surgeon general may have been referring to are the unknown long-term psychological effects on women who have
had an abortion. In addition, there are many unanswered questions concerning viability. As medical technology improves, the point of viability is moved
back. In 1973, viability was placed at some point between the 24th and 28th
week of pregnancy; now the theory is that viability is possible as early as 23 ½
to 24 weeks' gestation. During the litigation of *Webster vs. Reproductive Health
Services,* it was established that there may be a four-week error in estimating
gestational age, which means that viability in some pregnancies may occur
as early as the 20th week of pregnancy,

15: Missouri Regulation of Abortions

188.010: It is the intention of the general assembly of the state of Missouri to grant the right to life of all humans, born and unborn, and to regulate abortion to the full extent permitted by the Constitution of the United States, decisions of the United States Supreme Court, and federal statutes.

[**Amended in 1986:** Substituted "grant the right to life to all humans, born and unborn, and to regulate abortion to the full extent permitted by the Constitution of the United States, decisions of the United States Supreme Court and federal statutes" for "reasonably regulate abortion in conformance with the decisions of the United States Supreme Court."]

188.015: Definitions: Unless the language or context clearly indicates a different meaning is intended, the following words or phrases for the purpose of 188.010 to 188.030 shall be given the meaning ascribed to them:

(1) **ABORTION:** The intentional destruction of the life of an embryo or fetus in his or her mother's womb or the intentional termination of the pregnancy of a mother with an intention other than to increase the probability of a live birth or to remove a dead or dying unborn child.

(2) **ABORTION FACILITY:** A clinic, physician's office, or any other place or facility in which abortions are performed other than a hospital.

(3) **CONCEPTION:** The fertilization of the ovum of a female by a sperm of a male.

(4) **GESTATIONAL AGE:** Length of pregnancy as measured from the first day of the woman's last menstrual period.

(5) **PHYSICIAN:** Any person licensed to practice medicine in this state by the state board of registration of the healing arts.

(6) **UNBORN CHILD:** The offspring of human beings from the moment of conception until birth and at every stage of its biological development, including the human conceptus, zygote, blastocyst, embryo, and fetus.

(7) **VIABILITY:** That stage of fetal development when the life of the unborn child may be continued indefinitely outside the womb by natural or artificial life-supportive systems.

[**Amended in 1986:** Modified the definition of "conception" and interpolated "gestational age."]

188.020: No person shall perform or induce an abortion except a physician.

188.025: Every abortion performed at sixteen weeks gestational age or later shall be performed in a hospital.

188.027: No abortion shall be performed except with the prior, informed and written consent freely given of the pregnant woman.

188.028: No person shall knowingly perform an abortion upon a pregnant woman under the age of eighteen years unless:

(1) The attending physician has obtained the informed written consent of the minor and one parent or guardian; or

(2) The minor is emancipated and the attending physician has received the informed written consent of the minor; or

(3) The minor has been granted the right to self-consent to the abortion by order of the court pursuant to subsection (2) of this section and the attending physician has received the informed written consent of the minor; or

(4) The minor has been granted consent to the abortion by court order and the court has been given its informed written consent in accordance with subsection (2) of this section and the minor is having the abortion willingly, in compliance with subsection (3) of this section.

(5) The right of the minor to self-consent to an abortion under subdivision (3) of subsection (1) of this section or court consent under subdivision (4) of subsection (1) of this may be granted by a court order pursuant to the following procedures:

(1) The minor or next friend shall make an application to the Juvenile Court which shall assist the minor or next friend in preparing the petition and notices required pursuant to this section. The minor or next friend of the minor shall thereafter file a petition setting forth the initials of the minor; the age of the minor; the names and addresses of each parent, guardian, or, if the minor's parents are deceased and no guardian has been appointed, any other person standing in "loco parentis" of the minor; that the minor has been fully informed of the risks and consequences of the abortion; that the minor is of sound minor mind and has sufficient intellectual capacity to consent to the abortion; that if the court does not grant the minor majority rights for the purpose of consent to the abortion, the court should find that the abortion is in the best interest of the minor and give judicial consent to the abortion; that the court should appoint a guardian, an "ad litem" of the child; and if the minor does not have private counsel, that the court should appoint counsel. The petition shall be signed by the minor or the next friend;

(2) Copies of the petition and a notice of the date, time and place of the hearing shall be personally served upon each parent, guardian, or if the minor's parents are deceased and no guardian has been appointed, any other person standing in "loco parentis" of the minor listed in the petition by the sheriff or his deputy. If a parent or guardian or, if the minor's parents are deceased and no guardian has been appointed, any other person standing in "loco parentis" cannot be personally served within two days after reasonable effort, the sheriff or his deputy shall give constructive notice to them by certified mail to their last known address and the hearing shall not be held for at least forty-eight hours from the time of the mailing. In any case where there exists the potential or appearance of conflict of interests between the parents or guardian or next friend of the child and the child, the court shall appoint a guardian "ad litem" to defend the minor's interest. The court shall set forth, for the record, the grounds for such an appointment;

(3) A hearing on the merits of the petition, to be held on the record, shall be held as soon as possible within five days of the filing of the petition. If any party is unable to afford counsel, the court shall appoint counsel at

least twenty-four hours before the time of the hearing. At the hearing, the court shall hear evidence relating to the emotional development, maturity, intellect and understanding of the minor; the nature, possible consequences and alternatives to abortion; and any other evidence that the court may find useful in determining whether the minor should be granted majority rights for the purpose of consenting to the abortion or whether the abortion is in the best interest of the minor;

(4) In decree, the court shall for good cause:

(a) Grant the petition for majority rights for the purpose of consenting to the abortion; or

(b) Find the abortion to be in the best interests of the minor and give judicial consent to the abortion, setting forth the grounds for so finding; or

(c) Deny the petition, setting forth the grounds on which the petition is denied.

(5) If the petition is allowed, the informed consent of the minor, pursuant to a court grant of majority rights, or the judicial consent, shall bar an action by the parents or guardian of the minor on the grounds of battery of the minor by those performing the abortion. The immunity granted shall only extend to the performance of the abortion in accordance herewith and any necessary accompanying services which are performed in a competent manner. The costs of the action shall be borne by the parties;

(6) An appeal from the order issued under the provisions of this section may be taken to the court of appeals of this state by the minor or by a parent or guardian of the minor. The notice of intent to appeal shall be given within forty-eight hours from the date of issuance of the order. The record on appeal shall be completed and the appeal shall be perfected within five days from the filing of the notice to appeal. Because time may be of the essence regarding the performance of the abortion, the Supreme Court of this state shall, by court rule, provide for expedited appellate review of cases appealed under this section.

(7) If a minor desires an abortion, then she shall be orally informed of and, if possible, sign the written consent required by section 188.039 in the same manner as an adult person. No abortion shall be performed on any minor against her will, except that an abortion may be performed against the will of a minor pursuant to a court order described in subdivision (4) of subsection (1) of this section that the abortion is necessary to preserve the life of the minor.

188.030: Abortion of viable unborn child permitted, when, procedure-second attendant physician also required, duties.

(1) No abortion of a viable unborn child shall be performed unless necessary to preserve the life or health of the woman. Before a physician may perform an abortion upon a pregnant woman after such time as her unborn child has become viable, such physician shall first certify in writing that the abortion is necessary to preserve the life or health of the woman and shall further certify in writing the medical indications for such abortion and the probable health consequences.

(2) Any physician who performs an abortion upon a woman carrying a viable unborn child shall utilize the available method or technique of abortion most likely to preserve the life and health of the unborn child. In cases where the method or technique of abortion which would most likely preserve the life and health of the unborn child would present a greater risk to the life and

health of the woman than another available method or technique the physician may utilize such other method or technique. In all cases where the physician performs an abortion upon a viable unborn child, the physician shall certify in writing the available method or techniques considered and the reasons for choosing the method or technique employed.

(3) An abortion of a viable unborn child shall be performed or induced only when there is in attendance a physician other than the physician performing or inducing the abortion who shall take control of and provide immediate medical care for a child born as a result of the abortion. During the performance of the abortion, the physician performing it and subsequent to the abortion, the physician required by this section to be in attendance, shall take all reasonable steps in keeping with good medical practice, consistent with the procedure used, to preserve the life and health of the viable unborn child; provided that it does not pose an increased risk to the life or health of the woman.

188.029: Physician, determination of viability, duties:
Before a physician performs an abortion on a woman he has reason to believe is carrying an unborn child of twenty or more weeks gestational age, the physician shall first determine if the unborn child is viable by using and exercising that degree of care, skill and proficiency commonly exercised by an ordinarily skillful, careful and prudent physician engaged in similar practice under the same or similar conditions. In making this determination of viability, the physician shall perform or cause to be performed such medical examinations and tests as are necessary to make a finding gestational age, weight, and lung maturity of the unborn child and shall enter such findings and determination of viability in the medical record of the mother.

188.035: Death of child aborted alive deemed murder in the second degree, when: Whoever, with intent to do so, shall take the life of a child aborted alive, shall be guilty of murder in the second degree.

188.036: Prohibited abortions, those done with intent to use fetal organs or tissue for transplant, experiments or for consideration, exceptions.

(1) No physician shall perform an abortion on a woman if the physician knows that the woman conceived the unborn child for the purpose of providing fetal organs or tissue for medical transplantation to herself or another, and the physician knows that the woman intends to procure the abortion to utilize those organs or tissue for such use for herself or another.

(2) No person shall utilize the fetal organs or tissue resulting from an abortion for medical transplantation, if the person knows that the abortion was procured for the purpose of utilizing those organs or tissue for such use.

(3) No person shall offer any inducement, monetary or otherwise, to the mother or father of an unborn child for the purpose of conceiving an unborn child for the medical, scientific, experimental or therapeutic use of fetal organs or tissue.

(4) No person shall offer any inducement, monetary or otherwise, to the mother or father of an unborn child for the purpose of procuring an abortion for the medical, scientific, experimental or therapeutic use of the fetal organs or tissue.

(5) No person shall knowingly offer or receive any valuable consideration for the fetal organs or tissue resulting from an abortion, provided that nothing in this subsection shall prohibit payment for burial or other final

disposition of the fetal remains, or payment for a pathological examination, autopsy or postmortem examination of the fetal remains.

(6) If any provision in this section or the application thereof to any person, circumstance or period of gestation is held invalid, such invalidity shall not affect the provisions or applications which can be given effect without the invalid provisions or application, and to this end the provisions of this section are declared severable.

188.037: Experimentation with fetus, or child aborted alive, prohibited exception: No person shall use any fetus or child aborted alive for any type of scientific, research, laboratory or other kind of experimentation either prior to or subsequent to any abortion procedure except as necessary to protect or preserve the life and health of such fetus or child aborted alive.

188.039: Consent form, content-coercion prohibited-woman to be informed of certain facts, when:

(1) No physician shall perform an abortion unless, prior to such abortion, the physician certifies in writing that the woman gave her informed consent, freely and without coercion, after the attending physician had informed her of the information contained in subsection (2) of this section not less than forty-eight hours prior to her consent to the abortion, and shall further certify in writing the pregnant woman's age, based upon proof of age offered by her.

(2) In order to insure that the consent for an abortion is truly informed consent, no abortion shall be performed or induced upon a pregnant woman unless she has signed a consent form that shall be supplied by the state division of health, acknowledging that she and, if she is a minor, her parent or legal guardian or person standing in "loco parentis" have been informed by the attending physician of the following facts:

(1) That according to the best medical judgment of her attending physician she is pregnant;

(2) The number of weeks elapsed from the probable time of conception of her unborn child, based upon the information provided by her as to the time of her last menstrual period and after a history and physical examination and appropriate laboratory tests;

(3) The probable anatomical and psychological characteristics of the unborn child at the time the abortion is to be performed;

(4) The immediate and long-term physical dangers of abortion and psychological trauma resulting from abortion and any increased incidence of premature births, tubal pregnancies and still-births following abortion;

(5) The particular risks associated with the abortion technique to be used;

(6) Alternatives to abortion shall be given by the attending physician, including a list of public and private agencies and services that will assist her during her pregnancy and after the birth of her child.

(3) The physician may inform the woman of any other material facts or opinions, or provide any explanation of the above information which, in the exercise of his best medical judgment, is reasonably necessary to allow the woman to give her informed consent to the proposed abortion, with full knowledge of its nature and consequences.

188.040: Infant to be abandoned ward of the state, when;
In every case when a live born infant results from an attempted abortion which was not performed to save the life or health of the mother, such infant shall

be an abandoned ward of the state under the jurisdiction of the juvenile court wherein the abortion occurred, and the mother and father, if he consented to the abortion, of such infant shall have no parental rights or obligations whatsoever relating to such infant, as if the parental rights had been terminated. The physician shall forthwith notify said juvenile court of the existence of such live born infant.

188.045: Woman seeking abortion, information required to be given her, certification of the receipt of such information required. Any woman seeking an abortion in the state of Missouri shall be verbally informed of the provisions of section 188.040 by the attending physician and the woman shall certify in writing that she has been so informed.

188.047: Tissue sample authorized, pathologist to file report, copies furnished. A representative sample of tissue removed at the time of abortion shall be submitted to a board eligible or certified pathologist, who shall file a copy of the tissue report with the state division of health, and who shall provide a copy of the report to the abortion facility or hospital in which the abortion was performed or induced and the pathologist report shall be made a part of the patient's permanent record.

188.050: Relating to the use of saline amniocentesis. (Law was repealed in 1979, remainder of text not available.)

188.052: Physician's report on abortion and post-abortion care, when division of health to publish statistics.

(1) An individual abortion report for each abortion performed or induced upon a woman shall be completed by her attending physician.

(2) An individual complication report for any post-abortion care performed upon a woman shall be completed by the physician providing such post-abortion care. This report shall include: (1) date of abortion, (2) name and address of the abortion facility, and (3) nature of the abortion complication diagnosed or treated.

(3) All abortion reports shall be signed by the attending physician, and submitted to the state division of health within forty-five days from the date of the abortion. All complication reports shall be signed by the physician providing the post-abortion care and submitted to the division of health within forty-five days from the date of the post-abortion care.

(4) A copy of the abortion report shall be made part of the medical record of the patient of the facility or hospital in which the abortion was performed.

(5) The state division of health shall be responsible for collecting all abortion reports and complication reports and collating and evaluating all data gathered therefrom and shall annually publish a statistical report based on such data from abortions performed in the previous calendar year.

188.055: Forms to be supplied to health facilities and physicians.

(1) Every abortion facility, hospital and physician shall be supplied with forms by the division of health for use in regard to the consents and reports required by section 188.010 to 188.085. A purpose and function of such consents and reports shall be the preservation of maternal health and life by adding to the sum of medical knowledge through the compilation of relevant maternal health and life data and to monitor all abortions performed to assure that they are done only under and in accord with the provisions of the law.

(2) All information obtained by physician, hospital, or abortion facility

from a patient for the purpose of preparing reports to the division of health under section 188.010 to 188.085 or reports received by the division of health shall be confidential and shall be used only for statistical purposes. Such records, however, may be inspected and health data acquired by local, state, or national public health officers.

188.060: Records to be retained for seven years. All medical records, reports and other documents required to be kept under section 188.010 to 188.085 shall be maintained in the permanent files of the abortion facility or hospital in which the abortion was performed for a period of seven years.

188.065: Revocation of license, when: Any practitioner of medicine, surgery, or nursing, or other health personnel who shall willfully and knowingly do or assist any action made unlawful by section 188.010 to 188.085 shall be subject to having his license, application for license, or authority to practice his profession as a physician, surgeon, or nurse in the state of Missouri rejected or revoked by the appropriate state licensing board.

188.080: Abortion performed by other than a licensed physician is a felony. Any person who is not a licensed physician as defined in subdivision (1) of section 188.015, is guilty of a felony and upon conviction, shall be imprisoned by the division of corrections for a term of not less than two years nor more than seventeen years.

188.200: Definitions: As used in section 188.200 to 188.220, the following terms mean:

(1) **PUBLIC EMPLOYEE:** Any person employed by this state or any agency or political subdivision thereof.

(2) **PUBLIC FACILITY:** Any public institution, public facility, public equipment, or any physical asset owned, leased, or controlled by this state or any agency or political subdivision thereof.

(3) **PUBLIC FUNDS:** Any funds received or controlled by this state or any agency or political subdivision thereof, including, but not limited to, funds derived from federal, state, or local taxes, gifts or grants from any source, public or private, federal grants or payments, or intergovernmental transfers.

188.205: Use of public funds prohibited, when;
It shall be unlawful for any public funds to be expended for the purpose of performing or assisting an abortion, not necessary to save the life of the mother, or for the purpose of encouraging or counseling a woman to have an abortion not necessary to save her life.

188.210: Public employees, activities prohibited, when;
It shall be unlawful for any public employee within the scope of his employment to perform or assist an abortion, not necessary to save the life of the mother. It shall be unlawful for a doctor, nurse or other health care personnel, a social worker, a counselor or persons of similar occupations who is a public employee within the scope of his public employment to encourage or counsel a woman to have an abortion not necessary to save her life.

188.215: Use of public facilities prohibited when;
It shall be unlawful for any public facility to be used for the purpose of performing or assisting an abortion not necessary to save the life of the mother or for the purpose of encouraging or counseling a woman to have an abortion not necessary to save her life.

188.220: Taxpayer standing to bring suit, when, where;

Any taxpayer of this state or its political subdivisions shall have standing to bring out in a circuit court of proper venue to enforce the provisions of section 188.200 to 188.215.

Since 1974, the state of Missouri has, on three separate occasions, initiated a series of abortion laws, all of which have been appealed to the Supreme Court. The statutes enacted in 1974 were appealed before the Supreme Court in 1976 in *Planned Parenthood of Central Missouri vs. Danford.* The statutes enacted in 1979 were appealed before the Supreme Court in 1983 in *Planned Parenthood of Kansas City vs. Ashcroft.* The statutes enacted in 1986 were appealed before the Supreme Court in April 1989 in *Webster vs. Reproductive Health Services.*

Modified, Amended, and Repealed Statutes

188.010 was enacted in 1974 and amended in 1986: Substituted "grant the right to life to all humans, born and unborn, and to regulate abortion to the full extent permitted by the Constitution of the United States, decisions of the United States Supreme Court and federal statutes" for "reasonably regulate abortion in conformance with the decisions of the United States Supreme Court."

188.015 was enacted in 1974 and amended in 1986: Modified the definition of "conception" and inserted "gestational age."

188.025 was enacted in 1974 and amended in 1986: Substituted "at sixteen weeks gestational age or later" for "subsequent to the first twelve weeks of pregnancy."

188.028 was enacted in 1979 and amended in 1986: Deleted subdivision (2) of subsection (2), which pertained to the service of the petition required from minors who exercised the right of self-consent to abortion and redesignated former subdivisions (3) to (6) as subdivisons (2) to (5), respectively.

188.030 was enacted in 1974 and amended in 1979: Rewrote the section that previously read: "No abortion not necessary to preserve the life or health of the mother shall be performed unless the attending physician first certifies with reasonable medical certainty that the fetus is not viable."

188.039 was enacted in 1979 and amended in 1986: Deleted "not less than forty eight hours prior to her consent to abortion" following "subsection (2) of this section" in subsection (1); substituted "state department of health, acknowledging that she has" for "division of health, acknowledging that she and if she is a minor, her parents or legal guardian or persons standing in 'loco parentis' have" in the introductory fragment of subsection (2); substituted "whether she is or she is not" for "she is" in subsection (2)(1); deleted former subsections, (2)(2) to (2)(4), which required the attending physician to inform a woman seeking an abortion, the number of weeks elapsed since conception, the probable anatomical and psychological effects of the abortion; redesignated former subsections (2)(5) and (2)(6) as subsections (2)(2) and (2)(3) and in subsection (2)(3) deleted language that required physicians to provide a list of public and private agencies that will assist the person seeking an abortion during her pregnancy and after birth of her child.

188.040 was enacted in 1974, repealed in 1986.

188.045 was enacted in 1974, repealed in 1986.

188.047 was enacted in 1979 and was modified in 1986 to reflect the establishment of the Department of Health, which formerly constituted the Division of Health within the Department of Social Services.

188.050 was enacted in 1974, repealed in 1986.

188.052 was enacted in 1979 and modified in 1986 to reflect the establishment of the Department of Health, which formerly constituted the Division of Health within the Department of Social Services.

188.055 was enacted in 1974, amended in 1979, and modified in 1986: The 1979 amendment substituted "abortion" for "health" preceding "facility," inserted "hospital" and deleted "promulgated" following "forms," and inserted "for use in regards to consents and reports required by §§188.010 to 188.085" in the first sentence; deleted "The" and inserted "A" preceding "purpose"; substituted "such consents and reports" for "which" in the second sentence of subsection (1); deleted former subsection (2), which read: "The forms shall be provided by the state division of health." Renumbered former subsection (3) as subsection (2); deleted "clinic or other health" preceding "facility" and inserted "abortion" preceding "facility"; and substituted "§§188.010 to 188.085," for "this section," in that subsection.

188.080 was enacted in 1974 and amended in 1986: Inserted "Notwithstanding any other penalty provisions in this chapter"; substituted "class 'B' felony" for "felony"; and substituted "punished as provided by law" for "imprisoned by the division of corrections for a term of not less than two years nor more than seventeen years"; and added the second sentence.

Rulings of the Circuit Court of Appeals

The United States Circuit Court of Appeals for the Eighth Circuit affirmed many of the findings of the United States district court. Sections 188.205, 188.210, 188.215, 188.029, 188.025, and 1.205 were ruled unconstitutional by the district court, affirmed by the circuit court.

Rulings of the United States Supreme Court

On July 3, 1989, the United States Supreme Court, in what can best be described as a "lackluster" and almost predictable decision of conservatives versus moderates, overturned many of the rulings of the United States circuit court of appeals, but did not overturn *Roe vs. Wade*, as anticipated. Section 188.205 was overturned by a 6–3 vote. Section 188.210 was overturned by a 6–3 vote.

Section 188.215 was overturned by an identical 6–3 vote, section 188.029 by a slim 5–4 margin.

Section 188.025, which was ruled unconstitutional by the district and circuit courts, did not become part of Missouri's appeal before the Supreme Court. The Supreme Court refused to rule on section 188.205.

Webster vs. Reproductive Health Services

On January 10, 1989, the United States Supreme Court, with a conservative majority and encouragement from the Reagan administration, agreed to hear the appeal of a 1986 Missouri abortion law. In 1988, the Eighth Circuit Court of Appeals had ruled that certain provisions violated a woman's constitutional rights. This litigation was of profound importance since once again it tested the powers of a state in regulating abortion. But perhaps an even more critical aspect was in testing the new conservative majority of the Court that many had speculated was anxious to reverse direction on legalized abortions as set forth in *Roe vs. Wade* (1973).

Legal experts felt that there were no positive indications the Court would overturn *Roe vs. Wade* as a result of the challenge. Attorneys for Planned Parenthood and representatives for other women's-rights organizations, however, expressed much concern over the Court's decision to hear the appeal of the lower-court decision. In a combined statement, they asserted that it represented the most serious threat to legalized abortions since the Supreme Court declared the procedure for the most part constitutional in *Roe vs. Wade*.

Dawn Johnsen, litigation director for the National Abortion Rights League based in Washington, D.C., commented, "The threat to safe and legal abortions has never been greater since *Roe* was decided than it is today. The Court has before it a case in which they've been asked to overrule *Roe vs. Wade,* or at the very minimum to uphold very [burdensome] restrictions on a woman's access to abortions."

Most observers doubted that the action taken by the Court would result in a reversal of *Roe.* One of them, Roger Evans, director of litigation for Planned Parenthood who was assigned to argue the case before the Court, was quoted as saying, "The case does not mandate a genuine reconsideration of *Roe vs. Wade.*"

Evans stated that although *Roe* did not appear to be directly threatened, "the case could signal the beginning of a conservative swing of the abortion pendulum." The outcome would depend on the opinions of the two jurists who had not clarified their views on the issue, Sandra Day O'Connor and Anthony Kennedy.

Eve Paul, general counsel for Planned Parenthood, said, "This is a new

Court. Kennedy is new and has not previously expressed his views on the abortion issue. We are concerned that he may not be as committed in protecting fundamental rights of women as others. O'Connor, the only woman ever to sit on the Court, can be expected to play a crucial role in its deliberations. O'Connor is in the middle; she supports the right to abortion, but she may be willing to restrict it in some way.

For political observers it comes as no surprise that Missouri is the state which is appealing the July 1988 decision of the Eighth Circuit Court of Appeals because it boasts the largest population of "pro-life" followers. Not only does the state have the largest population of "pro-lifers," but they also have a state legislature that is purposely balanced in that direction. The state attorney general and the governor of Missouri subscribe to pro-life idealism. Recently, one Missouri state official was quoted as saying, "We work hard to get them [pro-lifers] elected."

The stage has been set and the curtain is about to rise on the beginning of a new era in judicial history. For after a decision is reached on this litigation, one can only speculate as to what additional changes will be made from the current regulations regarding abortion.

Health-care employees, clinics performing abortion services in the state of Missouri, a number of pregnant women seeking an abortive remedy, and members of the clergy filed a class action suit in the federal District Court for the Western District of Missouri, asking that appellees be granted both injunctive and declarative relief to prevent William Webster, attorney general of Missouri, from enforcing the state's restrictive abortion laws on grounds that they were unconstitutional. The district court's chief judge, Scott O. Wright, declared many of the provisions to be violations of constitutional rights and permanently prohibited the state from enforcing the abortion statutes. The state immediately appealed to the Eighth Circuit Court of Appeals. The court heard the case on January 12, 1988, and handed down a decision on July 13 of that year.

Chief Judge Donald Lay of the Eighth Circuit Court of Appeals, speaking for the court and his colleague Justice Arnold, affirmed in part and reversed in part the decision of the federal district court and held that section 188.205 relating to the use of public funds for nonemergency, elective abortions is constitutional. Section 188.210, which prohibits public employees from participating in abortions that are not related to saving of the mother's life, is unconstitutional. The court ruled section 188.025, requiring post–first-trimester (16th week of pregnancy and over) abortions be performed in a full-service hospital, unconstitutional. Section 188.029, requiring the physician to perform fetal testing in order to determine fetal viability but only after he has determined that his patient is in at least her 20th week of pregnancy, was ruled unconstitutional. Section 188.205, proclaiming that all human life begins at conception, was ruled unconstitutional.

In April 1989, the case was argued before the United States Supreme Court amid rumors that the Court would completely vacate the edicts set forth in *Roe vs. Wade.* On July 3, 1989, the long-awaited decision was revealed by the Court. The angry demonstrations and rhetoric prior to the decision of the Court proved to be more exciting than the decision itself. The ruling of the Supreme Court was predictable, overturning some of the findings reached by the lower courts while affirming others.

Post First Trimester Hospitalization

One of Missouri's abortion regulations included hospitalization for post–first-trimester procedures that were performed at the 16th week of pregnancy and thereafter. The primary stipulation was that this procedure be performed in a full-service hospital. The requirement was invalidated by the federal district court, and the invalidation was upheld by the Eighth Circuit Court of Appeals. Both lower courts found the requirement unconstitutional because a full-service hospital is less accessible and more costly than clinics, which may lead to placing a woman's health in jeopardy.

To date there is no tangible evidence that proves full-service hospitals are safer than abortion clinics for procedures performed during this stage of pregnancy. Laws that are specifically legislated to restrict a woman's access to abortion prior to the stage of viability can be constitutional only if they reasonably relate to concerns of maternal health.

Determining Viability

A section of Missouri's abortion regulations stipulates that if a woman is in her 20th week of pregnancy, her physician is required to administer tests of the fetus to determine if it is viable prior to performing an abortion. The fetal testing includes estimating gestational age, approximate weight, and lung development.

In previous judgments, courts have found fetal testing to be unconstitutional because it is considered legislative encroachment into an area of medical judgment and skills. In the Court's findings, it was stipulated that the state may not dictate either the tests or the findings that enter into a decision of whether or not a fetus is viable. A Supreme Court ruling in *Colautti vs. Franklin* (1979) said that neither the legislature nor the courts may proclaim one of the elements of viability, be it weeks of gestation, fetal weight, or any other single factor.

Regardless of the previous rulings on this issue, in 1989 the United States Supreme Court found Missouri's statute to be reasonable in ensuring that abortion procedures are not performed on viable fetuses. On this issue, the Court said that the section creates what is essentially a presumption of viability at 20 weeks, which the physician, prior to performing the abortion, must rebut with tests — including if feasible, those for gestational age, fetal weight, and lung capacity — indications that the fetus is not viable. While the district court found that uncontradicted medical evidence established that a 20 week fetus is not viable, and that 23½ to 24 weeks' gestation is the earliest point at which a reasonable possibility exists, it also found that there may be a four-week error in estimating gestational age, which supports testing at 20 weeks.

The Supreme Court further stated that the doubt cast on the Missouri statute by these cases is not so much a flaw in the state as it is a reflection of the fact that *Roe*'s rigid trimester analysis has proven to be unsound in principle and unworkable in practice. The *Roe* framework is hardly consistent with the notion of a Constitution like ours that is cast in general terms and usually speaks in general principles. The framework's key elements — trimesters and viability — are not found in the Constitution's text, and since the bounds of the inquiry are essentially indeterminate, the result has been a web of legal rules that have become increasingly intricate, resembling a code of regulations rather than a body of constitutional doctrine. There is also no reason why the state's compelling interest in protecting potential human life should not extend throughout pregnancy rather than coming into existence only at the point of viability. At this point, the Court called for abandoning of the trimester system.

In *Roe vs. Wade* the Supreme Court stipulated that it would not resolve the difficult question of when life begins when those in the respective disciplines of medicine, philosophy, and theology were unable to arrive at any consensus. The judiciary at this point in development of man's knowledge was not in a position to speculate as to the answer.

Regardless of the opinion issued by the Supreme Court, the Missouri General Assembly declared that (1) life begins at conception; (2) unborn children have protectable interests in life, health, and well-being; and (3) the natural parents of unborn children have protectable interests in the life, health, and well-being of their unborn child.

In addition, the Missouri statute declared that the unborn child from conception is entitled to the protection of all laws of the state, including rights, privileges, and immunities that are afforded to other residents of the state. The provision clearly defines the terms *unborn children* and *unborn child* to include all children from the moment of conception.

The lower court invalidated the statute because it found the declaration that all unborn children have the same rights as other citizens to be unacceptable. A state may not adopt one theory of when life begins to justify the regulation of abortions.

The United States Supreme Court, by a slim margin of 5 to 4, voted not to issue a judgment on the issue since it did not concern questions of constitutional irregularities or legal precedence. The Court stated, however, that at some time in the future it might want to investigate the issue in more depth.

Public Funding

The state of Missouri prohibited the use of public funds for the purpose of counseling and encouraging women to have an abortion. The United States district court found the law to be an infringement of a woman's Fourteenth Amendment rights to have an abortion. The Eighth Circuit Court of Appeals affirmed the ruling and added that the law represented an obstacle to abortion, especially for women who have had all of the precounseling and obtained all the pertinent information and thus are prepared to make their decision with full knowledge and intelligence.

In previous cases the Supreme Court has continually said that a state has no authority to interfere with an abortion decision that has been made intelligently by placing legislative obstacles in the path of a woman who has been fully informed on the procedure by her physician. In addition, the Court has held that a woman's total freedom of choice is contingent on the condition that her physician is free in making decisions concerning his patient that are based on his best medical judgment, not on government intrusion.

In *Colautti vs. Franklin* (1979), the Supreme Court made a more definitive assessment by carefully defining the term *physician's freedom*. The Court said that the physician's exercise of his best medical judgment encompasses both assisting the woman in the decision-making process and implementing her decision should she decide to have an abortion.

A woman should have the freedom to decide on abortion after consulting with her physician and the right to make that decision free of any state interference. This implied freedom should not be revoked until the stage of pregnancy is reached when state interest in maternal health is profound enough to warrant concern. This stage usually occurs when viability is reached, between the 24th and the 27th weeks of pregnancy. The district court interpreted Missouri's law as placing "roadblocks" between the patient and her physician by prohibiting him from providing his patient with certain pertinent information and advice that could be interpreted by Missouri law as "encouraging" his patient to have an abortion in situations where she feels that abortion is a medical necessity but not necessarily a life-threatening situation. In *Thornburgh vs. American College of Obstetricians and Gynecologists,* the Supreme Court invalidated a similar statute on grounds that it attempted to "structure the dialogue" between a woman and her physician.

The circuit court stipulated that the state's analogy of its ban on encouraging or counseling women on the abortion procedure, including prohibiting public funding of abortions, is completely inept. It seems that Missouri has gone beyond its intended boundaries of not using tax dollars to fund elective abortions to prohibiting doctors from discussing certain information with their patients who have chosen abortion over childbirth. Furthermore, the state has chosen to make it very difficult for a woman to exercise her constitutional rights by blocking the free flow of information that contains data on alternatives to childbirth. The state's limitation on doctor-patient discussion reflects the state's choice for childbirth over abortion in a manner that prevents the patient from making a fully informed and intelligent choice. The Supreme Court, in *Maher vs. Roe* (1977), said that states cannot constitutionally impose such burdensome obstacles to what is at the bottom a right to decide whether to terminate a pregnancy.

The opinion of the circuit court summed up the issue: Few obstacles are more burdensome to the right to decide than a state-imposed blackout of information necessary to make a decision. Therefore, the district court's judgment that a state ban on encouraging and counseling abortion patients is an infringement on the right to choose an abortion, protected by the Fourteenth Amendment, is affirmed.

The issue was appealed by Missouri to the United States Supreme Court. In July 1989, the Court ruled by a 6 to 3 margin that the matter was a moot point since it is not directed at the conduct of any physician or health-care provider, private or public, and is aimed only at those persons responsible for expending public funds. Appellees contended that they are not adversely affected under the state's interpretation of the statute, and therefore that there is no longer a case or controversy before the Court on this issue.

Missouri's statute, which bans public employees from aiding in or assisting an abortion procedure in a public facility, does not interfere with previous Court holdings on the abortion issue. The Due Process Clause, which has been interpreted to include a woman's right to have an abortion, does not guarantee that the government is responsible for funding of the procedure with tax dollars. The Court has upheld the government's decision to withhold public funds for nontherapeutic abortions, at the same time allowing payments for medical services that are related to natural childbirth, which understandably makes it an attractive alternative to abortion but in no way violates Court holdings in *Roe vs. Wade*.

The Supreme Court stressed that since Missouri has decided to use public facilities and employees to encourage natural childbirth over abortion, this decision may appear somewhat unfair and may lead to claims of constitutional improprieties; it nevertheless places no governmental obstacle in the path of women who choose abortion. The Court stated that the challenged provisions restrict only her ability to obtain an abortion to the extent that she chooses to use a physician affiliated with a public hospital. Nothing in the Constitution requires a state to enter into or to remain in the abortion business or entitles private physicians and their patients to access to public facilities for the performance of abortions.

The state of Missouri banned the use of public facilities for the purpose of performing abortions unless the procedure was necessary to save the life of the mother. The state defined the term *public facility* as any institution, public facility, public equipment or any physical asset owned, leased, or controlled by the state of Missouri or any agency or political subdivision thereof.

In a 1982 case that involved a similar restrictive law, the state of Virginia answered a challenge to a statute that prohibited doctors from using any public hospital or other facility for the purpose of performing a termination-of-pregnancy procedure unless it was necessary to save the mother's life. In that litigation, the Supreme Court ruled that a state could not restrict doctors from performing abortions in public facilities if the procedure was privately funded.

The Supreme Court has continually held that the government was not obligated to provide funds for elective abortions. In 1977 the Hyde Amendment, which prohibited federal Medicaid funding to indigent women for the purpose of providing payment for elective abortions but allowed Medicaid funding of natural childbirth, was passed by Congress. The issues may seem similar, but after taking a close look, it becomes evident that they are different. The Hyde Amendment prohibits the use of federal funds for the purpose of providing indigent women the means of obtaining an abortion, but the state of Missouri enacted a law that is stricter; it prohibits the use of public employees and facilities for the purpose of performing abortions, even for those patients who can afford to pay for the procedure.

Are states creating obstacles and undue burdens to hinder women seeking abortions by barring access to public facilities? To bar access to public facilities does more than demonstrate a political choice in favor of childbirth; it clearly narrows and in some cases forecloses the availability of abortions to women. This type of restrictive law could directly interfere with a woman's choice to select a physician who may be prohibited by law from performing an abortion at some hospitals, and only because of the language of the law. The result could be increased costs of abortion, inability to select a physician of the woman's own choosing, and a delay in performing the abortion procedure, which may have the effect of increasing the health risk to the patient.

Essentially, Missouri's law simply prevents a pregnant woman who desires to terminate her pregnancy from exercising her "right" in a public facility, even though she has offered to pay for it.

It seems almost a contradiction to forbid a state from interfering with an abortion decision made between a patient and her doctor, at the same time barring a woman access to a public hospital for the purpose of abortion. Because of the apparent contradiction of the law and the finding that prohibiting women from having abortions at public facilities is just another form of interfering with the abortion decision, the Eighth Circuit Court of Appeals found the restrictive law in violation of the Fourteenth Amendment.

The invalidation of the law by the circuit court was immediately appealed by the state of Missouri to the United States Supreme Court, which vacated the invalidation in July 1989. It stated that the challenged provision only restricts a woman's ability to obtain an abortion to the extent that she chooses to use a physician affiliated with a public hospital. This circumstance is more easily remedied and thus considerably less burdensome than indigency, which makes it difficult and in some cases, perhaps impossible for some women to have abortions without public funding. Having held that the state's refusal to fund abortions does not violate *Roe vs. Wade,* it strains logic to reach a contrary result for the use of public facilities and employees.

The circuit court misinterpreted the evidence presented as implying that all costs incurred for an abortion procedure at a public facility are eventually recouped after the patient pays for the service. Absent any expenditure of public funds, the lower court thought that Missouri was "expressing" more than "its preference for childbirth over abortions," but rather was creating an obstacle to exercise of the right to choose an abortion (that could not) stand absent a compelling state interest. The Supreme Court disagreed with the lower court's assessment of the provision and reversed the lower court's judgment by a slim margin.

Public Employees Assisting in Abortion

The state of Missouri prohibits public employees from assisting in any non-emergency abortion, as defined in section 188.210, which states that it shall be unlawful for any public employee within the scope of his employment to perform or assist in abortion not necessary to save the life of the mother.

The Due Process Clause of the Fourteenth Amendment grants to women the right to have an abortion free of government encroachment. The presumed "right," however, does not transcend its stated boundaries by providing funds for abortion procedures, but it does prohibit the use of any state-mandated obstruction or any attempt whatsoever to interfere with a woman's desire to have an abortion. Regardless of the stated guarantees of the Fourteenth Amendment, the state of Missouri has created a law that prohibits public employees from performing abortions, thus making a strong case in favor of invalidating the entire provision.

From the evidence presented before the circuit court, there is no tangible evidence that supports the claim that any public tax dollars are being lost if patients are willing to pay for the services of the facility and the employees involved in performing the abortion procedure. The lower court found that by refusing to permit public employees to perform or assist abortions, Missouri is not expressing its preference for childbirth over abortion by refusing to fund the latter. Rather the state is declaring that even women who can afford abortions cannot obtain them through the assistance of public employees, for no other expressed reason than the state's desire to discourage abortions. That Missouri has chosen to discourage abortion aggressively is not reason enough for the apparent obstacle the state has purposely placed in its restrictive abortion law. The circuit court therefore affirmed the judgment of the district court to invalidate the law that prohibits public employees from performing abortions.

The state disagreed with the finding of the circuit court and immediately appealed the decision to the United States Supreme Court. After listening to arguments, the Court overturned the judgment of the lower court and commented that the Constitution does not compel any state to provide facilities or funding for abortions: Nor do private physicians and their patients have some kind of constitutional right of access to public facilities for the performance of abortion. In previous decisions, the supportive view has been that the state need not commit any resources to facilitating abortions, even if it can turn a profit by doing so.

Opinion of the Court:
Read by Chief Justice Rehnquist (Paraphrase)

One of the more misconstrued of Missouri's abortion statutes was referred to by the state as a Preamble of its regulation of abortions. Known as section 1.205.1, it declared that state laws be interpreted to include provisions for unborn children with "all of the rights, privileges and immunities available to other persons, citizens, and residents of this state," subject to remaining within constitutional guidelines and precedents set by the Supreme Court.

When the Eighth Circuit Court of Appeals invalidated the law, it relied on previous directives of the Supreme Court, one of which stated that a state may not adopt one theory of when life begins to justify its regulation of abortions. The court of appeals completely rejected the argument of the law as "abortion-neutral." The court also rejected the opinion that it is a state "prerogative" to make a determination of when life begins if it so wishes and the word *abortion* does not enter the text of the law. The court of appeals' primary objection was in its belief that the state intended its abortion regulations to be understood against the backdrop of its theory of life.

Missouri countered with the argument that the wording of the Preamble is more advisory than directory; therefore, it does not interfere with a woman's decision to have an abortion, which renders appellees' arguments over the issue invalid, thus nullifying the entire pretense of their challenge. Appellees insist that the Preamble is an operative part of the act intended to guide the interpretation of the other provisions of the act. They feel strongly that the "definition of life" in the Preamble may influence some physicians to rethink their position on the issuance of birth-control and intrauterine devices.

In the view of the Supreme Court, the court of appeals incorrectly interpreted this Court's previous judgments on the matter. In a case that involved the city of Akron, the Supreme Court stipulated that a state could not justify an abortion regulation otherwise invalid under *Roe vs. Wade* on the grounds that it embodied the state's view about when life begins. Certainly the Preamble does not by its terms regulate abortion or any other aspect of appellees' medical practice.

The Supreme Court has held that the judgment in *Roe vs. Wade* has never denied to individual states the authority of making a value assessment favoring childbirth over abortion. In this case the wording of the statute should not be interpreted in any other way.

We think the extent to which the Preamble's language might be used to interpret other state statutes or regulations is something that only the courts of Missouri can definitively decide. The only presumed intention of Missouri's law is that it protects the unborn from personal harm and in matters of probate law, but beyond that, there is no tangible evidence that the state had anything else in mind.

We are thus invited to pass upon the constitutional validity of a state statute which has not yet been applied or threatened to be applied by the state courts to petitioners or others in the manner anticipated. Lacking any authoritative construction of the statute by the state courts, without which no constitutional question arises, unwilling to give such controlling construction ourselves, and with a record that presents no concrete set of facts to which the statute is to be applied, the case is plainly not one to be disposed of by the declaratory-judgment procedure.

It will be time enough for federal courts to address the meaning of the Preamble should it be applied to restrict the activities of appellees (physicians) in some concrete way. Until then, this Court is not empowered to decide abstract propositions or to declare for the government of future cases, principles, or rules of law that cannot affect the result as to the thing in issue in the case before it.

The next area of concern is section 188.210, which stated that it shall be unlawful for any public employee to perform or assist in an abortion not necessary to save the life of the mother. This and section 188.215 provide the state with a double shot in regulating abortions. Section 188.215 provides that it is unlawful for any public facility to be used for the purpose of performing or assisting an abortion not necessary to save the life of the mother. The circuit court of appeals felt that these statutes violated the holding of the Supreme Court in *Roe vs. Wade*. However, this Court disagrees with that interpretation.

In previous decisions made by this Court, we've adhered to the opinion that the Due Process Clause may indeed grant a woman the right to have an abortion, but at the same time we are of the opinion that the Due Process Clause confers no right for financial assistance to cover the costs of an abortion procedure. In *Maher vs. Roe* (1977), the Court agreed with the state of Connecticut when its welfare department refused to fund abortion with federal Medicaid payments, at the same time providing funding for natural childbirth. The Court rejected the claim that this unequal subsidizing of abortion and childbirth was impermissible under *Roe vs. Wade*. In *Maher vs. Roe,* the Court stipulated that the Connecticut regulation before us is different in kind from the laws invalidated in our previous abortion decisions. The Connecticut regulation places no obstacles, absolute or otherwise, in the pregnant woman's path to an abortion. An indigent woman who desires an abortion suffers no disadvantage as a consequence of Connecticut's decision to fund childbirth; she continues as before to be dependent on private sources for the service she desires. The state may have made childbirth a more attractive alternative, thereby influencing the woman's decision, but it has imposed no restriction on access to abortions that was not already there. The indigency that may make it difficult and in some cases perhaps impossible for some women to have abortions is neither created nor in any way affected by the Connecticut regulation.

The court of appeals, however, saw these provisions as discriminatory because they both prevent access to public facilities for abortion patients, which demonstrates a political choice in favor of childbirth; it clearly narrows and in some cases forecloses the availability of abortion to women. In reaching its conclusion, the circuit court of appeals strongly felt that to ban a woman from public facilities could severely hamper her choice of physician, because of his "unprivileged" status at public hospitals or because in the future private hospitals may adopt the same antiabortion stand. The court also felt that such a prohibition could increase the cost or delay the abortion.

This Court disagreed with the assessment of the lower court, however. The state's decision to use public facilities and staff to encourage childbirth over abortion placed no governmental obstacle in the path of a woman who chooses to terminate her pregnancy. Interpreting the position of the Supreme Court, prohibiting the use of public funds to indigent women for the purpose of abortion was akin to Congress's deciding not to subsidize health costs for any reason. In both cases the indigent woman would be left with identical choices. In respect to that interpretation, when Missouri decided to enact a law that would prohibit public employees from participating in any phase of the abortion decision and the inclusion in that law of barring public facilities from being used for abortions, the state essentially gave women the same choice as if it had decided not to operate any public hospitals or clinics.

Congress and the Supreme Court stand together in their constitutional interpretation of the Due Process Clause as including the right of women to have abortions, but no more than that.

Nothing in the Constitution requires states to enter or remain in the business of performing abortions. Nor, as appellees suggest, do private physicians and their patients have some kind of constitutional right of access to public facilities for the performance of abortions. Indeed, if the state does recoup all of its costs performing abortions and no state subsidy, direct or indirect, is available, it is difficult to see how any procreational choice is burdened by the state's ban on the use of its facilities or employees for performing abortions. The Constitution does not forbid a state or city, pursuant to democratic process, from expressing a preference for normal childbirth as the city of St. Louis has done. Thus we uphold the act's restrictions on the use of public employees and facilities for the performance or assistance of nontherapeutic abortions.

Regarding the issue of public employees' engaging in the process of either counseling or encouraging women on abortion, section 188.205 prohibits the use of public funds for this purpose unless the procedure is necessary to save the life of the pregnant woman. Language embodied in section 188.210 prohibits public employees from engaging in such discussions with women who desire an abortive remedy, and section 188.215 forbids any dialogue in public hospitals or clinics.

When it came time for the court of appeals to rule on sections 188.205, 188.210, and 188.215, it did not consider them separately but rather together as unconstitutionally vague, and that the ban on using public funds, employees and facilities to encourage or counsel a woman to have an abortion is an unacceptable infringement of the woman's Fourteenth Amendment right to choose an abortion after receiving the medical information necessary to exercise the right knowingly and intelligently.

Questions over the constitutionality of section 188.205 arose after the law was interpreted as going too far in interfering with a woman's right to have an abortion. However, the law is advisory and directed only at those primarily responsible for the disbursing of public funds. We accept for the purpose of decision, the state's claim that section 188.205 is not directed at the conduct of any physician or health care provider, private or public, but is directed solely at those persons responsible for expending public funds.

Many of the questions over the constitutionality of section 188.029 were raised over the interpretation of its language. The state reasoned that the law was enacted to ensure that a fetus of 20 weeks' gestational age will not be aborted alive. The circuit court felt that testing for viability of a fetus that is approximately 20 weeks of development would prove to be "unreliable and inaccurate," and would add additional costs to an already expensive procedure. The lower court added that amniocentesis, the only method available to determine lung maturity, is contrary to accepted medical practice until 28–30 weeks of gestational age, is expensive and imposes significant health risks for both the pregnant woman and the fetus.

The first order of business is to understand the "real" meaning of section

188.029. Usually the Court will abide by the lower court's interpretation of the construction of a particular state statute, but in this case the lower court has "fallen into plain error" in construing the statute in question.

We think the viability-testing provision makes sense only if the second sentence is read to require only those tests that are useful to making subsidiary findings as to viability. The provision required viability testing regardless of the relevancy of the tests or their potential danger to the mother or the fetus. If physicians were not allowed to make that determination using their best medical skill and judgment, the second sentence of the act would be contradictory to what is stated in sentence one of the act.

The concerns expressed in section 188.029 were actually extensions of the recognized interest in promoting potential human life rather than expressions of concern for maternal health. The act is designed to create an amount of awareness among physicians that a fetus of 20 weeks' gestation "may be" viable. However, viability at this stage in pregnancy can only be presumed until it is refuted by a physician who adheres to a state-mandated requirement of fetal testing.

The district court found that there is almost no possibility that a fetus of 20 weeks will be viable, that the earliest known to the medical profession is between 23½ to 28 weeks of development. But the Court also found that there may be a four-week error in estimating gestational age, which supports testing at 20 weeks.

In *Roe vs. Wade* (1973), the Supreme Court acknowledged that a state has a binding interest in the protection of maternal health and potential human life and that the implied interest becomes more profound as the pregnancy advances to term. During the second trimester of pregnancy, the state may closely monitor the abortion procedure, but only for reasons of concerns over maternal health. Even at this late stage in pregnancy, however, the ultimate judgment of viability is left to the medical skills of the attending physician. When the stage of viability is reached, the state may closely regulate the abortion procedure or prohibit it except where it is necessary, in appropriate medical judgment, for the preservation of the life or health of the mother.

The district court and the circuit court of appeals found that section 188.029 does indeed regulate the method for determining viability, that it does impose a medical judgment of determining that a particular fetus is viable. Both courts ruled the provision unconstitutional in citing previous Supreme Court findings. In *Planned Parenthood vs. Danford* (1976), it was stated that the determination of whether a particular fetus is viable is, and must be, a matter for the judgment of the responsible attending physician. And in *Colautti vs. Franklin* (1979), the Court commented that neither the legislature nor the courts may proclaim one of the elements entering into the ascertainment of viability, be it weeks of gestation or fetal weight or any other single factor as the determinant of when the state has a compelling interest in the life or health of the fetus.

We think that the doubt cast upon the Missouri statute by these cases is not so much a flaw in the structure of the statute as it is a reflection of the fact that the rigid trimester analysis of the course of a pregnancy as asserted in *Roe vs. Wade* has resulted in subsequent cases like *Colautti vs. Franklin* and *Akron vs. Akron Center* making constitutional law in this area a virtual Procrustean bed. Statutes specifying elements of informed consent, for example, were invalidated if they were thought to structure the dialogue between the woman and her physician. In a dissenting opinion in *Thornburgh vs. American College of Obs and Gyns* (1986), speaking on the subject of structuring of dialogue, Justice White commented that such a statute would have been sustained under any traditional standard of judicial review, or for any other surgical procedure except abortion.

At the center of our jurisprudence system is an important element known in legal circles as *stare decisis,* which means that most litigations are decided based on knowledge acquired from a previous case that set some form of legal precedent. But *stare decisis* has a lesser impact on cases that involve constitutional questions, where, besides Congress, this Court is the only body able to make needed changes. We have not refrained from reconsideration of a prior construction of the Constitution that has proven unsound in principle and unworkable in practice. The trimester system imposed as a result of the judgment in *Roe vs. Wade,* falls into the category of possible reconsideration.

The rigidity of some aspects of the *Roe* decision is inconsistent with the language of our Constitution, which is written in general terms and usually speaks in general principles. The primary elements involved in the *Roe* decision, trimesters and viability, would not be found in the text of the Constitution or in any place else one would expect to find a constitutional principle. Since the bounds of inquiry are essentially indeterminate, the result has been a web of legal rules that have become increasingly intricate, resembling a code of regulations rather than a body of constitutional doctrine. Justice White, in *Planned Parenthood vs. Danford,* said that the trimester framework has left this Court to serve as the country's *ex officio* medical board with powers to approve and disapprove medical and operative practices and standards throughout the United States.

It is unreasonable to forbid a state from protecting potential human life until the stage of viability was reached. The rigid line allowing state regulation after viability but prohibiting it before viability is unacceptable. Justice White, in *Thornburgh,* said that the state's interest, if compelling after viability, is equally compelling before viability. And in that case, Justice O'Connor, in a dissenting opinion, said that a state has compelling interests in ensuring maternal health and in protecting potential human life, and these interests exist throughout pregnancy.

To reiterate, the required fetal testing in section 188.029 mandates that physicians perform testing on the fetus to determine viability. The state here has chosen viability as the point at which its interest in potential human life must be safeguarded. Section 188.030, adopted in 1986, stipulates that no abortion of a viable unborn child shall be performed unless necessary to preserve the life or health of the pregnant woman. It is true that the tests in question increase the expense of abortion and regulate the discretion of the physician in determining the viability of the fetus. Since the tests will undoubtedly show in many cases that the fetus is not viable, the tests will have been performed for what were in fact second-trimester abortions. But we are satisfied that the requirement of these tests permissibly furthers the state's interest in protecting potential human life, and we therefore believe section 188.029 to be constitutional.

Viewpoint: Selected Views of Justice O'Connor, Concurring in Part (Paraphrase)

Although Justice O'Connor agreed with a majority of the provisions of Missouri's act, she did not concur entirely but did agree in full with the judgment of the Court.

Unlike the majority, I do not understand these viability-testing requirements to conflict with any of the Court's past decisions concerning state regulation of abortion. Therefore, there is no necessity to accept the state's invitation to reexamine the constitutional validity of *Roe vs. Wade*. Where there is no need to decide a constitutional question, it is a venerable principle of this Court's adjudicatory processes not to do so, for the Court will not anticipate a question of constitutional law in advance of the necessity of deciding it. Neither will it generally formulate a rule of constitutional law broader than is required by the precise facts to which it is to be applied. Quite simply, it is not the habit of the Court to decide questions of constitutional nature unless absolutely necessary to decide a case. The Court today has accepted the state's every interpretation of its abortion statute and upheld, under our existing precedents, every provision of the statute properly before us. Precisely for this reason, reconsideration of *Roe vs. Wade* falls not into any good-cause exception to this fundamental rule of judicial restraint. When the constitutional invalidity of a state's abortion statute actually turns on the constitutional validity of *Roe vs. Wade*, there will be time enough to reexamine *Roe* — and to do so carefully.

In assessing section 188.029, it is especially important to recognize that appellees did not appeal the district court's ruling that the first sentence of section 188.029 is constitutional. It is therefore safe to assume that none of the litigants are disputing the constitutionality of the presumption of viability at 20 weeks, as stated in the first sentence of section 188.029. If anything might arguably conflict with the Court's previous decisions concerning the determination of viability, I would think it is the introduction of this presumption. The stage of viability may vary with each individual; therefore, the responsibility of determining viability must be a medical judgment of the attending physician. The 20-week presumption of viability in the first sentence of section 188.029, it could be argued (though I think unsuccessfully), restricts the judgment of the responsible attending physician by imposing on that physician the burden of overcoming the presumption. This presumption may be construed as a massive imposition of state regulation on an important exclusive function of the medical profession, determining viability of a particular fetus, but if so, it is a restriction on the physician's judgment that is not before us. As the majority properly interprets the second sentence of section 188.029, it does nothing more than describe means by which the unchallenged 20-week presumption of viability may be overcome if those means are useful in doing so and can be prudently employed. But the majority's suggestion that this was the reason why the district court did not rule the second sentence of section 188.029 unconstitutional is in error. Rather, both the district court and the court of appeals thought the second sentence to be unconstitutional precisely because they interpreted that sentence to impose state regulation on the determination of viability that it does not impose.

I agree with the majority that it was plain error for the court of appeals to interpret the second sentence of section 188.029 as meaning that doctors must perform tests to find gestational age, fetal weight, and lung maturity. When read together with the first sentence of 188.029, which requires a physician to determine if the child is viable by using and exercising that degree of care, skill, and proficiency commonly exercised by the ordinary skillful, careful, and prudent physician engaged in similar practice under the same or similar conditions, it would be contradictory nonsense to read the second sentence as requiring a physician to perform viability examinations and tests in situations where it would be careless and imprudent to do so. The interpretation of the majority is correct that the viability-testing provision makes sense only if the second sentence is read to require only those tests that are useful to making subsidiary findings as to viability, and I would like to add, only those examinations and tests that it would not be imprudent or careless to perform in the particular medical situation before the physician.

I disagree with the lower court's interpretation of the second sentence of section 188.029 as imposing a degree of state regulation on the medical determination of viability that in any way conflicts with prior decisions of this Court. No decision of this Court has held that the state may not directly promote its interest in potential life when viability is possible. In *Thornburgh vs. American College of Obs and Gyns,* the Court was asked to decide on the validity of a Pennsylvania law that required a second physician to be in attendance during a postviability abortion. The statute was subsequently struck down by the Court on grounds that it made no exceptions for emergency situations and not because it found a constitutional difference between the state's promotion of its interest in potential life when viability is possible and when viability is certain. Despite the clear recognition by the *Thornburgh* majority that the Pennsylvania and Missouri statutes differed in this respect, there is no hint in the opinion reached by the *Thornburgh* Court that the state's interest in potential life differs depending whether it seeks to further that interest after viability or when viability is possible.

On this Court's interpretation of section 188.029 it is clear that Missouri has not substituted any of the elements entering into the determining of viability as the determinant of when the state has a compelling interest in the life and health of the fetus. The second sentence of section 188.029 clearly states that the requirement of performing those fetal tests, which are useful in determining viability, should be conducted only when it is proper to do so. Viability remains the critical point under section 188.029.

Finally, and rather halfheartedly, the majority suggests that the marginal increase in costs of an abortion created by Missouri's viability-testing provision may make section 188.029, even as interpreted, suspect under this Court's decision in *Akron vs. Akron Center,* striking down a second-trimester hospitalization requirement. I dissented from the Court's opinion in *Akron vs. Akron Center* because it was my view that even apart from *Roe's* framework, which I continue to consider problematic, the majority in *Akron* distorted and misapplied its own standard for evaluating state regulation of abortion, which had been applied by the Court with fair consistency in the past, that previability abortions be performed without state regulation, and that if the state was granted the permission to oversee the procedure, it would be constitutional only if the state did not directly interfere with the woman's right to have an abortion.

It is clear to me that requiring the performance of examinations and tests useful to determining whether the fetus is viable, when viability is possible, and when it would not be medically imprudent to do so does not impose an undue burden on a woman's abortion decision. On this ground alone I would reject the suggestion that section 188.029 as interpreted is unconstitutional. The judgment in the *Akron* case resulted in the invalidation of the requirement that second-trimester abortions be performed in a hospital setting, on grounds that it would unnecessarily burden the woman and nearly double the cost of a relatively "inexpensive and simple" procedure. By contrast, the costs of examinations and tests that could usefully and prudently be performed when a woman is at least 20 weeks pregnant to determine whether the fetus is viable would only marginally, if at all, increase the cost of an abortion. At 20 weeks' gestation, an ultrasound examination to determine gestational age is already standard medical practice. As a matter of fact, an ultrasound examination can determine all three of the state-mandated findings of fetal testing, as stated in sentence two of section 188.029. A finding of fetal weight can be obtained from the same ultrasound test used to determine gestational age. There are a number of different methods in standard medical practice to determine fetal lung maturity at 20 or more weeks' gestation. The most simple and most obvious is by observation. It is well known that fetal lungs do not mature until 33–34 weeks' gestation. If an assessment of the gestational age indicates that the child is less than 33 weeks, a general finding can be made that the fetal lungs are not mature. This finding can then be used by the physician in making his determination of viability under section 188.029. Another clinical test for gestational age, and by inference, fetal weight and lung maturity, is an accurate report of the last menstrual period.

Moreover, the examinations and tests required by section 188.029 are to be performed when viability is possible. This feature of section 188.029 distinguishes it from the second-trimester hospitalization requirement struck down by the *Akron* majority. As the Court recognized in *Thornburgh,* the state's compelling interest in potential life after viability renders its interest in determining the critical point of viability equally compelling. Accordingly, because the court of appeals misinterpreted section 188.029, and because section 188.029, when properly interpreted, is not inconsistent with any of this Court's prior precedents, I would reverse the decision of the court of appeals.

Viewpoint: Selected Views of Justice Blackmun, Concurring in Part, Dissenting in Part (Paraphrase)

Justice Blackmun was joined in his opinion by Justices Brennan and Marshall.

Today, *Roe vs. Wade* and the fundamental constitutional right of women to decide whether to terminate a pregnancy survive but are not secure. Although the Court extricates itself from this case without making a single, even incremental change in the law of abortion, the majority and Justice Scalia would overrule *Roe* (the first silently, the other explicitly) and would return to the states virtually unfettered authority to control the quintessentially intimate, personal, and life-directing decision whether to carry a fetus to term. Although today, no less than yesterday, the Constitution and the decisions of this Court prohibit a state from enacting laws that inhibit women from the meaningful exercise of that right, a plurality of this Court implicitly invites every state legislature to enact more and more restrictive abortion regulations in order to provoke more and more test cases, in the hope that sometime down the line the Court will return the law of procreative freedom to the severe limitations that generally prevailed in this country before January 22, 1973. Never in my memory has a plurality announced a judgment of this Court that so provokes disregard for the law and for our standing decisions. Nor in my memory has a plurality gone about its business in such a deceptive fashion. At every level of its reviews, from its effort to read the real meaning out of the Missouri statute to its intended evisceration of precedents and its deafening silence about the constitutional protections that it would jettison, the plurality obscures the portent of its analysis and leaves *Roe* "undisturbed," albeit "modified and narrowed." But this disclaimer is totally meaningless. The plurality opinion is filled with winks, nods, and knowing glances to those who would do away with *Roe* explicitly, but turns a stone face to anyone in search of what the plurality conceives as the scope of a woman's right under the Due Process Clause to terminate a pregnancy free from the coercive and brooding influence of the state. The simple truth is that *Roe* would not survive the plurality's analysis and that the plurality provides no substitute for *Roe's* protective umbrella.

I fear for the future. I fear for the liberty and equality of the millions of women who have lived and come of age in the 16 years since *Roe* was decided. I fear for the integrity of, and public esteem for, this Court.

I dissent.

The majority has chosen to parade through the Missouri statutes separately. I shall not do this, but shall relegate most of my comments as to those sections with more latitude.

Contrary to the majority I do not see how the Preamble, section 1.205.1, may realistically be construed as "abortion neutral." It declares that the life of each human being begins at conception and that unborn children have protectable interests in life, health and well-being. By the Preamble's specific terms, these declarations apply to all of Missouri's laws, which in turn, are to be interpreted to protect the rights of the unborn to the fullest extent possible under the Constitution of the United States and the decisions of this Court. As the court of appeals concluded, the Missouri legislature intended its abortion regulations to be understood against the backdrop of its theory of life.

In my view, a state may not expand indefinitely the scope of its abortion regulations by creating interests in fetal life that are limited solely by reference to the decisional law of this Court. Such a statutory scheme, whose scope is dependent on the uncertain and disputed limits of our holdings, will have the unconstitutional effect of chilling the exercise of a woman's right to terminate her pregnancy and burdening the freedom of health professionals to provide abortion services. In this case, moreover, because the Preamble defines fetal life as beginning upon the fertilization of the ovum of a female by a sperm of a male, it also burdens the use of contraceptive devices, such as IUDs and the morning-after pill.

As for section 188.210 and section 188.215, when looked at side by side, the statutes appear to give the state "permission" to "withdraw from the business of abortion" legally, by taking affirmative steps to "assure that abortions are not performed in private hospitals by private physicians." The law defined *public facility* as any public institution, public facility, public equipment, or any other physical asset owned, leased or controlled by this state, or any agency or political subdivision thereof. Missouri's statutes essentially prohibit the performance of abortions in institutions that in all pertinent respects are private yet are located on property owned, leased, or controlled by the government. Thus, under the statutes, no abortion may be performed at the Truman Medical Center in Kansas City, where in 1985, 97 percent of all Missouri hospital abortions at 16 weeks or later were performed, even though the center is a private hospital staffed primarily by private doctors and administered by a private corporation. The center is located on ground leased from a political subdivision of the state.

Missouri, in prohibiting the use of public facilities for the performance of abortions, goes far beyond merely offering incentives in favor of childbirth, or a straightforward disassociation of state-owned institutions and personnel from abortion services. Here by defining as "public" every health-care institution with some connection to the state, no matter how attenuated, Missouri has brought to bear the full force of its economic power and control over essential facilities to discourage its citizens from exercising their constitutional rights, even where the state itself could never be understood as authorizing, supporting, or having any other positive association with the performance of abortion.

The difference is critical. Even if the state may decline to subsidize or to participate in the exercise of a woman's right to terminate a pregnancy, and even if a state may pursue its own abortion policies in distributing public benefits, it may not affirmatively constrict the availability of abortions by defining as public that which in all meaningful respects is private. The majority has chosen to interpret Missouri's statute as giving a pregnant woman the same choice as if the state had chosen not to provide any public facilities. But as we have learned, this is an error since a large number of presumed private facilities actually fall into the category of public facilities and are therefore affected by any state prohibition on the performance of abortion. In essence, because of the wide-ranging area encompassed by Missouri's law, the ban on the use of public facilities has left pregnant women with fewer choices and in some cases, no choice at all. This aggressive and shameful infringement on the right of women to obtain abortions in consultation with their chosen physicians, unsupported by any state interest, much less a compelling one, violates the command of *Roe*.

Although I do not agree altogether with Justice O'Connor's approach in her interpretation of section 188.210 and section 188.215, I do concur with her comment of leaving open the possibility that some applications of the "public facilities" ban may be unconstitutional.

I am especially disturbed by the plurality's misapplication of our past decisions in upholding Missouri's ban on the performance of abortions at public facilities. The plurality's discussion of these provisions is merely prologue to its consideration of the statute's viability-testing requirement, section 188.029, the only section of Missouri's statute that the plurality construes as implicating *Roe* itself. There, tucked away at the end of its opinion, the plurality suggests a radical reversal of the law of abortion; and there, I direct my attention.

The majority opinion holds that section 188.029, the fetal-testing statute, is a method used by the state to place an additional burden on second-trimester abortions, while at the same time furthering its primary interest in protecting potential human life. "Since under the *Roe* framework, the state may not fully regulate abortion in the interest of potential life (as opposed to maternal health) until the third trimester, the plurality finds it necessary, in order to save the Missouri testing provision, to throw out *Roe's* framework. The opinion of the majority directly contradicts the holding by this Court in *Roe* by concluding that Missouri's interest in potential life is just as binding before viability as it is after the stage of viability, and as a result the majority has seen fit to uphold the fetal-testing requirement, because it permissibly furthers that state interest.

At the outset, I note that in its haste to limit abortion rights, the plurality compounds the errors of its analysis by needlessly reaching out to address constitutional questions that are not actually presented. The conflict between section 188.029 and *Roe's* trimester framework, which purportedly drives the plurality to reconsider our past decisions, is a contrived conflict, the product of an aggressive misreading of the viability-testing requirement and a needlessly wooden application of the *Roe* framework.

When the majority of this Court read the language of section 188.029, they quickly set aside the construction of the statute adopted by the district court and court of appeals as plain error; the plurality reads the viability-testing provision as requiring only that before a physician may perform an abortion on a woman whom he believes to be carrying a fetus of 20 or more weeks' gestational age, the doctor must determine whether the fetus is viable and, as part of that exercise, must, to the extent feasible and consistent with sound medical practice, conduct tests necessary to make findings of gestational age, weight, and lung maturity. But the plurality's reading of the provision, according to which the statute requires the physician to perform tests only in order to determine viability, ignores the statutory language explicitly directing that the physician shall perform or cause to be performed such medical examinations and tests as are necessary to make a finding of the gestational age, weight, and lung maturity of the unborn child and shall enter such findings in the mother's medical record. The statute's plain language requires the physician to undertake whatever tests are necessary to determine the three state-mandated findings, which include, age, weight, and lung development, without a hint of regard for the additional health risks the tests may bring upon the pregnant woman and the fetus she is carrying. In addition to increasing the costs of the procedure, which are absorbed by the patient, there are questions whether these tests are essential to the discovery of fetal viability.

Had the plurality read the statute as written, it would have had no cause to reconsider the *Roe* framework. As properly construed, the viability-testing provision does not pass constitutional muster under even a rational-basis standard, the least restrictive level of rule applied by this Court. By mandating tests to determine fetal weight and lung maturity for every fetus thought to be more than 20 weeks' gestational age, the statute requires physicians to undertake procedures, such as amniocentesis, that in the situation presented have no medical justification, impose additional health risks on both the pregnant woman and the fetus, and bear no rational relation to the state's interest in protecting fetal life. As written, section 188.029 is an arbitrary imposition of discomfort, risk, and expense, furthering no discernible interest except to make the procurement of an abortion as severe and difficult as possible. The majority worked in an assiduous and tortuous manner to avoid at all costs the plain language of section 188.029 and could have concurred with the findings of the lower courts by ruling the testing provision patently irrational, irrespective of the *Roe* framework. The plurality never states precisely its construction of section 188.029. I base my synopsis of the plurality's views mainly on the assertion that the entire provision must be read in light of its requirement that the physician act only in accordance with reasonable professional judgment and that the provision imposes no requirement that a physician perform irrelevant or dangerous tests. To the extent that the plurality may be reading the provision to require tests other than those that a doctor, exercising reasonable professional judgment, would deem necessary to a finding of viability, the provision bears no rational relation to a legitimate governmental interest and cannot stand.

No one contests that under the *Roe* framework the state, in order to promote its interests in potential human life, may regulate and even proscribe nontherapeutic abortions once the fetus becomes viable. If, as the plurality appears to hold, the testing provision simply requires a physician to use appropriate and medically sound tests to determine whether the fetus is actually viable when the estimated gestational age is greater than 20 weeks (and therefore within what the District Court found to be the margin of error for viability), I see little or no conflict with *Roe*. As convincingly demonstrated by Justice O'Connor, the cases cited by the plurality are not to the contrary. As noted in both *Colautti vs. Franklin* and *Planned Parenthood vs. Danford*, we stressed that the determination of viability is a matter for the judgment of the responsible physician. But section 188.029, at least as construed by the plurality, is consistent with this requirement. The provision does nothing to remove the determination of viability from the judgment of the attending physician; it merely instructs the physician to make a finding of viability, using tests to determine the gestational age, weight, and lung maturity when such tests are feasible and medically appropriate.

In *Akron* we invalidated a city ordinance requiring that all second-trimester abortions be performed in acute-care hospitals on the ground that such a requirement was not medically necessary and would double the cost of abortions. By contrast, the viability determination at issue in this case (as read by the plurality) is necessary to the effectuation of the state's compelling interest in the potential human life of viable fetuses and applies not to all second-trimester abortions but only to that small percentage of abortions performed on fetuses estimated to be of more than 20 weeks' gestational age.

None of the holdings in *Roe* or later abortion cases have suggested that a state is prohibited from exercising its mandated interest in protecting potential human life of a fetus that is viable. The Court felt that to avoid the inherent "pitfalls" of accurately determining viability, which is far from being an exact science, and to ensure that a viable fetus is not mistakenly aborted, the state should be allowed to retain its compelling interest.

A requirement that a physician make a finding of viability for every fetus that falls within the range of possible viability does more than preserve the state's recognized authority. Although the plurality correctly points out that such a testing requirement would have the effect of imposing additional costs on second-trimester abortions where the tests indicate that the fetus was not viable, these costs would be merely incidental to and a necessary accommodation of, the state's unquestioned right to prohibit nontherapeutic abortions after the point of viability. To reiterate, the fetal-testing requirement as interpreted by the majority is consistent with what we originally held in *Roe* and could continue to be held valid under our current laws.

How ironic it is, then, that the plurality scolds the court of appeals for adopting a construction of the statute that fails to avoid constitutional difficulties. By distorting the statute, the plurality manages to avoid invalidating the testing provision on what should have been noncontroversial constitutional grounds; having done so, however, the plurality rushes headlong into a much deeper constitutional thicket, brushing past an obvious basis for upholding section 188.029 in search of a pretext for scuttling the trimester framework. Evidently, from the plurality's perspective, the real problem with the court of appeals' construction of section 188.029 is not that it raised a constitutional difficulty but that it raised the wrong constitutional difficulty, one not implicating *Roe*.

Having set up the conflict between section 188.029 and the *Roe* trimester framework, the plurality summarily discards *Roe's* analytic core as unsound in principle and unworkable in practice. The majority took this stand because of their claim that not one of the key factors of the *Roe* construction is mentioned in the Constitution, the framework is more akin to a code of regulations than constitutional law, and under the framework the state's interest in potential human life is considered compelling only after viability when in fact that interest is equally compelling throughout pregnancy. However this is only presumption, since the plurality has never bothered to explain the flaws they allege are inherent in the *Roe* construction. What the majority has managed is to replace reasoning with many empty assertions.

The argument of the majority has not focused on the fact that the text of the Constitution does not mention a right to privacy; rather they have centered their attention on the issue pertaining to some very critical aspects of the *Roe* framework — more precisely, viability and the trimester system, the wording of which also will not be found in the language of the Constitution, which the plurality complains is not consistent with a Constitution that is cast in general terminology. Were this a true concern, we would have to abandon most of our constitutional jurisprudence. As the plurality well knows, or should know, the critical elements of countless constitutional doctrines nowhere appear in the Constitution text. The Constitution makes no mention, for example, of the First Amendment's actual-malice standard for proving certain libels of the standard for determining when speech is obscene. Similarly, the Constitution makes no mention of the rational-basis test or the specific verbal formulations of intermediate and strict scrutiny by which this Court evaluates claims under the Equal Protection Clause. The reason is simple. Like the *Roe* framework, these tests or standards are not and do not purport to be rights protected by the Constitution. Rather, they are judge-made methods for evaluating and measuring the strength and scope of constitutional rights or for balancing the constitutional rights of individuals against competing interests of the government.

With respect to the *Roe* framework, the general constitutional principle, indeed the fundamental constitutional right for which it was developed, is the right to privacy, a species of liberty protected by the Due Process Clause, which under our past decisions safeguards the rights of women to exercise some control over childbirth. The trimester framework simply defines and limits that right to privacy in the abortion context to accommodate, not destroy, a state's legitimate interest in protecting the health of the pregnant woman and preserving potential human life. Fashioning such accommodations between individual rights and the legitimate interests of the government, establishing benchmarks and standards with which to evaluate the competing claims of individuals and government, lies at the very heart of constitutional adjudication. To the extent that the trimester framework is useful in this enterprise, it is not only consistent with constitutional interpretation but necessary to the wise and just exercise of this Court's paramount authority to define the scope of constitutional rights.

One of the primary disputes the majority had with the construction of the trimester system was that it resembled a "code of regulations" and not a structure of "constitutional doctrines." They also felt it had become a tangle of "legal rules" that were becoming more ambiguous than a set standard. Again, if this were a true and genuine concern, we would have to abandon vast areas of our constitutional jurisprudence. The plurality complains that under the trimester framework the Court has distinguished between a city ordinance requiring that second-trimester abortions be performed in clinics and a state law requiring that these abortions be performed in hospitals, or between laws requiring that certain information be furnished to a woman by a physician or his assistant and those requiring that such information be furnished by the physician exclusively. Are these distinctions any finer or more "regulatory" than the distinctions we have often drawn in our First Amendment jurisprudence, where, for example, we have held that a "release-time" program permitting public school students to leave school grounds during school hours to receive religious instruction does not violate the Establishment Clause, even though a release-time program permitting religious instruction on school grounds does violate the clause?

Simply that many constitutional principles tend to cut a narrow path between the characterization of similar situations certainly should not be misconstrued as this Court vacating a judgment "in favor of regulation."

Finally, the plurality asserts that the trimester framework cannot stand because the state's interest in potential life is compelling throughout pregnancy, not merely after viability. The opinion contains not one word of rationale for its view of the state's interest.

In answering the plurality's claim that the state's interest in the fetus is uniform and compelling throughout pregnancy, I cannot improve upon what Justice Stevens wrote in *Thornburgh* — that the state's interest in the protection of an embryo, even if that interest is defined as protecting those who will be citizens, increases progressively and dramatically as the organism's capacity to feel pain, to experience pleasure, to survive, and to react to its surroundings increases day by day. The development of a fetus and pregnancy itself are not static conditions, and the assertion that the government's interest is static simply ignores this reality. Unless the religious view that a fetus is a person is adopted, there are fundamental and well-recognized differences between a fetus and a human being; indeed, if there is not such a difference, the permissibility of terminating the life of a fetus could scarcely be left to the will of the state legislatures. And if distinctions may be drawn between a fetus and a human being in terms of the state interest in their protection, even though the fetus represents one of those who will be citizens, it seems to me quite odd to argue that distinctions may not also be drawn between the state interest in protecting the freshly fertilized egg and the state interest in protecting the nine-month fully sentient fetus on the eve of birth. Recognition of this distinction is supported not only by logic but also by history and our shared experiences.

For my part, I remain convinced, as six other members of this Court 16 years ago were convinced, that the *Roe* framework, and the viability standard in particular, fairly sensibly, and effectively function to safeguard the constitutional liberties of pregnant women while recognizing and accommodating the state's interest in potential human life. The viability line reflects the biological facts and truths of fetal development; it marks the threshold moment prior to which a fetus cannot survive separate from the woman and cannot reasonably and objectively be regarded as a subject of rights or interests distinct from or paramount to those of the pregnant woman. At the same time, the viability standard takes account of the undeniable fact that as the fetus evolves into its postnatal form it loses its dependence on the uterine environment, the state's interest in the fetus's potential human life and in fostering a regard for human life in general becomes compelling. As a practical matter, because viability follows quickening, the point at which a woman feels movement in her womb, and viability occurs no earlier than 23 weeks' gestational age, it establishes an easily applicable standard for regulating abortion while providing a pregnant woman ample time to exercise her fundamental right with her responsible physician to terminate her pregnancy. Although I have stated previously for a majority of this Court that constitutional rights do not always have easily ascertainable boundaries, to seek and establish those boundaries remains the special responsibility of this Court. In *Roe,* we discharged that responsibility as logic and science compelled. The plurality today advances not one reasonable argument as to why our judgment in that case was wrong and should be abandoned.

Having contrived an opportunity to reconsider the *Roe* framework, and then having discarded that framework, the plurality finds the testing provision not objectionable because it permissibly furthers the state's interest in protecting potential human life. This newly minted standard is circular and totally meaningless. Whether a challenged abortion regulation permissibly furthers a legitimate state interest is the question that courts must answer in abortion cases, not the standard for courts to apply. In keeping with the rest of its opinion, the plurality makes no attempt to explain or justify its new standard, either in the abstract or as applied to this case. Nor could it.

The plurality pretends that *Roe* survives, explaining that the facts of this case differ from those in *Roe*; here, Missouri has chosen to assert its interest in potential life only at the point of viability whereas in *Roe* Texas had asserted that interest from the point of conception, criminalizing all abortions except where the life of the mother was at stake. If the Constitution permits a state to enact any statute that reasonably furthers its interest in potential life, and if that interest arises at conception, why would the Texas statute fail to pass muster? One suspects that the plurality agrees. It is impossible to read the plurality opinion without recognizing its implicit invitation to every state to enact more and more restrictive abortion laws and to assert their interest in potential life as of the moment of conception. All these laws will satisfy the plurality's nonscrutiny until sometime a new regime of old dissenters and new appointees will declare what the plurality intends: That *Roe* is no longer good law.

Thus, "not with a bang, but a whimper," the plurality discards a land-mark case of the last generation, and casts into darkness the hopes and visions of every woman in this country who had come to believe that the Constitution guaranteed her the right to exercise some control over her unique ability to bear children. Those who represent the majority opinion of this Court have chosen to follow a heartless path by creating a sense of insecurity for thousands of women with their campaign of using scare and pressure tactics in a continuing attempt to overturn *Roe vs. Wade*. The result has been that numerous women have given up their career goals and plans to start families. Apparently, the plurality is ready to clear the path for government intrusion, to force women to bear labor while adhering to strict rules and policies that will follow them through the various stages of pregnancy to term, without regard to the psychological harm it may cause a woman who is forced to carry to term a pregnancy she may not want.

If *Roe* was overturned, the presumption is that conditions would return to those "horrifying" days of yesteryear when women who were desperate defied the law by procuring "illegal" abortions in filthy back-alley clinics operated by untrained practitioners who mutilated and murdered many young women anxious to terminate a pregnancy, regardless of the risks to life and health. The only other option for women who are desperate to terminate a pregnancy is to "self-abort," but this is not only a dangerous option; it can also be a disastrous one. Have we already forgotten those "statistics of horror" of the years prior to the *Roe* decision when women, especially indigents and minorities, died or suffered severe emotional and physical trauma all in the name of enforced morality or religious dictates or a lack of compassion, as it may be?

To overturn a constitutional decision is a rare and grave undertaking. To overturn a constitutional decision that secured a fundamental personal liberty to millions of persons would be unprecedented in our 200 years of constitutional history. Although the doctrine of *stare decisis* applies with somewhat diminished force in constitutional cases generally, even in ordinary constitutional cases any departure from *stare decisis* demands special justification. This requirement of justification applies with unique force where, as here, the Court's repudiation of precedent would destroy the people's firm belief, based on past decisions of this Court, that they possess an unbridgeable right to undertake certain conduct.

As discussed in perhaps too great length above, the plurality makes no serious attempt to carry the heavy burden of persuading that changes in society or in the law dictate the abandonment of *Roe* and its numerous progeny, much less the greater burden of explaining the vacating of a fundamental personal freedom. Instead, the plurality pretends that it leaves *Roe* standing and refuses to discuss the real issue underlying this case. Whether the Constitution includes an unenumerated right to privacy that encompasses a woman's right to decide to terminate her pregnancy.

This comes at a cost. The doctrine of *stare decisis* permits society to presume that bedrock principles are founded in the law rather than in the disposition of individuals, and thereby contributes to the integrity of our constitutional system of government, both in appearance and fact. Today's decision involves the most politically divisive domestic legal issue of our time. By refusing to explain or to justify its proposed revolutionary revision in the law of abortion and by refusing to abide not only by our precedents but also by our canons for reconsidering those precedents, the plurality invites charges of cowardice and illegitimacy at our door. I cannot say that these would be undeserved.

For today, at least, the law of abortion stands undisturbed. For today, the women of this nation still retain the liberty to control their destinies. But the signs are evident and very ominous, and a chill wind blows.

Viewpoint: Selected Concurring Views of Justice Scalia (Paraphrase)

I share Justice Blackmun's view, that section 188.029 effectively would overrule *Roe vs. Wade.* I think that should be done but would do it more explicitly. Since today we contrive to avoid doing it, and indeed to avoid almost any decison of national import, I need not set forth my reasons, some of which have been well recited in dissents of my colleagues in other cases.

The outcome of today's case will doubtless be heralded as a triumph of judicial statesmanship. It is not that, unless it is statesmanlike needlessly to prolong this Court's self-awarded leadership over a field where it has little proper business since the answers to most of the cruel questions are political and not judicial, a preeminence which therefore quite properly, but to the great damage of the Court, makes it the object of the sort of organized public pressure that political institutions in a democracy ought to receive.

Justice O'Connor speaks of a "fundamental rule of judicial restraint," which in a sense obligates the Court to refrain from reviewing *Roe vs. Wade,* but this "rule" should not be taken seriously. By finessing *Roe* we do not, as she suggests, adhere to the strict and venerable rule that we should avoid deciding questions of a constitutional nature. We have not disposed this case on some statutory or procedural ground but have decided, and could not avoid deciding, whether the Missouri statute meets the requirements of the United States Constitution. The only choice available is whether, in deciding that constitutional question, we should use *Roe vs. Wade* as the benchmark or something else. What is involved, therefore, is not the rule of avoiding constitutional issues where possible but the quite separate principle that we will not formulate a rule of constitutional law broader than required by the precise facts to which it is to be applied. The latter is sound general principle, but one often departed from when good reason exists.

It would be wrong in any decision to ignore the reality that our policy not to formulate a rule of constitutional law broader than is required by the precise facts has a frequently applied good-cause exception. But it seems particularly perverse to convert the policy into the absolute in the present case in order to place beyond reach the inexpressibly broader than was required by the precise facts structure established by *Roe vs. Wade.* The real question, then, is whether there are valid reasons to go beyond the most stingy holding today. It seems to me there are not only valid but compelling ones. Ordinarily, speaking no more broadly than is absolutely required avoids throwing settled law into confusion; doing so today preserves a chaos that is evident to anyone who can read and count. Alone sufficient to justify a broad holding is the fact that our retaining control through *Roe* of what I believe to be, and many of our citizens recognize to be, a political issue continuously distorts the public perception of this Court. We can now look forward to at least another term with carts full of mail from the public and streets full of demonstrators, urging us, their unelected and life-tenured judges who have been awarded this extraordinary undemocratic characteristic precisely in order that we might follow the law despite the popular will, to follow the popular will. Indeed, we can look forward to even more of that than before, given our indecisive decision today. And if these reasons for taking the unexceptional course of reaching a broader holding are not enough, then consider the nature of the constitutional question we avoid: In most cases, we do no harm by not speaking more broadly than the decision requires. Anyone affected by the conduct that the avoided holding would have prohibited will be able to challenge it and have his day in court to make the argument. Not so with respect to the harm that many states believed pre–*Roe,* and many may continue to believe, is largely caused by unrestricted abortion. That will continue to occur if the states have the constitutional power to prohibit it and would do so, but we skillfully avoid telling them so. Perhaps those abortions cannot constitutionally be proscribed. That is surely an arguable question, the question that reconsideration of *Roe vs. Wade* entails. But what is not at all arguable, it seems to me, is that we should decide now and not insist that we run into a corner before we grudgingly yield up our judgment. The only sound reason for the latter course is to prevent a change in the law, but to think that desirable begs the question to be decided.

It was an arguable question today whether section 188.029 of the Missouri law opposes this Court's understanding of *Roe vs. Wade.* In *Roe vs. Wade* the Court stipulated that the physician has the right to administer medical treatment according to his professional judgment up to the point where important state interest provides compelling justification for intervention. The Court has also made the point that the point of viability is exclusively a medical judgment. This is an important point since viability varies with each individual pregnancy. In addition, section 188.029 conflicts with the purpose and hence the fair import of this principle because it sometimes requires a physician to perform tests that he would not otherwise have performed to determine whether a fetus is viable. It is therefore a legislative imposition on the judgment of the physician and one that increases the cost of an abortion.

Justice O'Connor departs from the opinion of the Court's "conservative block," concurring with the Court's holding as stated in the above paragraph, but Justice O'Connor would uphold the law because it does not impose an undue burden on a woman's abortion decision. This conclusion is supported by the observation that the required tests impose only a marginal cost on the abortion procedure, far less of an increase than the cost-doubling hospitalization requirement invalidated in *Akron vs. Akron Center for Reproductive Health.* Since the cost of the tests required by section 188.029 were less than costs invalidated by the Court in earlier litigations, this case could not be decided on the basis of a previous decision. It does not tell us whether the present requirement is an undue burden, and I know of no basis for determining that this particular burden (or any other for that matter) is "due." One could with equal justification conclude that it is not. To avoid the question of *Roe vs. Wade's* validity, with the attendant costs that this will have for the Court and for the principles of self-governance on the basis of a standard that offers no guide but the Court's own discretion merely adds to the irrationality of what we do today.

Justice O'Connor was "irrational" when she introduced her new concept into the law in order to achieve her result, the notion of a state's interest in potential life when viability is possible. Since viability means that mere possibility (not certainty) of survivability outside the womb, "possible viability" must mean the possibility of a possibility of survivability outside the womb. Perhaps our next opinion will expand the third trimester into the second even further by approving state action designed to take account of "the chance of possible viability."

I would have preferred examining *Roe* rather than examining the contradictions. Given the Court's new restraint, what will it take, one must wonder, to permit us to reach that fundamental question? The result of our vote today is that we will not reconsider that prior opinion, even if most of the justices think it is wrong, unless we have before us a statute that in fact contradicts it, and even then (under our newly discovered no-broader-than-necessary requirement) only minor problematic aspects of *Roe* will be reconsidered, unless one expects state legislatures to adopt provisions whose compliance with *Roe* cannot be argued with a straight face. It thus appears that the mansion of constitutionalized abortion law, constructed overnight in *Roe vs. Wade,* must be disassembled doorjamb by doorjamb and never entirely brought down, no matter how wrong it may be.

Of the four courses we might have chosen today—to reaffirm *Roe,* to overrule it explicitly, to overrule it silently without fanfare, or to avoid the question — the last is the least responsible. On the question of section 188.029, I concur in the judgment of the Court and strongly dissent from the manner in which it has been reached.

Viewpoint: Selected Views of Justice Stevens, Concurring in Part, Dissenting in Part (Paraphrase)

Justice Stevens joined in the majority opinion of section 188.205, which prohibited the use of public funds for the purpose of encouraging or counseling women on abortion, and because of his stand on the issue, Justice Stevens would not comment further. Stevens also agreed with the opinion of Justice Blackmun in his evaluation of section 188.210 and section 188.215, provisions that prohibited the use of public facilities and employees for the purpose of counseling, encouraging, or performing abortions.

Justice Stevens, however, was in agreement with the court of appeals invalidation of section 188.029, the fetal-testing statute and the Preamble, section 1.205.1, the provision that affords the fetus protection of the law from the point of conception. Because of his opinion on these issues, Stevens felt that additional explanation of his views was appropriate.

It seems to me that in its opinion of section 188.029, the plurality strains to place construction on section 188.029 that enables it to conclude, we would modify and narrow *Roe* and succeeding cases. That statement is ill-advised because there is no need to modify even slightly the holdings of prior cases in order to uphold section 188.029.

I cannot accept the construction of section 188.029 (2) as interpreted by Justice O'Connor because it is foreclosed by two controlling principles of statutory interpretation. First, it is our settled practice to accept the interpretation of state law in which the district court and the court of appeals have concurred even if an examination of the state-law issue without such guidance might have justified a different conclusion. Second, the fact that a particular application of the clear terms of a statute might be unconstitutional does not provide us with a justification for ignoring the plain meaning of the statute. In this case I agree with the court of appeals and the district court that the second sentence of section 188.029 is too plain to be ignored. The sentence twice uses the mandatory term *shall* and contains no qualifying language. If it is implicitly limited to tests that are useful in determining viability, it adds nothing to the requirement imposed by the preceding sentence.

My interpretation of the plain language is supported by the structure of the statute as a whole, particularly the Preamble, which "finds" that life begins at conception and further commands that state laws shall be construed to provide the maximum protection to the unborn child at every stage of development. The district court's interpretation was correct that obviously, the purpose of this law is to protect the potential life of the fetus, rather than safeguard maternal health. A literal reading of the statute tends to accomplish that goal. Thus it is not unreasonable to assume that the Missouri legislature was trying to protect the potential human life of nonviable fetuses by making the abortion decision more costly. On the contrary, I am satisfied that the court of appeals, as well as the district court, correctly concluded that the Missouri legislature meant exactly what it said in the second sentence of section 188.029. I am also satisfied with Justice Blackmun's opinion concerning the fetal-testing provision as clearly unconstitutional.

Concerning the Preamble, section 1.205.1, and the definition of *conception* as stated in section 188.015, the fertilization of the ovum of a female by a sperm of a male (even though standard medical texts equate conception with implantation in the uterus occurring about six days after fertilization): Missouri's declaration implies regulation not only of pre-viability abortions but also of common forms of contraceptives such as the IUD and the morning-after pill. Because the Preamble, read in context, threatens serious encroachments upon the liberty of pregnant women and the health professional, I am persuaded that these plaintiffs, appellees before us, have standing to challenge its constitutionality.

Several decisions of this Court make clear that freedom of personal choice in matters of marriage and family life is one of the liberties protected by the Due Process Clause of the Fourteenth Amendment. As recently as last term, we recognized the right of the individual, married or single, to be free from unwarranted governmental intrusion into matters so fundamentally affecting a person as the decision whether to bear or beget a child. That right necessarily includes the right of a woman to decide whether to terminate her pregnancy. Certainly the interests of a woman in giving of her physical and emotional self during pregnancy and the interests that will be affected throughout her life by the birth and raising of a child are of a far greater degree of significance and personal intimacy than the right to send a child to private school or the right to teach a foreign language.

Clearly, therefore, the Court today is correct in holding that the right asserted by *Roe vs. Wade* is embraced within the Fourteenth Amendment.

It was quite evident that the Missouri legislature, when enacting the Preamble, had intended to promote a religious conviction in its declaration that life begins at conception and that conception occurs at the moment of fertilization. Under the edicts of the First Amendment's Establishment Clause, which states that "Congress shall make no law respecting an establishment of religion, or prohibiting the free exercise thereof . . . ," the Preamble's primary section becomes invalid. This conclusion does not and could not rest on the fact that the statement happens to coincide with the conviction of certain religions or on the fact that the legislators who voted to enact it may have been motivated by religious considerations. Rather, it rests on the fact that the

Preamble, an unequivocal endorsement of a religious tenet of some but by no means all Christian faiths, serves no identifiable religious purpose. That fact alone compels a conclusion that the statute violates the Establishment Clause.

St. Thomas Aquinas (1225–1274), was an Italian Dominican theologian, scholastic philosopher, and Doctor of the Church. He attempted to reconcile Christian faith and human reason. His arguments to prove the existence of God have been very influential, and the Roman Catholic Church recognizes him as one of its most important theologians. The position of St. Thomas Aquinas is summarized in a report entitled "Catholic Teaching on Abortion" prepared by the Congressional Research Service Library of Congress. It states in part that the disagreement over the status of the unformed as against the formed fetus was crucial for Christian teaching on the soul. It was widely held that the soul was not present until the formation of the fetus 40 or 80 days after conception, for males and females, respectively. Thus, abortion of the "unformed" or "inanimate" fetus was something less than true homicide, rather a form of anticipatory or quasi-homicide. This view received its definitive treatment in St. Thomas Aquinas and became for a time the dominant interpretation in the Latin Church.

For St. Thomas, as for mediaeval Christendom generally, there is a lapse of time, approximately 40 to 80 days, after conception and before the soul's infusion. Seed and what is not seed is determined by sensation and movement. What is destroyed in abortion of the unformed fetus is "seed," not man. This distinction received its most careful analysis in St. Thomas. It was the belief of Christendom, reflected for example, in the Council of Trent (1545–1563), which restricted penalties for homicide to abortion of an animated fetus only. If the views of St. Thomas were held as widely today as they were in the Middle Ages, and if a state legislature were to enact a statute prefaced with a "finding" that female life begins 80 days after conception and male life 40 days after conception, I have no doubt that this Court would promptly conclude that such an endorsement of a particular religious philosophy is violative of the Establishment Clause.

In my opinion the difference between that hypothetical statute and Missouri's Preamble reflects nothing more than a difference in theological doctrine. The Preamble to the Missouri statute endorses the theological position that there is the same nonreligious interest in preserving the life of a fetus during the first 40 or 80 days of pregnancy as there is after viability; indeed, after the time when the fetus has become a "person" with legal rights protected by the Constitution. To sustain that position as a matter of law, I believe Missouri has the burden of identifying the secular interests that differentiate the first 40 days of pregnancy from the period immediately before or after fertilization when, as related cases establish, the Constitution allows the use of contraceptive procedures to prevent potential life from developing into full personhood.

Focusing our attention on the first several weeks of pregnancy is especially appropriate because that is the period when the vast majority of abortions are performed.

As a nonreligious matter, there is an obvious difference between the state interest in protecting the freshly fertilized egg and the state interest in protecting a nine-month fully sentient fetus on the eve of birth. There can be no interest in protecting the newly fertilized egg from physical pain or mental anguish because the capacity for such suffering does not yet exist; respecting a developed fetus, however, that interest is valid. In fact whether one separates the theological concept of ensoulment or accepts Aquinas's view that ensoulment does not occur for at least 40 days, a state has no greater secular interest in protecting the potential life of an embryo that is still "seed" than in protecting the potential life of a sperm or an unfertilized ovum.

There have been many times in history when military and economic interests would have been served by an increase in population. No one argues today, however, that Missouri can assert a societal interest in increasing its population as its nonreligious reason for fostering potential life. Indeed, our national policy, as reflected in legislation the Court upheld last term, is to prevent the potential life that is produced by pregnancy and childbirth among unmarried adolescents. If the secular analysis were based on a strict balancing of fiscal costs and benefits, the economic costs of unlimited childbearing would outweigh those of abortion. There is, of course, an important and unquestionably valid (nonreligious) interest in protecting a young pregnant woman from the consequences of an incorrect decision, although that interest is served by a requirement that the woman receive medical and, in appropriate circumstances, parental advice. After all is considered, it seems nonsensical for a state legislature to enact a law containing language that many would construe as having religious overtones, as is the case with section 1.205.1.

The state's suggestion that the finding in the Preamble is, in effect, an amendment to its tort, property, and criminal laws is not persuasive. The court of appeals concluded that the Preamble is simply an impermissible state adoption of a theory of when life begins to justify its abortion regulations.

Bolstering my conclusion that the Preamble violates the First Amendment is the fact that the intensely divisive character of the national debate over the abortion issue reflects the deeply held religious convictions of many participants in this debate. The Missouri legislature may not inject its endorsement of a particular religious tradition into this debate, for the Establishment Clause does not allow governing bodies to format such disagreement.

In my opinion the Preamble is unconstitutional for two reasons. It has substantive impact on the freedom to use contraceptive procedures, it is inconsistent with the central holding in previous related cases. To the extent that it merely makes legislative findings without operative effect, as the state argues, it violates the Establishment Clause of the First Amendment. Contrary to the theological finding of the Missouri legislature, a woman's constitutionally protected liberty encompasses the right to act on her own belief that, to paraphrase St. Thomas Aquinas, until a seed has acquired the powers of sensation and movement, the life of a human being has not yet begun.

The Court's Decision

The speculation was that *Webster vs. Reproductive Health Services* would ultimately lead to the complete invalidation of *Roe vs. Wade* by the Supreme Court, but that did not happen. Although the arguments were brisk and heated, they did not come close to matching the angry politicking that transpired between opposing factions in the public sector. Supreme Court justices are not oblivious to public opinion; they are aware of the controversies that are created by public awareness over disputable issues like abortion. In this case, public debate penetrated the halls of the Supreme Court chambers, to the extent that it became the center of the argument presented by Justice Scalia. An important issue concerning how public pressure affects the judgment of the Court was raised.

After heated debates, confusion, and much speculation over the probable holding in the case, the Supreme Court announced a judgment in *Webster vs. Reproductive Health Services* on July 3, 1989. There were only a few surprises as voting on the various issues ran along conservative and moderate lines. *Roe vs. Wade* was not overturned, although its importance was narrowed.

Chief Justice Rehnquist announced the judgment of the Court and read an opinion of the Court in respect to sections 188.205, 188.210, 188.215, and the Preamble, section 1.205.1. In addition, he read a concurring opinion in regard to section 188.029, which was joined by Justices White and Kennedy.

Justice O'Connor, who expressed some opinions that were contradictory to those of her conservative colleagues, concurred in the judgment of the Court and wrote a concurring opinion in respect to section 1.205.1, the Preamble, section 188.210, section 188.215, and section 188.205. Although O'Connor did concur with the judgment on section 188.029, she was not in total agreement with the Court opinion on the issue.

Justice Scalia joined the opinion of the Chief Justice in respect to sections 1.205.1, 188.210, 188.215, and 188.205. Regarding section 188.029, Scalia joined the opinion of Justice Blackmun that it could effectively lead to the overturning of *Roe vs. Wade*.

Justice Blackmun concurred in part and dissented in part. Justice Blackmun was in complete disagreement with the plurality's opinion in regard to section 188.029 but did concur with some comments made by Justice O'Connor in her opinion.

Justice Stevens concurred with the Court opinion of section 188.205 and joined the opinion expressed by Justice Blackmun with respect to Missouri section 188.210 and section 188.215. Stevens, however, dissented from the plurality's view of section 188.029, the viability-testing provision, and the Preamble, section 1.205.1. On these issues he chose to adopt the court of appeals' assessment and judgment of invalidation. Justice Stevens split from the plurality on this issue because he was not in favor of their "ill-advised statement" concluding that they could modify and narrow the scope of *Roe* by validating these statutes.

The justices of the Supreme Court voted by a 6 to 3 margin to ban the use of tax dollars for encouraging and counseling women on the abortion procedure, and by an identical margin of 6 to 3, voted that states do possess the authority to prohibit the use of public clinics or hospitals or any other taxpayer–supported facility for the purpose of counseling, encouraging, or performing abortions. On these two issues, Chief Justice Rehnquist, Justices O'Connor, Scalia, White, Kennedy, and Stevens concurred, while Justices Blackmun, Marshall, and Brennan dissented.

On the issue of fetal testing at 20 weeks' gestation, section 188.029, Justices Stevens, Marshall, Blackmun, and Brennan dissented, while Chief Justice Rehnquist, Justices O'Connor, Scalia, White, and Kennedy formed the plurality in validating the provision. The vote was 5 to 4. Concerning the Preamble, by a margin of 5 to 4, the plurality voted not to respond to the provision since it did not have a legal impact. The dissenters were Justices Stevens, Marshall, Blackmun, and Brennan.

16: Pending Cases

Just as the dust was settling over the stormy session and difficult judgment in *Webster vs. Reproductive Health Services,* a new twist was formed over the interpretation of Missouri's Preamble, section 1.205.1, which proclaims that life begins at conception. Since the Court did not rule on the constitutionality of this provision, the resultant backlash has been an "open season" on interpretations and applications. There are more questions over the statute's meaning now than when it was presented before the Court for review. The primary issue is that the language of section 1.205.1 says that life begins at conception and that the unborn fetus from time of conception has all of the rights, privileges, and immunities available to other persons, citizens and residents of the state.

This issue has raised several interesting questions, including the following: (1) A lawsuit filed with the United States district court contends that a fetus is illegally imprisoned because his mother is an inmate serving time. The argument centers on the issue that the fetus is not charged with any crime. Attorney Michael Box, who filed the action on behalf of the fetus, said, "If life begins at conception, then fetuses are supposed to be like anyone else; they're persons and they have constitutional rights." (2) A 20-year-old, charged with driving while intoxicated and possession of alcohol while under the legal drinking age of 21, argued that since state law says that life begins at conception, he has added nine months to his age, making him 21, the legal drinking age.

Timothy Heinsz, dean of the University of Missouri–Columbia School of Law, said recently, "I think you are going to have to make a close relationship between the abortion statute and whatever other statute the court or attorneys are trying to apply. The argument is limited only by the creative mind of the attorney."

Michael Boicourt, the assistant attorney general of Missouri who helped in the defense of the statute before the Supreme Court, issued a statement that claimed the provision does nothing in creating rights for the unborn fetus, that it is just a declaration of legislative strategy. Boicourt stipulated that the statute's only intent is protection of the fetus in respect to property rights, personal injury, or criminal proceedings. As for the legal questions now pending,

Boicourt did not consider them serious, but they do provoke interesting discussions for public debate.

Missouri state Representative Sue Shear has asked the attorney general to issue an opinion on the scope of the Preamble, if indeed it can be applied to other state laws that involve having knowledge of a person's age. Representative Shear felt that without specific guidelines, lawyers will have a "heyday," applying a variety of cases to the Preamble since in its present state interpretations are practically unlimited.

Attorney Frank Susman of St. Louis, who argued against the statute before the Court, said, "The law demonstrates the total absurdity of what the legislature did and of not having thought things through on a piece of legislation." He stated that he anticipated the consequences of the Preamble would be unknown and many.

St. Louis attorney Andrew Puzder, in a recent interview, said, "It's almost like the Supreme Court put its stamp of approval on it by not striking it down, and that makes it easier to utilize. This law was never intended to change the time by which you compute a person's age by their date of birth. Nobody has the right to have that date moved up or back. Nothing that says life begins at conception changes how the state computes age."

There are three abortion cases working through the legal system, eventually headed for the Supreme Court for constitutional review.

1. *Hodgson vs. Minnesota:* Dr. Jane Hodgson, a physician in that state, is challenging a Minnesota law that requires women under 18 years of age to notify their parents prior to having an abortion.

2. *Ohio vs. Akron Center for Reproductive Health:* An abortion clinic in Akron is challenging an Ohio law that requires women under the age of 18 years to notify their parents prior to having an abortion. The state contends that parents should have a voice in the decision because it involves the termination of a potential life.

3. *Turnock vs. Ragsdale:* Dr. Richard Ragsdale, a physician in Illinois, is challenging an Illinois law that requires clinics that perform abortions to be regulated by the state. The state claims the law is necessary to improve standards of medical care.

References

CHAPTER 2:   *Roe vs. Wade* (410 United States Reports 113)

CHAPTER 3:   *Doe vs. Bolton* (410 United States Reports 179)

CHAPTER 4:   *Planned Parenthood of Missouri vs. Danford* (428 United States Reports 52)

CHAPTER 5:   *Bellotti vs. Baird* (428 United States Reports 132)

CHAPTER 6:   *Maher vs. Roe* (432 United States Reports 464)

CHAPTER 7:   *Bellotti vs. Baird (II)* (443 United States Reports 623)

CHAPTER 8:   *Colautti vs. Franklin* (439 United States Reports 379)

CHAPTER 9:   *H.L. vs. Matheson* (450 United States Reports 398)

CHAPTER 10:   *City of Akron vs. Akron Center for Reproductive Health* (462 United States Reports 416)

CHAPTER 11:   *Planned Parenthood of Kansas City, Missouri vs. Ashcroft* (462 United States Reports 476)

CHAPTER 12:   *Simopoulos vs. Virginia* (462 United States Reports 506)

CHAPTER 13:   *Thornburgh vs. American College of Obstetricians and Gynecologists* (476 United States Reports 747) (851 Federal Reporter (2nd series) 1071)

CHAPTER 15:   *Webster vs. Reproductive Health Services* (89 Daily Journal 8724) (109 Supreme Court Reporter 3040)

Index

abortion: adolescent 5, 34, 36; back
  alley clinics 1, 151, 189; blanket
  laws 49, 78; defined 1; elective 26,
  54–56; fundamental right 56; "gray"
  area (pregnancy) 45; illegal 1, 189;
  incest 2, 113, 149; medical judgment 36, 85; nontherapeutic 52, 54,
  168, 185; personal choice 14; post-
  abortion (depression) 81; potential
  life 23, 43–44, 97, 175–177, 179–180,
  188, 192, 196; rape 2, 113, 149; regulation 40, 171; religious concept 1; right
  to privacy 15, 26–27, 65, 77, 85, 94,
  98; self-abortion 151; statistics 7, 156
*Akron vs. Akron Center for Reproductive
  Health* (1983) 90–99, 108, 135, 137,
  142, 176, 179–180, 184, 192
American Civil Liberties Union 148
American College of Obs and Gyns 123
American Law Institute (ALI) 20, 25;
  Model Penal Code (Section 230.3
  Abortion) 19–20
amniotic fluid 72
amniotic sac 72
Aquinas, St. Thomas (1225–1274) 196,
  197

Bellotti vs. Baird (1976) 47–50
Bellotti vs. Baird II (1979) 58–67, 78
Bill of Rights 14, 26
Blackmun, Harry Andrew 3, 13–14, 16,
  24–25, 29, 39–40, 44, 49–50, 57, 66,
  72–73, 75, 86, 99, 109, 114, 145–146,
  148, 180–190, 193, 197–198
Bork, Robert H. 146
Brennan, William Joseph 16, 29, 45,
  55–57, 66, 75, 86, 99, 109, 114,
  145–146, 198

Burger, Warren Earl 16, 25–26, 29, 45,
  55, 57, 66, 75, 79–80, 86, 99, 109,
  114, 132–134, 145–146
Bush, George 147, 149, 150, 152

Catholic Teaching on Abortion 195
Colautti vs. Franklin (1979) 68–75, 165,
  167, 175–176, 184
Conn vs. Conn (1988) 151–152
Connecticut: regulation 56, 57; Welfare
  Abortion Regulation (Sec. 275) 51;
  Welfare Department 51, 54
consent: adolescent (minor) 62, 63, 79,
  80, 81, 84, 85, 102; adult 38–39,
  49–50, 125; alternative 65–66; court
  ordered 108, 148; emancipated 36, 78,
  82, 83, 108; husband (spouse) 4, 5,
  35–36, 39, 151; immature 109; informed 124, 126, 127, 132–133, 136,
  137, 143; joint (married) 5, 39; mature
  62, 63, 64, 65, 82, 92; parental (guardian) 5, 36–37, 39, 41, 42, 43, 48–49,
  50, 51, 65, 66, 95, 108, 133; substitute 65–66, 104, 108–109; "third"
  party 36, 49, 61, 65–66, 70, under 10
  34, 36, 37, 49, 59, 65–66, 77; unmarried 34, 36, 37, 49, 59, 65–66, 77,
  78, 82, 95, 110–111; written 35, 39,
  95
conservative majority 68
Constitution 54, 55, 176; Due Process
  Clause (14th Amendment) 11, 82, 94,
  129–130, 134, 168, 170, 181, 186, 194;
  interpreting 3; "Right to Privacy" (4th
  Amendment) 3, 94, 96, 186
Constitutional Amendments: first 186,
  194 196–197· fourteenth 11, 12, 13, 14,
  21, 22, 25, 27, 41, 48, 50, 51, 54, 61,

64, 83, 93–94, 98, 130, 134, 136, 167,
    170, 174; fourth 3, 14, 21; fifth 60;
    ninth 3, 11, 21; tenth 130
Constitutional Articles: Article III
    (1787) 8; Council of Trent
    (1545–1563) 195; Department of
    Health, Education, and Welfare 6

dilation and evacuation (D&E) 4, 91,
    95, 104, 107–108
disposing of fetal remains 93–94
Doe vs. Bolton (1973) 2, 20–22, 29, 40,
    55, 56, 57, 73, 83, 86, 132
Douglas, William Orville 16, 26–27, 29
Dukakis, Michael 149

Eisenhower, Dwight David 10
Equal Protection Clause 186
Equal Rights Clause 6
Establishment Clause 187, 195–196
Exon Amendment 149

Feminist Woman's Health Center 150
fetal survival 4, 72, 74, 107, 124, 135,
    139–140, 144
fetal-testing 164–165, 174–178, 183–185,
    191–194
first trimester 95–97, 106, 111

Georgia: statutes on abortion 17–19
Ginsburg, Douglas H. 146
Griswold vs. Connecticut (1962) 130–131

H.L. vs. Matheson (1981) 5, 76–86
Hippocratic Oath (Ancient) 1
Hospital Committee 5, 22, 23, 24, 25,
    113
hospitalization 4, 22, 23, 24, 25, 95,
    97–98, 103–104, 108–109, 112–114, 165,
    179
Hyde Amendment 6, 150, 169
hysterotomy (cesarean section) 4, 40,
    71–72

indigent: pregnant women 6, 53–57,
    149, 173–174, 189

Joint Commission on Accreditation of
    Hospitals (JCAH) 22, 23, 24, 25,
    113
Judiciary Act (1789) 8, 94

Kennedy, Anthony M. 146, 147, 148,
    163–164, 197–198
Kennedy, John Fitzgerald 10
Koop, C. Everett 152–153

late (third) trimester procedure 6,
    107–108, 126, 129, 134, 139–140,
    183

Maher vs. Roe (1977) 51–57, 132, 168, 173
Marshall, Thurgood 16, 29, 45, 66, 75,
    81–85, 86, 99, 109, 145–146, 198
Massachusetts Abortion Statute (Sec.
    12P) 47–50, 58
Massachusetts Abortion Statute. (Sec.
    12S) 58–67
Medicaid 51, 52, 53, 54
medical judgment 2, 6, 57, 79, 95–96,
    140–142, 167, 174–175, 191–192
medical records 38, 126, 128
Medicare 6
Missouri Statutes on Abortion (1974)
    30–33; Sec. 2(2) 40; Sec. 2(3) 39;
    Sec. 3(2) 40; Sec. 3(3) 41, 43; Sec.
    3(4) 40, 43; Sec. 6(1) 38, 45; Sec.
    9 41, 45
Missouri (Kansas City) Statutes
    (100–102) Sec. 188.025 102, 104, 109;
    Sec. 188.028 102, 109; Sec. 188.030.3;
    102, 109; Sec. 188.047 102, 109;
Missouri Regulation of Abortion (1986)
    rulings: Circuit Court of Appeals 162;
    U.S. Supreme Court 162–163; Sec.
    1.205.1 164, 171, 181, 193–194, 196,
    197–198; Sec. 188.015(3) 181, 194; Sec.
    188.025 164; Sec. 188.029 164,
    175–180, 183–185, 190, 191–194, 197–

198; Sec. 188.029(2) 193, 194; Sec. 188.030 177; Sec. 188.205 164, 174–175, 193, 197–198; Sec. 188.210 164, 172, 174, 181–182, 193, 197–198; Sec. 188.215 173–174, 181–182, 193, 197–198

National Abortion Federation 106
National Abortion Rights League 163
natural childbirth 56, 168
normal childbirth 57, 136

O'Connor, Sandra Day 95–99, 109, 114, 132, 135, 142–144, 163–164, 176, 178, 182, 190, 192, 193, 197–198
Ohio (Akron) Abortion Ordinances 87–89; Sec. 1870.05 90; Sec. 1870.06 90; Sec. 1870.7 90; Sec. 1870.16 90; Sec. 1870.03 99

pathologist report 103–107
Pennsylvania Abortion Control Act (1974) 68; Sec. 5(a) 69, 73, 74, 75; Sec. 5(d) 70, 74, 75
Pennsylvania Abortion Control Act (1982) 115–123; Sec. 3205 124–125, 126–127, 144; Sec. 3205(a) 143; Sec. 3205 (a)(v) 143; Sec. 3208 124, 126–127; Sec. 3208(a)(1) 125; Sec. 3208(a)(2) 125; Sec. 3210(b)(c) 124; Sec. 3210(b) 126–128, 144; Sec. 3210(c) 126–129, 144; Sec. 3211(a) 124, 126–127; Sec. 3214 127; Sec. 3214(a) 124, 126–127; Sec. 3214(a)(b) 126, 144; Sec. 3214(e) 139; Sec. 3214(e)(2) 127; Sec. 3214(h) 124, 126–127; Sec. 3241(a) 127 Sec. 3241(h) 127
physician's judgment 22, 80, 81, 127
Planned Parenthood vs. Danford (1976) 4–5, 33–46, 49, 64, 65, 66, 73, 74, 78, 81, 83, 84, 86, 98, 128, 133, 151, 175–176, 184
Planned Parenthood of Kansas City (Missouri) vs. Ashcroft (1983) 102–109, 126, 138, 110, 111
Powell, Lewis Franklin, Jr. 16, 29, 45, 54–55, 57, 62–64, 66, 75, 80–81, 86, 94, 99, 109, 114, 145–146

postviability abortions 107–108, 125–126, 128, 133, 139–141, 178
potential life 43, 57, 72–73, 135–136, 145, 175–177, 179–180, 183–185, 187–188, 192, 196
preserving fetal life 11, 37–38, 107, 133, 140, 186, 195
prostaglandin amniocentesis 4, 40–41, 44–45
public employees 168–169, 172, 173–174, 193
public facilities 169–170, 173–174, 181–182, 193, 198
public funding 6, 51–57, 168, 170, 173–175

quickening 188

Reagan, Ronald 99, 123, 148, 149, 152, 163
Rehnquist, William Hubbs 3, 14, 16, 28, 29, 46, 57, 64, 67, 75, 86, 95, 99, 109, 114, 145–146, 151, 197–198
residency requirement 24
Right to Life League 150
Roe vs. Wade (1973) 2, 6, 10, 11–16, 20, 22, 28, 29, 39, 40, 41, 43, 53, 55, 56, 57, 64, 72, 74, 83, 84, 86, 91, 96, 112, 113, 123, 129, 130, 131, 132, 133, 134, 135, 136, 138, 139, 140, 141, 142, 145, 146, 147, 148, 152, 162, 163, 165, 166, 168, 169, 172, 173, 175, 176, 177, 179, 180, 181, 182, 183, 184, 185, 186, 187, 188, 189, 190, 191, 192, 193, 194, 197, 198
Roosevelt, Franklin Delano 10

saline amniocentesis 4, 37, 40, 44, 71, 110–111, 174
Scalia, Antonin 145, 146, 180, 190–194, 197, 198
second physician 102–103, 104–109, 125–126, 128–129, 133, 141, 144
second trimester abortion 4, 95–96, 97, 104, 105–109, 110, 111–112, 113–114, 177–180, 183, 185, 187
Simopoulos vs. Virginia (1983) 110–114
Social Security Act (Title XIX) 51
standard of care 34, 38, 71, 73, 74–75, 129
stare decisis 148, 176, 189–190

Stevens, John Paul 3, 16, 41–42, 45, 57, 64–65, 66, 81, 86, 99, 109, 114, 126, 129–132, 145, 146, 151, 187, 193–197, 198
Stewart, Potter 29, 40–41, 45, 57, 66, 75, 86
Supreme Court: appeals 9; appointments 9–10; branches of government 8; convened (1789) 8; formation 8; functioning 9; Judiciary Act (1789) 8; landmark ruling 1–2; number of cases 9; number of justices 9; philosophical balance 2; writ of certiorari 9

Texas Abortion Statutes 10; Article 1196 15; theological concept of ensoulment 196; theory of idealism 83–84
Thornburgh vs. American College of Obstetricians and Gynecologists (1986) 123–146, 167, 176, 178, 179, 187

Utah Annotated Code Sec. 76-7-304 77; Sec. 76-7-305 76; Sec. 76-7-304(2); 77, 79, 80, 81, 82, 85–86

viability (viable) 2, 12, 26, 34–35, 39, 40, 43, 69–71, 72, 73, 74, 75, 96, 97, 103, 104, 105, 107–108, 125–126, 128, 135–136, 139–141, 164–166, 175–180, 183–188, 191–194, 195
Virginia Abortion Ordinance 110–111; class 4 felony 111

waiting period (24-hours) 93, 98–99
waiting period (48-hours) 147
Washington, George 10
Webster vs. Reproductive Health Services (1989) 152, 163–198, 199
White, Byron Raymond 16, 28, 29, 42–45, 46, 65–66, 73–74, 75, 86, 95, 99, 109, 114, 129–131, 134–142, 144, 145, 146, 198
writ of certiorari see Supreme Court